W9-BNY-178

Dying the Good Death

Dying the Good Death

The Pilgrimage to Die in India's Holy City

Christopher Justice

State University of New York Press

Cover photograph: Patricia Seymour

Cover design: Charles Martin

Published by
State University of New York Press, Albany

Printed in the United States of America

For information, address State University of New York Press, State University Plaza, Albany, N.Y. 12246

Production by M. R. Mulholland
Marketing by Fran Keneston

Library of Congress Cataloging-in-Publication Data
Justice, Christopher.
Dying the good death : the pilgrimage to die in India's Holy City / Christopher Justice.
p. cm.
Includes bibliographical references and index.
ISBN 0-7914-3261-0 (HC : alk. paper). — ISBN 0-7914-3262-9 (PB : alk. paper)
1. Death—Religious aspects—Hinduism. 2. Hinduism—India—Vārānasi—Customs and practices. 3. Vārānasi(India)—Religious life and customs I. Title.
BL1214.72.J87 1997
294.5'23—dc20 96-17471
CIP

10 9 8 7 6 5 4 3 2 1

Contents

Illustrations

Map of India

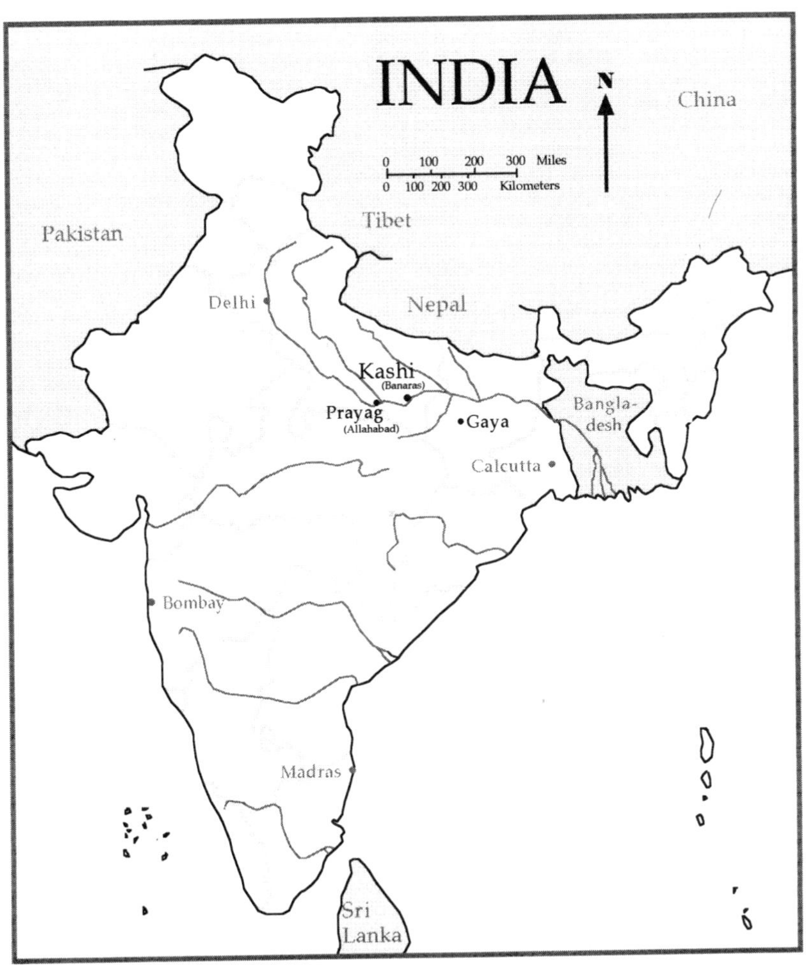

INDIA
N
0 100 200 300 Miles
0 100 200 300 Kilometers
China
Pakistan
Tibet
Delhi
Nepal
Kashi
(Banaras)
Prayag
(Allahabad)
Gaya
Bangla-
desh
Calcutta
Bombay
Madras
Sri
Lanka

Preface

I had half expected that the *Kashi Vishvanath Express,* the train we had boarded in Delhi en route to Kashi (Varanasi), would be full of old, dying people on their way to relinquish their bodies in the holy city. Patricia—then my fictive, now my real wife—and I had chosen to go "1st class, non A.C." realizing only later that this, in fact, is a synonym for 3rd class and means a constant stream of dust and people. As we watched miles of beautiful farmland and picturesque villages roll by, our compartment gradually filled up. We were joined by a middle-class, traveling, pharmaceutical salesman and then by seven uniformed police who filled the compartment beyond capacity. The police entertained themselves at our expense, mocking our protests and laughing as one or another grabbed our maps or books. Later, the businessman, who had become quite drunk, solaced me with a glass of his "Ayurvedic medicine" and shared with us the meal of spicy vegetables his wife had prepared for his journey.

We were on our way to Kashi, the holy city. I had come to India in order to study the experience of dying. My interest in the interplay of culture and physiology had lead me to consider a study of aging and dying as biological universals, modified by cultural environment. I had been to India several years before and had become enchanted by its complexity and mystical feel. I was hooked the moment that David Kinsley, whom I had kept in touch with since taking his *Health, Healing and Religion* course several years before, suggested I study the pilgrims going to the Hindu holy city to die.

Though I had been to India, I had not been to Kashi. I had, however, heard about it from other travelers. Kashi is definitely on the traveler's circuit. I had heard that it was awesome; that it was a place of death where you could see bodies burning on open fires and catch sight of bloated corpses floating down the holy Ganges. This image of Kashi is also captured in the literature: Diana Eck wrote that "No other city on earth is as famous for death as is Banaras (Kashi). More than for her temples and magnificent *ghats,* more than for her silks and brocades, Banaras, the Great Cremation Ground, is known for death" (1981, 324). I was particularly intrigued by the writing of Jonathan Parry, who has done research on death in Kashi since the early seventies. Parry's focus has broadly emphasized the significance and structure of Kashi as a place for dying, and has specifically focused on the ritual surrounding death and the priests that deal with death. I would study not death, but dying; specifically, the dying of pilgrims who go to Kashi when they feel their lives coming to an end in order to achieve the spiritual reward of *moksha.*

That pilgrims go to Kashi to die is well documented. From several sources, I knew that there were institutions in Kashi in which dying pilgrims regularly stayed. Parry (1981) wrote that there were "several" hospices in Kashi and mentioned three by name. He said that they kept records of the people who died in them and that in 1976, 558 people had "passed through these institutions" (350). Eck (1981, 329) wrote that the pilgrims are brought to hospices "at the eleventh hour." There, she wrote, "they may die in peace, for dying a good death is as important as living a good life."

Scholars such as David Counts have written on ideas of good and bad deaths and how they reflect society's cosmogony and morality. One of the foci of my research would be how conceptions of what it is to die a good death influence the way people actually die. Parry's conception of what a good death is to a Hindu is very interesting from this perspective. On the basis of Parry's research, Bloch and Parry (1982, 16) wrote that the good death for the pious Hindu is

> that of a man who, having fulfilled his duties on this earth, renounces his body (as the ascetic has earlier renounced his) by dying at the right place at the right time, and by making it a sacrifice to the gods. "Bad" death, by contrast, is the death of the person who is caught short, his body still full of excrement, and his duties unfinished. It is the death of one whose youthfulness belies the likelihood of a conscious and voluntary renunciation of life, or of one whose body is contaminated by a disease which makes it unfit as a life-creating sacrifice.

In the same volume, Parry (1982, 82) characterized the ideal Hindu death as follows:

> In the ideal case, the dying man . . . forgoes all food for some days before death, and consumes only Ganga water and *charan-amrit* (the mixture in which the image of a deity has been bathed), in order to weaken his body in order that the "vital breath" might leave it more easily; and in order—as I would see it—to make himself a worthy sacrificial object free of foecal matter. . . . Hav-

> ing previously predicted his time of going and set his affairs in order, he gathers his sons about him and—by an effort of concentrated will—abandons life. He is not said to die, but to relinquish his body.

To what extent a Hindu might actually share in this ideal of a good death, one which is based in ancient scriptural writings, would be another matter for investigation.

India, from what I had read, seemed a place where it was clear that dying is steeped in culture. There, ascetics perform their own death rituals and live the rest of their lives as a type of "living dead." There, it is written, "life was thought to consist of a conjunction of various elements such as hearing, sight, locomotion and substance. . . . There was no notion of the overriding importance of the activity of the heart or brain" (Bayly 1981, 158). The loss of sight or hearing or the ability to move around by oneself, Bayly argued, was regarded as a stage of "physical dissolution" as opposed to the manifestation of some illness which might eventually lead to death. In India, it seemed, death was regarded as process and not event. The idea that a good death is a process, and one that is conscious and controlled on the part of the dying person, suggested to me that India might be a fruitful place to see the relationship between physiology and culture.

I had also read that the Hindu's "different" ideas of what death is had been responsible for some conflicts between Hindu and British culture at the time the British were ruling India (Bayly 1981, 172). For instance, in the 1820s, Baptist missionaries in Bengal mounted an attack on what they called "ghat murders." Apparently, people who were thought to be terminally ill were sometimes carried down to the side of the river and left there to die. The missionaries seem to have revived some of these people and, charging that the practice was willful manslaughter, they managed to have legislation passed which forbade the exposure of those still alive (in Western physiological terms). Here was a clear example of the disjuncture between social and physiological death where the social death had preceded and was precipitating the physiological death.

I vividly remember standing with my head out of the window as the train slowly creaked its way through the outskirts of the city. Kashi's train station is enough to shake even the most seasoned traveler. Before we had descended from the train, porters had whisked our bags off through the crowds. We struggled after them, fighting off aggressive taxi drivers, past cows and deformed beggars. In the station, there was hardly room to walk for the hundreds of pilgrims camping on the floor, either waiting for an empty train home or having just arrived. Our bags were surrounded by a crowd of rickshawwalas who moved toward us as we emerged from the station and yelled prices and places and pulled on our shirt sleeves. We made the mistake of going with the man we judged to be the most honest looking of the lot, and enjoyed a two-hour tour of the city, arriving at a place we later discovered was only fifteen minutes away from the station.

Our first few days in Kashi can only be described in terms of sensory overload. Patricia wrote this account of our first visit to the river at Harischandra ghat, just down the street from the small hotel we initially settled in.

> There were several bodies being cremated on the steps going down to the river. We leaned over the railing of a tiny Shiva temple feeling bursts of heat from the pyres fifteen feet below and breathing air tinged with the distinctive, acrid smell of burning bodies. There seemed nothing somber or ceremonial about the scene around the pyres: the parties of mourners lounged around, occasionally poking the fires with long sticks, to ensure a thorough cremation; children laughed and played, splashing in and out of the water a few feet away from the pyres; dogs and cows wandered around grazing on whatever they could find. The sun was setting behind the ghats, lighting up the far banks of the river. The river was high and wide, filled by the monsoon rains, and the ghats stretched northward, following the slight curve of the river, as far as the eye could see. It was so like I had expected it would be from all the photographs I had seen at home. For some reason, this only reinforced my dissociated state.

Our time in Kashi coincided with a period of general political unrest throughout India. Banaras Hindu University, where I had arranged to be a research associate of the department of sociology, was closed down for many of the first few weeks we were there. Student protests—as extreme as self-immolations—were going on over proposed government policy of "reserving" jobs and university positions for the 'backward' castes. In the months that followed, we witnessed a violent resurgence of the long-running conflict between Hindus and Muslims over the disputed Babri Masjid mosque in Ayodhya which was said to stand over the site of the Hindu god Rama's birthplace and has since been demolished at the cost of hundreds of lives. We watched worshippers of Rama rioting in the streets and endured many subsequent days of curfew. Later in the year, the Indian general election was held and Rajiv Gandhi was assassinated, plunging much of India into renewed violence and more curfews. In the end more than a month of my thirteen in India was spent under curfew, many days of which we were forced to stay inside twenty-four hours. Many more days were disturbed by all the shops in Kashi spontaneously shutting down as waves of fear and sometimes violence swept through the city.

Despite the difficulties the time we spent in Kashi was remarkably alive, rich with new friends and the challenges of living and researching in a strange environment. In retrospect I see that first train journey to Kashi as symbolic of much that would happen. While the police who invaded our compartment on the train presaged the violence we witnessed in India, the businessman foreshadowed the schism I would confront in my analysis between ideal Hinduism (in which one should not drink) and lived reality (where many actually do). Though there were no old, dying people on the train, I realize now that we, too, had been pilgrims—travelling like all the others to Kashi and its wonderful rewards.

Acknowledgments

It is with great pleasure that I thank the many people who have assisted me in the research, analysis, and writing of this book. First of all, I am deeply indebted to the many people whom I met in Kashi and at the Muktibhavan who shared their thoughts, stories, and experiences with me. Many of the subjects of this book are no longer living. I hope their families see this book as testaments to their lives. I am grateful to several people in Kashi who made the research possible. Omji, my friend and research assistant, provided encouragement, logistic support, and a network of knowledgeable people. The manager of the Muktibhavan, Shuklaji, graciously allowed me access to the people staying and working at the institution, and shared with me his village, family, and spiritual understandings. Thanks to my many friends in Kashi, especially Manoj, Tulsi, and my compatriot Hillary Rodrigues, who made my time in Kashi so wonderful.

I am thankful to David Counts, my advisor, who provided me with a fine balance of intellectual guidance and freedom to think during the writing of the dissertation on which this book is based. I am very grateful to Bill Rodman, who taught me to find a voice and enjoy writing. He provided prompt, constructive criticism and continual encouragement from the start. I am also beholden to Paul Younger for sharing with me his deep understanding of India, his enthusiasm for the study of popular Hinduism, and his personal experiences of life and death. Paul offered unwavering support to me from the beginning. Wayne Warry, Angela Streather, and David Kinsley all carefully read and provided helpful comments on various drafts.

My research was supported by a Shastri Indo-Canadian Institute doctoral fellowship; thanks to the many warm and helpful people in Shastri's Delhi office. The research was also financially supported by doctoral fellowships from the Social Sciences and Humanities Research Council of Canada and Ontario Graduate Scholarships. The department of sociology, and Professor S. N. Tripathi, at Banaras Hindu University graciously allowed me to act as research associate there during my time in Kashi.

My most intimate debts are to members of my family. My mother and father have encouraged me to move in weird and wonderful directions throughout my life. They have my love and thanks. I owe my deepest debt of gratitude to my wife, Patricia Seymour, who went to some trouble to accompany me to the field and has patiently and lovingly helped me as I have struggled to think and write since returning home. She has provided many insights and her sharp eye and command of the English language were strenuously exercised in the editing of this work.

Notes on Transliteration

As is the common practice in books in English that deal with Hindi and Sanskrit words, many names and terms are transliterated from their Devanagari form. I have omitted the use of diacritical marks, however, and several other simplifications of the usual transliteration system have been employed. The "short a" at the ends of words is sometimes eliminated (as in *nark*), sometimes kept (as in *karma*). Nasalized plurals are not indicated but occasionally nouns are pluralized with the English "s" (as in one *rogi,* two *rogis*). Proper names of people, places, and castes appear in their usual English forms.

अ,आ	= a	क	= k	ज	= j	ब	= b	श,ष	= sh
इ,ई	= i	ख	= kh	झ	= jh	भ	= bh	व	= v, w
उ,ऊ	= u	च	= ch	ट,त	= t	ल	= l	ह	= h
ए,ऐ	= e, ai	छ	= chh	ठ,थ	= th	य	= y	न,ण	= n
अे,ओ	= o, au	च्छ	= cch	ड,द	= d	र,ड़	= r	ङ,ञ	= n
ऋ	= ri	ग	= g	ढ,ध	= dh	ढ़	= rh	म	= m
		घ	= gh	प	= p	स	= s		
				फ	= ph				

The term "Hinduism" is a convenient and accepted term for the religion of the "Hindus." However, many of the people I met in Kashi do not use the term "Hinduism" to refer to their religion but instead use the term *"sanatana dharma."*

1

Perspectives on Death and Dying

The research on which this book is based is situated in a sociohistoric moment in which there is a proliferation of academic and popular literature on death and dying, and a growth of social movements to change the way in which people can die. Counterpoised with societal concerns about the cost of extended care and keeping people "artificially" alive, are concerns about the lack of control people have over the way they die and the apparent meaninglessness of death. Recently we have witnessed the reemergence and growth of hospices and living wills, seen the emergence of groups such as the Hemlock Society arguing for the legality of assisted suicide, and heard arguments that withholding active treatment should not be considered passive euthanasia. Broadly speaking, the concerns and initiatives are focused on what some have called "death with dignity" (Roy 1986) and are aimed, in part, at making dying more "natural" (Marshall 1985, 58). The current concern about the way we die is reflected in the thanatological literature of recent years which has attempted to define Western attitudes toward death and identify their underlying causes.

Western Perspectives on Death and Dying

The use of the term "Western" requires a few words. I find it an unsatisfactory label for just one level of the entire complex culture of the geopolitical West. Among other things, it denies the significant variation both within the mainstream and amongst more obviously culturally distinct groups living in "the West"; a variability mirrored, incidentally, in the complexity of death practices in India. For example, Hutterians living in the Canadian prairies, have a process of dying which in idealizing a long, drawn-out death, markedly contrasts with the mainstream ideal (Stephenson 1983–84). Further, the term "Western" used in comparison suggests a more absolute distinction with others than there probably is—there are very few places on earth without "Western" structures or ideals and classes of people who aspire to be more or less "Western." With these hesitations I use the term in order to look at the literature which use it as common currency.

Most treatments of the subject begin with the Philip Ariès's history of changing "attitudes" to death in the West (Ariès 1974, 1981). Death prior to the Middle Ages, he argued, was less something which happened to an individual than an assault on the community. Now, Ariès argued, death has become a personal drama which is "shameful" and "forbidden." More generally, the Western "attitude" toward death has been described as one of "denial." This idea was fully developed by Ernest Becker (1973) who, assuming universal fear of death, argued that it has manifested in modern Western culture as the proclivity to pretend death does not exist. As one example of how this popular conception is used, Palgi and Abramovitch (1984, 410) speculate that the central position of the restored corpse in Western funerals has to do with the fiction of the deceased as peacefully sleeping. Much of the sociological and psychological literature on death assumes the validity of the premise that people in Western societies "deny" death and attempts to explain this attitude on the basis of one or another social-structural condition. Much of it assumes that there has been some change for the worse, and, explicitly or implicitly, makes comparison to either the past or to simpler societies.

Blauner (1966) wrote that the key determinant of the social impact of mortality is the age and social situation of those who die. Death, he said, is particularly disruptive when it strikes persons who are most relevant to the functional and moral activities of the social order. Riley (1983, 191), speaking more specifically of the West, argued similarly that death has taken on new meaning with the recent trend that death now generally occurs not among the young but among the old. Kaistenbaum and Aisenburg (1972, 205–8) called this trend the "transposition" of death and speculated that as death and old age have become equated in the Western psyche, death has come to be regarded, at least in the early years, as a distant and remote possibility. Death has become a social problem, in part, because the living find it hard to identify with the dying (Elias, 1985, 3).

Other literature finds the explanation for Western attitudes to death in our mode of societal arrangement. Stannard (1975) reasoned that when societies were smaller, more integrated, and consisted of extended families, death had more meaning for both individual and community. Further, he argued that factors such as specialization and diversification in commerce, individuality, and the recent mobility in social relations have led to a sense of insignificance when faced with death. Similarly Badone (1989, 18–19) has argued that the denial of death is most likely to be found "in a secular society where humanist ethical values are emphasized and where face-to-face social interaction is minimized."

One specific societal change which has been linked to the shift in Western attitudes toward death is the location in which dying occurs. Between the 1930s and the 1950s, the site of death changed from at home, with the family, to alone in a hospital. Kaistenbaum and Aisenburg (1972, 207) suggested that when people die in hospitals, those outside the hospital are protected from the sights of death. Thus, from the perspective of society, the institutionalization of death has allowed for the denial of death. From the perspective of a dying individual, it has been pointed out repeatedly that the hospital is not a good place to die. Mauksch (1975) argued that hospitals are committed to the recovery process, not to dying, and Sudnow (1967) demonstrated that among hospital staff efficiency is more highly valued than human dignity. Though according to Seale (1989) the attitudes of hospitals are changing with regard to death, a recent sociological study of dying in an oncology ward (Moller 1990) made the point that caregivers are often not comfortable dealing with death, and as a result handle dying patients quite poorly.

Other literature has suggested that the loss of symbols of continuity is responsible for new Western attitudes to death. Robert Jay Lifton in *The Broken Connection* (1979, 17) argued that people are on a "compelling and universal inner quest for continuous symbolic relationship to what has gone before and what will continue after our finite individual lives." Lifton felt that catastrophes associated with World War II, the subsequent Cold War, and the more recent threat of nuclear annihilation has raised doubts and loss of faith in the modes of continuity. Kaistenbaum and Aisenburg (1972) expressed a similar argument, associating a surge of interest in death with "multilateral development of overkill capabilities" which has confronted us with "the prospect that in one swift cataclysm we will lose not only our own lives, but all posterity" (1972, 234).

The spread of secularization throughout Western society is a common theme in understanding Western attitudes to death and dying. Palgi and Abramovitch (1984, 405) pointed out that secularization has weakened belief in an afterlife. Similarly, Jackson (1977) argued that, as a result of secularization, in the present century, the dead in American society have lost their social importance and visibility. Marshall (1980, 58) argued that, with the loss of religious meaning, people have focused their efforts at making death meaningful by making death and dying more "natural," as in the death with dignity movement.

As Moller (1990, 15) has observed, those very scholars who have been writing about death denial have, over the last couple of decades, created or initiated a huge body of literature on death and dying which itself is evidence that we might not be as death denying as is generally assumed. Moller tried to see this recent fascination with death and the proclivity to deny death as aspects of the same thing. He linked them to the dominant themes of American life: namely technocracy, materialism, individualism, and self-actualization. Technocratic and materialist society, he argued, is characterized by individuals with a "having" orientation. Life itself is experienced as a possession, something that is *lost* with death. It is the loss of this most prized of possessions that is the source of the tremendous fear of dying. The human potential movement, efforts at self-realization, and the recent concern for dying a dignified death are not a drastic parting of the way with this attitude: the improvement of one's most precious possession—the self—and the desire that it not deteriorate during the dying process, follow logically. Moller wrote: "If . . . ways can be found to transform the experience of dying into a process of growth, dignity and enrichment, a final triumph—a final victory—is amassed for the self" (10).

Moller's analysis has the advantage of offering an explanation for the recent social movements concerning death. Moller's own research was with cancer patients; his analysis highlights the fact that much of the thanatological literature, and, I would argue, the death with dignity issue, is about young people. Though some of the explanations for death denial lie in the demographic changes which have associated death with old age, most of the research which has been done on Western attitudes toward death is based on people dying of terminal illness before the end of the life cycle (Marshall, 1980, 69). It is quite possible that the entire postulate of the denial of death in the West and the assumption of universality of the fear of death is based on the fact that research, such as that of Kubler-Ross (1969), is on *young* dying individuals.

Whereas in many other societies, people tend to die throughout the life span, in Western society people tend to die when they are old (Counts and Counts 1985a, 1). In the United States for example people over the age of 85 account for only 1% of the population but for 17% of all deaths (cited in Riley 1983, 192). In my view, a basic distinction must be made between "premature death," such as death from a terminal illness like HIV/AIDS or an accident, and "natural death" at the end of the life cycle. Many anthropological accounts have shown that such a separation is made in other societies. McKellin (1985), for example, reported that the Managalase of Papua New Guinea distinguish between, and react quite differently to "loss of life" and "passing away" in old age. Counts and Counts (1992, 277) made the point that the perspectives on death held by many societies are shaped by the fact that most death is premature. I believe that the perspectives of death in the West may also be shaped by premature deaths, though not because they are in the majority, but because, as a result of our own disengagement with our elderly people, premature deaths remain the most visible.

On the basis of the literature reviewed above and in the face of the social movements to modify the way we die, it seems that there is general agreement that the meaning of death is ambiguous in North American society. As Marshall (1985, 269) argued, it is dying at the end of the life cycle which requires redefinition and understanding:

> If it is necessary to make sense of death, then the nature of what must be made sense of has changed. Not capricious death, but predictable death; not death at an early age, but death as the culmination of life, calls out for new meaning in the North American context, since older systems of meaning were accommodated to a form of death that is now increasingly rare.

This research was carried out under the assumption that cross-cultural research is essential to understanding anything that is affected by cultural factors (Palmore 1983). Specifically, I believe that studies of dying at the end of the life cycle which show how it is conceived and experienced by various peoples can elucidate the potential for responding to and shaping this biological universal.

Anthropology and Dying

Much of the anthropological literature on death is rooted in functionalism and is about how society responds to the death of an individual. Here I am following in a smaller and newer ethnographic tradition in which the problem shifts in emphasis from how society responds to death, to how individuals die and make sense of dying within a particular social and cultural environment. I refer to the anthropological literature which deals with societal and survivor response to death as an "anthropology of death," and to that which deals with the way it is done and conceptualized by dying people within a cultural and societal context as an "anthropology of dying." In practice this distinction is not clear; it is a matter of emphasis. The anthropology of dying, and some of the basic insights which have led to some of the issues I am concerned with here, have deep roots in some of the early work on death.

Here I rely on Palgi and Abramovitch (1984) for a basic organization of the topic. The very early anthropological work on death, such as that of Fraser and Tylor, sought to account for the origin of religion and beliefs about 'man's' posthumous fate. Themes which followed and continue to the present day are the socially restorative functions of funeral rites (Hertz [1905] 1960; Malinowski 1929; Radcliffe-Brown 1964; Mandelbaum 1965; DeCoppet 1981; Danforth 1982), the significance of death behaviour as an expression of the cultural value system (Hertz [1905] 1960; Bachofsen 1967; Bloch and Parry 1982; Humphrys 1981) and the theme of transition and concept of liminality (Hertz [1905] 1960; van Gennep 1960; Turner 1967). In another organization of the literature of anthropology of death, Goody (1971) argued that the evolutionists used organizational aspects to get at the conceptual realm, while the functionalists used conceptual aspects to get at social organization. In this schema, the lasting contribution of Hertz, van Gennep, and Turner was to *interrelate* the belief system and mortuary practice (Palgi and Abramovitch 1984).

Van Gennep's *Rites of Passage* (1960) dealt with death to the extent that he recognized in all rites of passage the common theme that between two categories there are three stages; between being alive and being dead there is a stage which is dying. This transitional stage is the hardest for the living to handle, as was shown by Turner's (1967) elaboration on this "liminal" stage. Robert Hertz (1960) had earlier recognized this idea of liminality by concentrating on the large number of societies in which death is not considered to be instantaneous. These societies enact a second burial with elaborate rites in order to assist the dead from their place on the margins of human habitation to the stable world of the ancestors. Rivers (1926, reprinted in Slobodin 1978) demonstrated the arbitrariness of the categories and boundaries between life and death.

The recognition that dying is best regarded as a process is based, in part, on such observations by anthropologists studying the views of other societies. These views were noticed and considered interesting because back home death was popularly conceived to be a singular, nonreversible event—an attitude which is part of a cultural bias toward rigid categorization. However, Western clinicians now recognize that, physiologically, death does not come to all organs simultaneously and, with technological intervention, the process of dying can be greatly extended. From a psychological perspective, dying is understood as beginning at the self-recognition of terminal status and pro-

FIGURE 1.1

A body on ice awaiting the arrival of family members before being carried to the burning ghat

ceeding (through stages, according to Kubler Ross 1969) to final unconsciousness. From a social perspective, death is most clearly processual, and as Counts and Counts (1991, 278) have pointed out, it is often regarded as a transformative process that can extend well past the end of the body's vital signs.

Dying in a Social and Cultural Context

The early research on how individuals die and make sense of dying within a particular social and cultural environment occurred in Western institutional settings. Glaser and Strauss (1965, 1968) first suggested that in hospitals people can die socially, in the sense of being considered and treated as if dead, before they die biologically. Sudnow (1967) documented examples of what he considered social death preceding biological death in Western hospitals. As one example, he noted that "near death" patients, at admission to the hospital where he was conducting research, were sometimes left in the supply room throughout the night. If in the morning they were still alive, nurses quickly assigned them beds before the arrival of physicians and/or relatives (1967, 83). This is an outrageous situation but dramatically illustrates the idea that people near to death can be considered, and thus treated as already dead. Similarly, at a nursing home Watson documented that people, once they were defined as dying, were consistently removed from the visual and social presence of the well, with the result that they had decreased access to medical services commonly available to the sick (1976, 122).

The idea of social death has been elaborated by anthropologists, who have noticed that in many societies there is a disjuncture between the physical body and the social persona. The social persona and physical body may have different life spans and the social death or birth of a person may not coincide with his or her physical birth or death (Counts and Counts 1990, 280). For instance, Counts and Counts (1985b, 145) told of a Kaliai man who attended his own mortuary service (while alive) at the completion of which he was considered socially dead. Scaletta (1985) described the death of a Kabana woman who when dying was installed in a lean-to on the perimeter of the village and, as her condition worsened, began to be referred to by others, and then herself, as already dead.

Social and biological deaths are causally connected but have an uncertain temporal relationship. Though it seems to be obvious that biological death will cause social death, social death can occur before, during, or after biological death. The widespread occurrence of ancestor cults and entities we tend to gloss as ghosts may be regarded as manifestations of biological death preceding social death; although biologically dead, people can play an active societal role, carry on conversations, or simply be remembered; Keesing pointed out of the Kwaio that their world is one in which "the living and the dead are coparticipants in everyday life" (1982, 112). Social death may also precede biological death and, in some circumstances, social death may cause or accelerate biological death. A striking instance of this is provided by W. H. R. Rivers (1926, reprinted in Slobodin 1978), who recounted that in the Solomon Islands, people were sometimes buried when in the condition known as *mate,* a category which includes both the dead and people very near death, even when they were still moving and vocalizing.

Other celebrated examples of biological deaths connected to the social realm are those that have been called "voodoo death" or "magical death." Cannon (1942) recounted many early reports of spells, sorcery, and "black magic" resulting in deaths often of apparently perfectly healthy individuals within just one or two days of the curse. These reports have been from various geographical locations, though Arnhem Land in Northern Australia is where most cases have been documented. Basedow (1925, 178–79) in *The Australian Aboriginal* described voodoo death thus:

> The man who discovers he is being boned (cursed) by any enemy is, indeed, a pitiable sight. He stands aghast, with his eyes staring at the treacherous pointer. . . . His cheeks blanch and his eyes become glassy. . . . He attempts to shriek but usually the sound chokes in his throat. . . . He sways backward and falls to the ground. . . . From this time onwards he sickens and frets, refusing to eat and keeping aloof from the daily affairs of the tribe . . . his death is only a matter of a comparatively short time.

Warner (1937), in his book *A Black Civilization: A Social Study of an Australian Tribe*, documented withdrawal of the victim's social group immediately following a curse. He argued that the cause of death in these circumstances is this withdrawal of social support from the cursed individual combined with stimuli from the group which positively suggest death to the victim. Unsatisfied by this "ultimate" explanation of voodoo death, Cannon (1942), and then others, have looked for more proximate causes. Cannon speculated that an individual on whom a supernatural curse had been placed often died as a result of extreme fear which, through the actions of the autonomic nervous system, results in prolonged shock (174). The shock, he argued, would be exacerbated by dehydration resulting from the victim refusing food and drink "in his terror . . . a fact which many observers have noted" (178).

More recently, Eastwell, who visited Arnhem Land regularly to conduct psychiatric clinics, argued that the belief that death is inevitable on both the parts of the cursed individual and his immediate social group, leads, sometimes passively sometimes actively, to no fluid intake on the part of the victim, who then quickly dies of dehydration in Arnhem's very hot climate (1982, 14). Because of the difficulty in observing actual cases of voodoo death, Eastwell argued by analogy. In fact, what he used were cases of deaths of *elderly* aboriginal people. The pattern that he pieced together, based on reports from his "health-worker informants" and some hospital records, is as follows: The relatives and/or the elderly person conclude that death is inevitable. The relatives withdraw and begin public mourning including wailing and chanting the dying person's ancestral songs. Though his informants are "adamant that chanting is requested by the dying person," Eastwell believed this to be not so in all cases, and stated that sometimes it is against the will of the dying person who is, however, powerless to prevent the sequence from continuing (12). At this point the person is "socially dead" and the social group denies him or her any fluids. Eastwell felt that such deaths range from "desirable euthanasia," in which a person is mercifully kept from dying a prolonged death, to outright "senilicide" (14).

The phenomenon of voodoo death has been generalized in two different ways, the first of which concentrates on societal motivation, the second on mechanism. Glascock (1983, 1990) considered voodoo death just one of the ways in which societies hasten the deaths of individuals who are decrepit or, in some other way, liminal or problematic. On the basis of a sample taken from the Human Relations Area File, he argued that death-hastening behavior, including abandoning, forsaking, and outright killing exists in about half of all societies, including the modern West. From a different perspective, Davis (1988, 197–212) argued that voodoo death is a recognizable phenomenon and is best called psychogenic death, a term which points to psychological factors as an intermediary between the social and biological processes (see also Lachman 1982–83).

The idea that important events in an individual's life can affect the timing of death is generally taken for granted (Kalish and Reynolds 1976, 38). For example, it is popularly understood that death of one member of a long lived couple may lead quickly to the death of the other, and that people can sometimes delay their death in anticipation of some important event such as the birth of a grandchild. These two phenomena differ in that the first is an acceleration of death and the second a retardation of death. Generally speaking, acceleration of the dying process has been largely substantiated by scientific inquiry (Shulz and Bazerman 1980, 260) which has shown a higher than expected mortality rate among the recently bereaved, and among persons who have undergone stressful events including divorce and job loss.

Retardation of death has been a much more elusive phenomenon, though there is popular agreement that the process occurs. As an example, Counts and Counts (1983–84, 104) reported the death of a man who appeared to hold on to life for a couple of weeks, anticipating the arrival of his eldest daughter, and then died within a couple of hours of her arrival. There have been several attempts to find statistical links between death and ceremonial occasions, especially birthdays: the "birthday-deathday" phenomenon (Phillips and Feldman 1973; Baltes 1977–78; Schulz and Bazerman 1980; Harrison and Moore 1982–83; and Zusne 1986–87). The results of studies are contradictory and seem to be highly dependent on methodology. For instance Phillips and Feldman (1973) found that there are fewer deaths than would be expected immediately *before* birthdays, suggesting postponement of death until after the anticipated event. Harrison and Moore (1982–83), on the other hand, found fewer deaths immediately *after* birthdays and speculate that the birthday is a dreaded event. Harrison and Kroll (1985–86), who studied deaths around Christmas, found what they call a "clear dip" in deaths the week before, and a "highly pronounced surge" during the two weeks after Christmas. They speculated that anticipation of Christmas produced a "positive mood" which acts to "delay death" and that there is essentially the opposite effect after Christmas.

Though the literature cited above is based on relatively minor demographic phenomena, its theoretical significance is far-reaching as it points to the linkage between self and society. This literature points to two interrelated processes whereby individuals are sometimes motivated to manage the time of their own deaths, often to fulfill some social commitment, and society sometimes exerts control over the death of its constituents.

Good and Bad Deaths

Counts (1976–77) argued that the death-related behavior of the Kaliai is based on a set of ordered principles which define the nature of death and the relationship of the dead to society. Death-related behavior is performed with the objective of avoiding dying a bad death. Individuals draw on their cultural knowledge to make sense of death and dying, and some deaths are considered more appropriate than others. To the extent that an individual can shape his or her dying process, he or she will shape it into an appropriate one.

Ideas of what are good deaths are thus of some importance in understanding the dying process and have been looked at cross-culturally. People can often express what a good or bad death is. In the social realm the distinction between good or bad deaths is underlined by differential ritual activity. Bad deaths often receive more elaborate ritual treatment (Counts and Counts 1985a), an activity which can be interpreted as a sense-making behavior (Marshall 1985, 269).

One common element in people's ideas of good death seems to be that of control. Bloch and Parry (1982) argued that the pervasive distinction between good and bad death is a response by society to the challenge of the deaths of its members: "Both the impulse to determine the time and place of death and the dissociation of social death from the termination of bodily function, clearly represent an attempt to control the unpredictable nature of biological death and hence dramatize the victory of order over biology" (15). A good death, in this view, is one "which suggests some degree of mastery" over the biological occurrence by "replicating a prototype to which all such deaths conform." A bad death, in contrast, demonstrates the absence of such controls. Counts and Counts (1983–84) also argued that the good death for the Kaliai is one in which there is a degree of control, adding public participation and lack of disruption as important factors. Badone (1989, 56) suggested that an important part of the good death among certain people in a region of rural Brittany is awareness that one is going to die, though this, she says, is changing. The distinction between a good and bad death is also commonly a moral one; death at an old age in much of Oceania is considered good because old age is equated with a morally correct life (Counts and Counts 1985a; Scaletta 1985).

The position I take in this study is that dying is a process occurring at social, individual (or psychological), and physiological levels but that there may be a disjuncture between the various levels such that one can die socially before or after biological death. Social processes can affect the biological process of dying both directly and indirectly. The very category of "dying" is a social one: the length of time someone spends in it and how it is shaped depends on how it is defined. Cultural ideas of, for instance, what is a good or bad death are implicit in the physiological dying process.

In much anthropological literature, the physiological process is considered immutable; the social and cultural effect on the physiological dying process is seen as the *interpreting* of the physiological response and the *defining* of the behavior that is appropriate. Here I am also interested in exploring the other half of the dialectical relationship between culture and physiology, namely, the effect that the cultural interpretations and definitions can have on the physiological process itself. The major theoretical aim of this book is to document the relationship of an individual's understanding of a good death—seen in relationship to the spectrum of Hindu possibilities—to the individual's actual multifaceted experience of dying.

Other Theoretical Considerations

This is a topic-oriented, person-centered ethnography which focuses on the experience of dying in the context of the Hindu holy city, Kashi. Broadly, the ethnographic goals are to discover the cultural knowledge people are using to organize their behavior and interpret their experiences, and to contribute to general theoretical statements about the process of dying in the context of cultural and social life. Specifically, I provide empirically based descriptions of the process of the dying of pilgrims who are brought by their families at the last moment to die in Kashi, and attempt to understand the behaviour in terms of the beliefs, understandings, values, and attitudes which the behaviors are based upon and reproduce.

At the basis for my choice in this research topic is an interest in the interplay of culture and biology, especially in terms of how societal processes affect physiological processes. I see this as one aspect of what I consider to be a deep concern of humankind as to the features and quality of human nature. Though my concerns are both culture and biology, a synthesis of cultural and biological perspectives is difficult due to basic methodological differences. In the biological perspective, life is viewed and not engaged (Peacock 1986, 98): subject studies object. I prefer an interpretive cultural perspective stressing holism and a concern for culture which are enhanced by capturing the interplay *between* subject and object. The recognition of this interplay, of the necessary subjectivity of the work, is ultimately for the purpose of striving *toward* objectivity, an unattainable goal which has its reward in the journey.

I take a life-course perspective which sees dying as the culmination of a life-long process of aging and which assumes that there are three processes—biological, psychological, and social—which interact over the course of life and during dying (Marshall 1985, 253). Though I emphasize the social and cultural milieu, I do not see socialization or cultural prescription as causal, but rather as providing a range of possibilities in which an individual can struggle to find meaning and act on the basis of what makes sense (Counts and Counts 1985a). My theoretical perspective fits largely into the framework of symbolic interactionism. Following Blumer (1969, 2), I accept that:

1. People act not on things themselves but the meaning that those things embody.
2. Meaning derives from interaction with others.

3. Meanings are reinterpreted and change, and actions are not automatic responses but are evaluations based on cultural knowledge.

I feel that my first responsibility in writing is to document the human phenomenon I studied in all its complexity and variability, in a way that reveals meaning to the reader. I see ethnographic meaning existing primarily at the two levels Charlsley (1987) has identified as indigenous and anthropological exegesis. Most basic to this research is the meaning that individuals see in what they are doing, that they have conveyed to me and that I have struggled to understand. The content of each chapter of the book is based on this level of meaning. A second level of meaning is created by my analyses and juxtapositions of ideas on the basis of plausible connections between them. These connections form the organization of the book and the topics of the chapters.

Both the indigenous and anthropological exegesis are connected to bodies of texts. In this chapter, I have attempted to situate the book in the anthropological and other literature which has informed it. One of the underlying themes of the chapters that follow is to show how the meaning expressed by the individuals who informed me is also situated in a complex body of texts—though these are scriptural—which act as a pool from which individuals and small groups can draw in different ways and degrees. A concern for how the "system" is produced and reproduced places the book in the margins of what Ortner (1984, 146) describes as the diverse "practice approach" in anthropology.

In the next chapter, after introducing the city of Kashi, I describe how I deal with the problem of the place of the scriptural texts in the cultural knowledge which informs people about going to Kashi to die. Chapters 3 and 4 describe the historical and present contexts in which the pilgrims spend their final days and hours. The following four chapters are more analytically focused. Chapters 5, 6 and 7 look at the place of tradition, spiritual knowledge, and morality in the pilgrimage to Kashi to die. Chapter 8 describes aspects of the physiological dying process and my concluding chapter ties the physiological process into the tradition of coming to Kashi and its spiritual and moral implications. I return from the field in the final chapter and briefly discuss the implications of the book for the way "we"—in Fabian's (1973) universal sense of the word—die.

2

Kashi and Studying Hinduism

[Kashi is] older than history, older than tradition, older even than legend.

—Mark Twain

Kashi

Kashi is one of the names of what is often called *the* holy city of the Hindus. The official name for the city, the one that must be written on a piece of mail, is Varanasi, a name which reflects the city's geographical setting in between where the Varana and Asi rivers flow into the Ganges. Most residents of the city refer to it as Banaras. But Kashi is the oldest name and it is the name which tends to be used by pious Hindus who go there on pilgrimage. As it is this perspective of the city that is most pertinent here, Kashi is the name I will use in this account.

Kashi is one of the oldest living cities in the world. To a large degree the ancient history of the city is merged with mythology and as anthropologist Bhaidyanath Saraswati (1975, 5) wrote: "Mythology dates this ancient city to the early period of creation." Kashi is mentioned in many early scriptures, though this does not provide an accurate age as the dates of origin of these texts are not secure and many things have been added subsequent to their original composition. However, archaeological excavations reveal significant structures which are thought to be the early Kashi and are dated to as early as the eighth century BC.

The population of Kashi as of the 1991 census was just over one million. This is a significant jump from the figure of a little under six hundred thousand reported for 1971 by Vidyarthi and co-workers (1979), who noted that, even at that time, Kashi was one of the most crowded cities in India. It is crowded because it is quite small; Kashi occupies about a three-mile stretch of the bank of the Ganges River, which it has transformed from mud and sand into hundreds of stone steps and temples, many of which are under water half the year when the river is in flood. Kashi is on the west bank of the Ganges; its density of buildings and humanity form a striking contrast to the east bank, just opposite, where not a soul resides. People in Kashi say this is so because if you happen to die on the east bank, instead of getting *moksha* as in Kashi, you will be reborn as a jackass.

Kashi, according to Saraswati (1975), like Rome and Mecca, needs no introduction, surpassing all the "civilizational" centers of the world. Nevertheless, Saraswati provided an introduction to Kashi which captures some of the complexity and colour of the city,

> On entering the holy city of Kashi (Banaras or Varanasi as it is also known) one is struck by the crowds of pilgrims followed by rapacious *pandas,* hustling through narrow stinking lanes, infested with dreadful fighting bulls and insidious monkeys, to small untidy temples. If a visitor goes . . . from the Varanasi railway station to the Dashashwamedha *ghat* he will meet, while gambling with his life during the 20-minute ride in a cycle rickshaw, at least, half a dozen *sanyasis* in ochre robes and one or two naked *babas* trailing the rickshaw. Right on Dashaswamedha *ghat* he will find *Akhara Gadhanath,* with young robust Ahirs wrestling, and some distance away is another kind of *akhara, Awhana Akhara Dasnam Shambu Panch,* the seat of the once-fighting *Dasnami Naga Sanyasis.* In the neighbourhood is yet another *akhara, Sri Yogiraj Sri 108 Bhagwandasjika Akhara Khak Chauk* where the visitor can see *Ramawat sadhus* smoking *charas* and *ganga.* More than these, the beauteous bathing scenes of pilgrims, the activities of the *ghatias* sitting under huge bamboo umbrellas, the boatmen haggling with the tourists for a ride offering a charming view of the colossal *ghats* on the Ganges, and again the bulls and beggars and the lepers cannot escape his notice. Straying into the city, the visitor may enter the *Kachauri gali* with its small, dirty, rotten shops serving *kachauri* and *rabri* to their crowded clientele. If he is unable to come out of the *chakravyuha* lanes, the visitor may at once follow a funeral procession carrying a decorated bier and shouting *Ram-nam sat hai* to the everburning cremation *ghat* of Manikarnika and there meet strange looking Domas claiming descent from Kalua Doma, the legendary king of Kashi. From there the visitor may take a boat and conveniently reach Dashaswamedha *ghat* once again, counting the massive monasteries, magnificient palaces of the Hindu princes from all over India,

and the countless spires of temples and mosques during the ride. On disembarking at the *ghat* if the visitor wants to return to his camp through Godolia, the heart of the city, flooded by the streams of uncanny traffic, he will definitely spoil his clothes, on being a little careless, from the reckless spitting of betel juice by the passers-by, who are so unconcerned about others. On loitering in Godolia even for 10 minutes he is destined to bump into, if not collide with, a robust man with red *gamachha* on his shoulder, and not unlikely by the semi-naked, funny dressed hippies who have recently taken a refuge in this sacred city. All these may at once drive away the casual visitor from this mad city. (1975, 1–2)

In this passage, Saraswati was trying to describe the phenomenal Kashi; the daunting and nerve-racking Kashi, the city which would be seen by a non-Hindu visitor to the city. The devout Hindu, in contrast, sees Kashi in a different way. He sees it with "so much love, so much charm and so much adoration" (1975, 2).

Seeing is an appropriate metaphor because, as Diana Eck (1983, 20) has pointed out, in the Hindu tradition the eyes have been entrusted with the apprehension of the holy; when Hindus go to the temple they say they are going for *darshana* (seeing) of the divine image. Pilgrimage too is done for *darshana* of the sacred sights. Eck, like Saraswati, presented her Kashi from two opposed perspectives; a Western (phenomenal) view and the view of Hindus for whom Kashi is "not only the city that meets the eye; it is also the city that engages the religious imagination . . . through the eyes of collective imagination and religious vision" (1983, 22–23). It is the Kashi of the religious imagination that must be envisioned for it is this Kashi which religious pilgrims, including those coming to die, act upon.

Two Kashis: Banarsi and Pilgrim

There are another two significantly different, though interconnected, Kashis; Kashi, the city in which people live and work; and Kashi, the pilgrimage destination.

Kashi, the city, is multicultural. People from all over India have settled in Kashi and they live in neighborhoods, each of which retains some of its original identity and linguistic flavor. People from outside have had a great impact over the centuries; so much so that Saraswati (1975) argued that "the history of Kashi's classical culture is the history of Gujarathi, Marathi, Tamil, Bengali and Maithili *pandits* (learned

FIGURE 2.1

An auspicious bathing day on the bank of the Ganges in Kashi

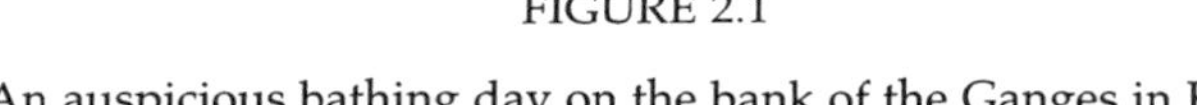

men) in Kashi" (50). Kashi, despite being a holy *Hindu* city, is also multireligious. In addition to Hindus, a significant percentage of the population is Muslim. Kashi, too, is multispecific; a huge number of creatures such as cattle, buffalo, pigs, donkeys, dogs, chickens, and monkeys live and wander freely through the city.

Kashi is a center of excellence in a variety of arts. Vidyarthi and co-workers (1979) argued that this is a direct result of Kashi's preeminence as a pilgrimage center, as opposed to the other way round, and that over the centuries pilgrims have essentially functioned as patrons of Kashi's arts. It is certain that pilgrims buy Banarsi *saris*, toys, and scented oils and perfumes, for which the city has become famous. But Kashi is also known as a center of Indian classical music and a center of learning excellence. As Eck (1982, 4) pointed out, Kashi has for over 2,500 years, been famous as a place of spiritual education and has attracted seekers from all over India. Sages such as the Buddha, Mahavira, and Shankara—famous teachers of Buddhism, Jainism, and Hinduism, respectively—all came to teach in Kashi. Even now Kashi has several universities which draw students to the city and as well as this, students still come from all over India to find a *guru* and learn in the traditional manner.

Kashi has its own way of life. Several of my friends in Kashi identify themselves to some degree as being *banarsi*, a term which Saraswati said describes the "self-identifiable mass culture" of Kashi. I find the observations of Saraswati, an Indian who lived as an anthropologist in Kashi for many years, interesting because, as an Indian, he has a perspective of what is and is not shared with a more regional or national culture. He found the *banarsi* culture peculiar and having "no rational explanation"(50). He said that it is a place where the social image of the *gundas* (thugs) is colorful, where poets compose poetry in brothels and prostitution is no social evil, and where people are totally insensitive to social evils and suffering (51). My strongest impression is of people taking *bhang* (an intoxicant) and lazily standing around chewing *betel pan* and chatting. In my experience, it is enjoyment of life, rather than the pursuit of a spiritual reward at death, that is the dominant theme of *banarsi* culture.

This in itself is significantly different from the understandings of the pilgrims who come to Kashi. While they are after worldly things too, the most significant thing about a pilgrimage to Kashi is the rewards which will accrue only after death. There are four big drawing cards: Pilgrims come because Kashi is the city of Vishvanath (Shiva) and they want to worship in the famous Vishvanath temple. Pilgrims also come because Kashi is said to be India in microcosm and a trip to all the shrines of Kashi is described by many scriptures as equivalent in merit to a trip to all the shrines of India. Pilgrims come to bathe in the Ganges, which is particularly potent near Kashi where it rounds a bend and flows auspiciously from south to north. And pilgrims come because Kashi is the *mahasmasham*—the great cremation place, and to leave one's body there is to attain *moksha.*

From childhood, the pilgrims coming to Kashi have heard about Kashi through a type of traditional literature called *mahatmya*—hymns of praise and glorification—which are statements of faith about the sacred city and descriptions of the Kashi of the religious imagination. The *mahatmyas,* echoed by pilgrims and taught to them by the city's *pandas,* describe Kashi as being the whole world but outside the world, as embodying all time, but being timeless. It is the home of Shiva and the City of Light, where reality and truth are illuminated. And it is the final pilgrimage stop on a long journey through a series of lives, for in Kashi death means *moksha* (Eck 1983).

But, as I will discuss in the following chapter, the promotion of the envisioned Kashi, the pilgrimage spot *par excellence,* cannot be seen as having been a wholly unconscious historical process. Pilgrimage supports a wide variety of priests (Eck 1983, 21). In addition to *pujaris* who officiate in temples, there are *ghatias* who look after bathers, *pandas* who organize pilgrims, *karmakhandis* who assist in particular rites, and those who specialize in death rites, the *mahapatras.* All of these people and countless others in Kashi have a material interest in the sacredness of the city. As Jonathan Parry argued in his paper *"Death and Cosmogony in Kashi"* (1981), the transcendental identity of Kashi is both seen and promoted by the sacred specialists who earn their livings on or around the burning ghats of the city (337).

According to these sacred specialists, Manikarnika ghat, the center of the city, is the place where the universe is created at the beginning of time and the place where the universe burns at the end of time. The city circumference is marked by the *panch kroshi* pilgrimage route, a five-day pilgrimage around the boundary within which all who die are granted *moksha.* Kashi is outside of the rest of the world, but at the same time contains the rest of the world. It stands on the trident of Shiva above the earth. All the gods can be found in Kashi as can all the famous places of pilgrimage; the *panch kroshi* pilgrimage around Kashi is also a circumambulation of the entire cosmos. It is always Satya Yuga in Kashi: the golden age of original time. Time does not flow in Kashi and in the same sense karmic retribution does not operate.

There are, however, obvious signs that it is no golden age in Kashi, and a lot of people act as if *karma* does operate. The Kashi of the religious imagination, as described by Parry, Eck, and others, is, in the end, the Kashi of the scriptural texts, and the Kashi described by the people who are well versed in the texts. Parry's (1981) adept analysis of cremation as a sacrifice, for instance, is really an analysis of this "book view." He suggests that as in Hindu thought there is a homology between body and cosmos, there is an equivalence between the burning of a body and the burning of the universe at the end of time, and that this is (in both cases) simultaneously an act of creation. "Since cremation is a sacrifice, since sacrifice regenerates the cosmos, and since the funeral pyres burn day and night at Manikarnika ghat, creation here is continually replayed" (340).

The connection of these types of ideas to the pilgrims coming to Kashi is complex. They hear of the spiritual Kashi from the sacred specialists. They have heard about it before coming from other people who have been there before and, to some degree, the spiritual Kashi is part of a more general cultural knowledge. The degree to which pilgrims coming to Kashi know about and believe all the wonderful properties of the city is, no doubt, variable. I will show later in this chapter that there is some variability in the understanding of what *moksha* is—the very motivating force which brings people to die in Kashi. In chapter 6 I will deal more thoroughly with the subject of how and what the pilgrims coming to Kashi to die know.

Though it may be difficult to know what all the people involved with Kashi believe, there are some things about Kashi and its uniqueness for death that are easily observable. Throughout India, the cremation ground *(shmashana)* is located outside of the city, usually to the south, and is regarded as an inauspicious place (Eck 1983, 32–33). But in Kashi the cremation grounds are right in the city; Manikarnika ghat, perhaps the most famous of cremation grounds, is in the very center of the city and is a most auspicious place. Corpses are brought into Kashi by the thousands in order to be burned there (in 1989 over 24,000 dead bodies were brought in from outside the city to be burned). Even packets of bones and ash are mailed to Kashi by people too far away to bring a body, to have a rite done over them and for final disposal in the Ganga (Parry 1981, 35). For a lot of people, however, being burned in Kashi or having one's bones and ash dumped into the Ganga at Kashi, is just not quite enough. These people want to die there and so they come when alive on a one-way pilgrimage to "abandon their bodies" in Kashi.

If the pilgrims and the residents of Kashi have quite different perspectives on the city, it is also true that their perspectives are inextricably linked. One estimate is that as many as three-quarters of the residents of Kashi are dependent on the pilgrim industry (Saraswati 1975, 45). The sacred is, to some degree, a secular industry. As Saraswati put it:

> what is more revealing about the sacred complex is that those who are professionally involved in it consider sacred as a mere means of livelihood and not something to be treated in a special manner. This attitude towards sacred is discerned by any conscious observer visiting a temple or observing a priest conducting rituals. This is so conspicuous in their behaviour that everyone knows what they are after.

A vivid example of the business side of the sacred complex are the *bhaddars* or "pilgrim hunters" (Vidyarthi et al. 1979). These people pick up unwary pilgrims at the train or bus station and arrange their stay in Kashi. They have contracts with other sacred specialists whom they "sell" the pilgrims to. They also take the pilgrims to *sari* shops and other places where they will get a commission on whatever the pilgrims buy. Another context in which the nature of the industry is clear is the cutthroat negotiations for price between funeral priests and mourners (Parry 1994, 80).

Another Type of Pilgrim

Many people have accepted the view of the scriptural texts that Kashi is "a microcosm of Indian civilization." This phrase is the subtitle of an anthropological work on Kashi (Vidyarthi et al. 1979), *The Sacred Complex of Kashi.* People are drawn to Kashi for a distilled and concentrated Hinduism. Also, Kashi is regarded as a seat of Indian large "C" Culture and people are drawn there for the classical music and the Sanskrit. Consequently, Kashi has become one more thing in addition to a residential city and a pilgrimage destination; Kashi is a city of researchers and foreign students. At any one time there will be several in Kashi. For the last twenty odd years the "Wisconsin program," which is run out of the University of Wisconsin in Madison, has been bringing in ten or so students to Kashi each year for eight-month stints. More recently, the American Institute of Indian Studies has put an office in Kashi and students come to study Hindi and Sanskrit. Banaras Hindu University, too, attracts students from all over, some of whom are in graduate programs and conducting research in Kashi.

People from many disciplines have worked in Kashi, but the majority are interested in religious studies, language (especially Sanskrit), textual studies, and anthropology. A few of the more significant researchers who have worked in and about Kashi are the following. Baidyanath Saraswati, under the initiative of L. P. Vidyarthi, went to study Kashi as a "sacred complex" in 1959, though most of the fieldwork was done in the late sixties and early seventies (Saraswati 1975, 1983, 1985; Vidyarthi et al. 1979). Diana Eck, a scholar of religion, first went to Kashi in the sixties. Her 1981 book *Banaras: City of Light,* essentially a *mahatmya,* or hymn of praise of Kashi aimed at the West, has probably attracted many students and researchers to the holy city. Nita Kumar went to Kashi in 1981 from the University of Chicago to look at Kashi from the perspective of popular culture, rather than a receptacle for pilgrims (cf. Kumar 1986, 1992). And in the late eighties Lawrence Cohen worked on old age in Kashi, looking at the city both as a "gerontopolis" that attracts old people from elsewhere in India, and as a home to old people whose normative understandings of age are influenced by the city's sacred institutions (Cohen 1995).

The most significant researcher of Kashi, however, from the perspective of this project, is Jonathan Parry who went to Kashi in the early seventies and studied various aspects of death (Parry 1980, 1981, 1982, 1985, 1994). He has been pursuing this topic now for about twenty years. Parry's research has influenced my own in several respects. It was on the basis of Parry's published research that I was able to formulate a research plan and I have been able to rely on Parry for a lot of background and detail, and thus focus much more specifically than would otherwise be possible. Perhaps even more significantly, I was assisted in conducting my research by a man named Om Prakash Sharma, otherwise known as Omji, who was originally hired, trained, and brought to Kashi as an anthropological research assistant by Parry. Omji has been in Kashi ever since. It is testimony to the number of students and researchers visiting Kashi that he has been employed there as a research assistant of various kinds for over twenty years now.

There are several parallels between pilgrimage and research in Kashi. *Pandits* of old composed the *mahatmyas,* the hymns of praise, of Kashi which attracted pilgrims to the city. The inflow of these pilgrims sparked the creation of a class of sacred specialists, such as *pandas* and *shraddha* priests, among others, who make their living by assisting the pilgrims. In the same way, Parry and other researchers, but especially

Eck (1983), have composed sociological praises of Kashi which have attracted other students and researchers. The inflow of these researchers and students has created an infrastructure of research specialists, like Omji and a few others, who assist them and derive a living from them.

Methodological Issues

While in Kashi, I lived in the world of the *banarsi,* but the realm I was interested in was that of the pilgrim. The point where the two cultures met, for me, was the institutions which house dying pilgrims and their families. Most of my time in Kashi was spent at one of these institutions, the Kashi Labh Muktibhavan, which I will refer to as simply the Muktibhavan.

I may not have been able to do the research without the help of Omji. The manager of the Muktibhavan, Shuklaji, is not particularly interested in the people who drop by from time to time to see the "place where people come to die." However, Omji had spent some time there over twenty years before, copying down some of the *bhavan*'s records for Parry. This was long before the present manager came to be there but Omji makes a point of keeping up with all contacts and forging new ones; networking in Kashi is, essentially, his profession. When I met Omji and explained what I wanted to do, he simply smiled and said "That is not a problem. We will use our power." We went to the Muktibhavan together the first time and Omji was received there as a celebrity. After tea and pleasantries, Omji's power had its effect and I was welcomed to come as often as I wanted and learn what I could.

In the first few months, Shuklaji was not interested in being interviewed. However, as time went by and I became less someone to put up with and more of an interesting diversion, Shuklaji changed his mind and insisted that I tape-record certain things that he said. My impression is that, initially, he was doing Omji's bidding by having me there, but later we developed a friendship and he decided I could be "helpful" to him. At one point he said to me:

> I know you are interested in all this and so you have come. My family does not understand where you have come from: this is the great difficulty. But I think that if more people come it is better. You are all forms of the divine soul and you will write some things and tell people about things. In this way some of my obligation will be lessened.

In conducting the research, I used what amounts to a standard anthropological methodology for data collection and analysis, adapted from a holistic methodology which Younger (1982) articulated nicely in his interpretation of the meaning of a Hindu religious festival. This involves understanding, and eventually integrating, meaning at three levels which are related to three techniques of inquiry: participant-observation, interviewing, and historical analysis. These levels of meaning correspond to three general anthropological questions: What do people appear to be *doing?* What do they *say* they are doing? And what do they say they *should* be doing? Participant-observation provides access to events and scenes, sometimes highly patterned, which may be relevant to the meaning and experience of dying but which any one person may not be fully aware of. Interviewing provides access to people's conscious level of understanding. What, for instance, do people say about the meaning of dying and the importance of dying a "good" death? Finally, historical analysis elucidates a level of meaning of which an individual may be fully unconscious; the understanding that dying in Kashi results in *moksha* is a product of an historical process. Kashi, itself, and the institutions for the dying are also embedded in a complex and textual history.

The majority of my time and energy was dedicated to understanding the experiences of the families bringing someone to die in Kashi. I spent most of my days in Kashi hanging around at the Muktibhavan watching and waiting. Most of the dying people arriving at the Muktibhavan are well beyond the point of being able to converse, but I would get to know accompanying family members and have conversations with them. Through these I began to understand how people were feeling and the difficulties they were going through as well as specific details of how they came and how long they thought they might have to stay. When it was appropriate, I conducted formal interviews, translated by Omji, with one or two members of the family.[1] I had the opportunity to interview dying people themselves on only three occasions. However, all three of these people left the Muktibhavan and returned to their villages alive. As it turns out, those who have come when they can still talk have misjudged the times of their deaths.

In addition to what I learned from observing and talking to people, I spent some time going through the institutions' records. Both the Kashi Labh Muktibhavan and another institution, the Kashi Gangalabh Bhavan, have kept records of the people coming to die there since they began operation. The records document such things as where the people are from, their sex, caste, age, and sickness, their date of arrival, date of death, and the number of accompanying kith and kin. The Kashi Labh Muktibhavan has records going back to 1958, and has recorded the visits of some 8,500 dying people.[2] The Kashi Ganga-labh Bhavan, which dates back to the mid-1930s was (in 1990) assigning registration numbers higher than 20,000 to the people arriving to die.

At both places getting permission to look at these records was relatively easy; at the Kashi Ganga-Labh Bhavan, however, actually getting hold of the records was a different matter. Everybody involved said that someone else actually had possession of them. Eventually, the manager "found" them in the cupboard where they are normally kept, but only those records since 1975. It seems that all the pre-1975 records had long ago been confiscated by a court somewhere in Bihar in connection with a fraudulent property inheritance case. Apparently, these records have never been returned.

Though there was this and some other difficulties with records, they provide a quantitative and historical perspective to the research and the understanding of these institutions. The results of my analysis of them are contained in chapters 4 and 5.

Finally, in order to supplement the recorded data and to provide a more detailed profile of the population of people who use the *muktibhavans,* I developed a survey instrument, with the help and advice of Omji and Shuklaji, designed to target between 75 and 100 families. The survey covered a couple of important demographic variables such as education level and occupation of the dying person but focused on such issues as the family's previous knowledge of the Muktibhavan and aspects of the dying experience such as whether or not the dying person has seen a doctor, whether or not he or she was eating food or taking any medicine and who had made the decision to come to Kashi. I ran this survey exclusively at Kashi Labh Muktibhavan. It was administered, at the insistence of the manager, by the priest-workers at the time that they were registering a new arrival. I discuss this survey and results more fully in chapter 4.

A Methodological Problem: The Relationship of Texts to Experience

Anthropologists, who have traditionally studied small and defined communities, generally have a "they" about whom generalizations can be made. However, the people coming to the Muktibhavan to die are connected at various levels and they share certain views, but "they" do not exist as a *defined* group other than being those who come to the Muktibhavan to die. In many respects the variation among them is as interesting as what unites them. It has been my feeling since doing the research, that a lot of the on-the-ground variability of the sort that I found has been covered up or ignored by some researchers in India because of their overreliance on scriptural texts in their analyses.

India is a place with a long and complicated textual tradition that exists in some sort of dialectical relationship with the many levels and layers of popular culture. The relationship between the textual tradition and lived Hinduism has long been a basic problem for anthropology in India. Though this is probably best seen as an instance of the more general problem of the relationship between official and popular religion—or "religion as prescribed" and "religion as practiced" (Badone 1990, 6)—in the scholarship on India specific concepts have been developed to deal with the disparity.

The concept of "Sanskritization," first articulated in Srinivas' (1952) monograph on the Coorgs, but fully developed in his *Social Change in Modern India* (1968), is a theory about how textual prescription enters lived reality. Sanskritization was developed to explain the (upward) social mobility of a caste by adopting the customs, rites, and beliefs of Brahmins, but later came to refer to "the process by which a 'low' Hindu caste, or tribal or other group, changes its customs, rituals, ideology, and way of life in the direction of a high, and frequently 'twice-born' caste" (Srinivas 1968, 6), who, themselves, are thought to rely directly on the Sanskrit texts.

To differentiate between two apparently different cultural processes, Robert Redfield (1955) developed the concepts of "great" and "little" traditions in conjunction with Srinivas's concept of Sanskritization (Sarkar 1978, 94). "Great" traditions referred to those Hindu traditions which are based in Sanskritic texts, the scriptural gods, and worship of those gods on a "high" or "pure" plane. "Little" tradition, on the other hand, referred to the traditions of worship of local deities (those not mentioned in the sacred literature), for some more "worldly" reason such as the alleviation of illness. The terms were often used in a manner that implied they are autonomous and discreet spheres, that a given group or caste belongs to either the great or little tradition and that there is a *one way* process by which the textually based knowledge of the great tradition percolates down to the groups of the little tradition. These concepts have been widely used, though in modified form. For instance, Mandelbaum (1961) preferred the terms "transcendental" and "pragmatic" complexes which imply that an individual may use both great and little traditions for "long term welfare" and "immediate exigencies"' respectively. McKim Marriot used these concepts in a study of a North Indian village, introducing the idea of the reverse of Sanskritization, the flow of little tradition elements into the great tradition (Sarkar 1978, 94).

As Fuller (1992, 257) has pointed out, the distinction between great and little traditions is the product of an indigenous ideological discourse of evaluation among members of the higher castes. Caroll (1977) argued that these concepts were accepted and used largely to integrate empirical data from field studies with an anthropological model of Indian society which is based in Brahmanical *texts.* The texts stress caste, the importance of ritual values, harmony, cooperation, and stability; aspects of the social scene often not really stressed outside, and in some cases within, Brahmin social groups. Sanskritization acts to integrate the disturbing elements into the model without requiring critical reevaluation of the model itself.

For the above reasons, these conceptual tools are not helpful in grappling with the problem of the relationship of textual tradition to lived reality. An even more basic flaw, however, is the assumption that there is a great tradition in the first place. I consider the idea of *the* (one) great tradition a gross simplification of the body of Hindu literature written over several thousand years and reflecting several philosophical streams of thought.

Textual analyses

This section deals primarily with a methodological problem of interpreting Hindu society. The problem concerns the relationship of lived experience to prescriptive texts. It became obvious from my first interviews that some sort of familiarity with the textual tradition is imperative for understanding the popular culture, though probably not as much as most textually based scholars would argue. Looking at the texts is, of course, necessary as they are important in day-to-day Hinduism. However, the relationship of text to life is complicated. The following should be regarded as a step toward dealing with this complex relationship. I start at the beginning of perhaps the most famous of texts:

It is the beginning of the huge fratricidal war between the Pandavas and the Kauravas. The vast armies are lined up on either side of the field of Hastinapura awaiting the start of the fighting. Arjuna, the Pandava leader, and his charioteer Krishna, God incarnate, pull out into the field. Then they stop. Arjuna suddenly becomes pensive, and begins a monologue on the misery of having to kill his kin and old friends who are lined up against him. He concludes by declaring that he will not fight. . . . Thus begins one of the most important scriptures of Hinduism, the *Bhagavadgita,* in which Krishna explains to Arjuna why he *must* fight. He begins with an epistemology of life and death. Smiling, Krishna said:

> Thou grievest for those whom thou shouldst not grieve for. . . . Wise men do not grieve for the dead or for the living. Never was there a time when I was not, nor thou, nor these lords of men, nor will there ever be a time hereafter when we all shall cease to be. . . . Know that that by which all this is pervaded is indestructible. . . . He who thinks that this slays and he who thinks that this is slain; both of them fail to perceive the truth; this one neither slays or is slain. . . . He is never born nor does he die at any time, nor having come to be will he again cease to be. He is unborn, eternal, permanent and primeval. He is not slain when the body is slain. . . . Just as a person casts off worn-out garments and puts on others that are new, even so does the embodied soul caste off worn-out bodies and take on others that are new. (Radhakrishnan 1982, 102–7)

For some writers, this is the Hindu view of death. However, in truth it is *not* the only Hindu view; Hindus have many more "possibilities." In addition to being reborn into a new body, a Hindu may become an ancestor, go to heaven or hell, turn into a ghost, or, as I will discuss, obtain the spiritual reward of *moksha.* And each of these categories of potential experience exists in myriad possibilities. Though all these ideas can be found in the scriptural texts, they are differentially favoured by particular texts and they are accepted differentially by region, cultural group, caste, and sect. These ideas can also be found all at once in one individual's conception.

Textual scholars, such as Carse in his work (1980, 109–35) on what he calls "the Hindu understanding of death," completely ignore this complexity. There are serious implications of such overreliance on the scriptures. Carse's chapter, for instance, entitled "Death as Illusion" suggests that, for a Hindu, death is somewhat less than real. Death may be an illusion in Hindu scripture, but death is *not* an illusion for most Hindus. To suggest it is is to deny Hindus somewhat of their humanness.

Textual scholars are not the only ones who take Hindu philosophy for Hindu life. Anthropologists also ignore this variability and confuse lived reality for textual prescription. The reason lies in the fact that followers of popular Hinduism are in a complicated relationship with a huge and complex body of sacred texts. These texts vary in their degree of sacredness, philosophical level of analysis, subject matter and even religious affiliation. Furthermore, they have been written over a period of several thousand years. Some of these texts are taken to be prescriptions for both behaviors and beliefs for certain segments of Hindu society. Other segments of society, which are not mutually exclusive of one another, rely on different texts in different relationships.

Many people in India probably do not, themselves, directly read these texts, but they hear this one being read and see that one being performed. More significantly, the traditional teachers and learned men are (traditionally) completely immersed in particular texts and give lessons according to them and relate narratives directly from them. Wrapped up in the old idea of the "Sanskritization" of lower castes is the idea that lower castes incorporate textually based behavior into their cultures by imitating the high-caste people who, supposedly, live elements of the sacred texts. The complexity of the relationship between texts and lived reality is *ultimately* responsible for the confusion of the one for the other. Here, I will give several examples of the manifestation of this confusion and more *proximate* reasons.

There are some anthropologists who see a straightforward relationship between text and lived reality. Traditionally, the Hindu is supposed to be bound in his or her day-to-day actions to an enormous extent; there are rules for everything in the scriptures. The ultimate source of all the rules is a body of texts which together form a corpus of works known as the sacred law or *dharmashastra*. Bhaidyanath Saraswati, in his book *Traditions of Tirthas in India: The anthropology of Hindu Pilgrimage* (1983), claimed that "[t]he clockwise circumambulation of a holy place or of several *tirthas* is believed to have the (equivalent) effects of (performing) a horse-sacrifice (*ashvameda*)." The implication of the word "believed" is that it is the pilgrims themselves who believe this. But this is simply one thing that one scriptural text has had to say about the way pilgrimage can and should be performed. Pilgrims probably don't believe this; they probably have never heard about it.

Many observers of Hinduism have commented on the degree to which Hindus follow the rules. It is thought by some such as Chaudhuri (1979, 191) that people either follow these rules consciously or the rules have become so well known that they have simply become custom. Either way, according to this view, the rules of actual behavior —of lived experience—can all be found in the texts. Often too, studies of Hinduism boil down to an analysis of the prescriptive texts and the degree to which they are actually followed.

Another reason for relying on the texts is to present a unified account of Hinduism; to find order in apparent diversity. There are not many anthropological attempts at finding commonality in other diverse groups of nearly a billion people, but the texts make India particularly favorable for such an analysis. Scholars such as Biardeau (1981) make the assumption that Hindus have embedded in them the core of their texts. An analysis of the texts, therefore, provides that core of Hinduism against which all the variation makes sense. This is the kind of thing that many synthesizers of Hinduism have done, but few explicitly. In *Hinduism: The Anthropology of a Civilization*, Biardeau describes her endeavor as "taking literally the desire of a whole society, as expressed by its scribes, but also no doubt with a broad consensus, to present itself as a well-ordered whole" (1981, 2). The assumption was expressed as follows: "In one way or another, by a more or less distant reference, and through endless reinterpretations . . . these texts live on in the Indian collective consciousness." She is aware of the risks of such an analysis. "How," she asked "can one be sure that the reduction of the fact to the norm does not conceal the intrusion of a historical contingency the data of which elude us?" (3). Nevertheless, she proceeded, citing the need for an overall system with which to frame the meaning found in its partial manifestations.

Finally, anthropologists rely too much on the texts not by looking at them directly, but by talking to people who are well versed in the texts. This is actually hard to avoid as such people seem to be the ones who are most expert in the "culture" and they are also probably the types of people likely to become main informants. The work of Jonathan Parry (1981) provides an example. In his analysis of cremation rites, he concluded that cremation is in fact a type of sacrifice. However, nobody I talked to in Banaras could understand cremation as a sacrifice, even after I explained the theory to them. That his analysis might baffle even his own learned informants was not important to Parry. It is as irrelevant as "whether the man on the Clapham omnibus recognizes that the values of individualism inform his ideas of romantic love" (1994, 189). As Parry himself recognized, his analysis is at a very esoteric level.

Many of Parry's informants were the sacred specialists of Banaras: high-caste men who were extremely well versed in various scriptures. His analysis is really at a textual level, looking for implicit logic and connections between things written at different times and for different reasons, even though his information came from live people. This, perhaps, is the hardest methodological pitfall to avoid. In fact, you probably cannot find anybody in India who is not familiar with the texts—it is a matter of degree—and often people are more comfortable telling what they know from the texts, than what they may consider to be their own "mistaken" and "incomplete" understandings.

FIGURE 2.2

A young priest at Kashi Labh Muktibhavan

Moksha and Levels of Connection

Now I will briefly look at the concept of *moksha* or *mukti,* which is the justification for coming to Kashi given by virtually everybody who comes there to die. Death in Kashi, they say, is *moksha.* The terms *moksha* and *mukti* are used interchangeably for the ultimate spiritual goal of classical Hinduism. As Parry (1981, 352) pointed out, they are also used in everyday Hindi speech to mean freedom from something, such as a debt. A problem, he stated, arises when one inquires what death in Banaras is liberation *from.* This question, itself, is text-driven, for the classical textual understanding of *moksha* or *mukti* is liberation from the eternal cycle of death and rebirth. As I shall demonstrate, and as Parry himself pointed out, there is a huge variation in individual understandings of the meaning of *moksha,* some of which do not suppose freedom from something so much as a gain of something.

Swami Shivishvaranand, who is both a renouncer and surgeon in a medical hospital which operates homes for the long-term dying in Banaras, explained *moksha* to me in the following manner:

> The soul is a conscious entity which is inherently separate from the body and the mind. But in its ignorance it considers itself to be body and mind. When this ignorance goes away and the soul realizes that it is separate from body and mind, this is called *moksha.* Now as long as the soul thinks it is part of body and mind it is reborn again and again. By purification of your mind you get over this ignorance.

What happens to the soul after *moksha?* Basically, nothing happens. "It is like the sea," he says, "and a particular wave is going along saying 'I am . . . I, I, I.' The wave finally realizes, that no, I am not a wave, I am the sea. Nothing really happens." As Shivishvaranand himself told me, his is essentially the monistic view of *moksha* developed by Shankaracharya in the early ninth century known as Advaita Vedanta (Kumar 1984, 98–115).

According to the founder of the Muktibhavan, Mr. Dalmia, *moksha* is also exemption from the cycle of birth, death, and rebirth. He said that this is desirable because life for most (meaning the poor) is miserable and there are much better places to be than this world. *Moksha,* in his view, has two dimensions. It is escape from this world and it is entry into another world. One's dying thoughts determine the *type* of *moksha* one can get: the state in which one will exist for all eternity. One can reside in the same world as god, remain near to god, take the same form as god, or—best of all—actually become merged with god. This view of *moksha* fits with the more dualistic understanding of *moksha* put forward by the philosopher Ramanuja in the early twelfth century (Kumar 1984, 115–23) and is more typical of Vaishnavas who give high priority to devotion *(bhakti).*

As I will fully elaborate in chapter 6, most of the people coming to Kashi institutions to die also explain *moksha* as being a residence in heaven, near God. To some extent this is seen as a positive thing (as Mr. Dalmia saw it). To an even greater extent, not getting *moksha* is seen as a negative thing and probably this is the main motivational factor in seeking *moksha.* As I shall show, many people coming to the Muktibhavan to die expect an almost endless period of painful nonhuman rebirths if they do not get *moksha* during this attempt. It is the avoidance of painful rebirths and not the promise of a heavenly reward which motivates their pilgrimage to Kashi. Like the understandings of Dalmia and Shivishvaranand, mentioned above, this understanding of *moksha* is also related to a particular set of scriptural texts, as I will show.

Finally, another explanation of *moksha* offered by people coming to die at the Muktibhavan was that it is not liberation from rebirth at all. *Moksha* is a *good* rebirth: rebirth as a rich landholder or as a holy man. This view is liberation to the extent that it is freedom from the immediate troubles of the present life, for the promise of a better next life. I have not been able to specifically relate this view to any scriptural or philosophical texts, though it is probably connected to the important scripture *Garuda Purana* which argues that heaven *(svarg)* and hell *(nark)* are here on this earth and represent good and bad lives respectively.

As I have briefly demonstrated, there is a wide variety of understandings of *moksha* and these understandings can be related to a variety of texts. The methodological problem is how to deal with this variability in lived experience and its relationship to a complex textual tradition. I have argued that the conceptual distinction between Great and Little traditions, and the process of Sanskritization, however modified, are not helpful. Among other criticisms, these concepts are based in a small selection of prescriptive texts and ignore a significant amount of important and interesting variation.

My approach in this book is not to attempt to synthesize *a* Hindu world view about dying nor to show the difference between the view on the ground and the view in the classical texts. Rather I attempt to emphasize variability by focusing on individuals and small groups. In terms of the way people die in institutional settings, what is important is the interaction of people with different worldviews through direct personal contact or through the structures they have created. Of more general interest is the process by which an ancient and complex body of scriptures participates in the ongoing creation of variability, in addition to uniting Hindus. Where I am able, the views of people are related to the texts but, in such cases, individual views are related specifically to those texts that their proponents have direct familiarity with.

I think that Biardeau (1981, 15) was correct when she said that what remains of traditional India, and is observed by anthropologists, is greatly clarified by reference to what she calls the classical tradition and that this is the way to move beyond the epistemological duality between "armchair" Indologists and "field-working" anthropologists. The question is—how? I do not agree with her that it is by bringing flesh and blood to the texts through conversations with learned Brahmins (15). People's ideas can be tied in with, and clarified by, the specific aspects of the textual tradition to which they are connected. This approach avoids assuming that the textual tradition is in any way unified, that different segments of the population do not tie into different texts, and that people do not tie into them to varying degrees.

On Constructing My Own Text

I spent just over a year doing fieldwork, but spent the best part of two years constructing my experiences into a book. Just as my fieldwork involved a lot of writing, writing has been a type of fieldwork to the extent that I have been reexperiencing, evaluating, and recording the field experience through my notes and memories. I believe that I have learned more about the subject in the two years of writing than during my time in Kashi. Certainly, I have constructed a much more coherent experience than I actually had in the field.

In writing this text, I have tried to take the lead of such ethnographers as Kirin Narayan, whose 1989 work *Storytellers, Saints and Scoundrels* contains evocative descriptions of people and atmosphere, and includes, as much as possible, the narrative form with which people tend to relate their experiences. Also following Narayan, I have tried to include theory as an illumination of people's lives rather than an end in itself. I have, to a limited degree, included myself, the ethnographer, in the text, as opposed to portraying myself as a distant observer. I am conscious that many of the things I struggled to learn are things which some of my informants know much better than I do. I have, I hope, at times merely orchestrated their voices. I have tried to make it obvious at these times that the interpretations are only mine because they were generously given to me.

The central theoretical theme of the text is the area of interaction between culture and physiological process, especially in terms of notions of good and bad deaths and their ties to spiritual goals and moral injunctions. There are other themes, however, which run through this text. It is secondly about Hindu tradition and society. Specifically, I try to deal with the complex relationship between lived Hindu reality and the rich Hindu textual tradition. Thirdly, this text is a collection of small portraits of a number of families who each brought one of their relatives to die in Kashi, and who were generous enough to share their experiences with me.

3

The Historical Context of Dying in Kashi

Sri Hridyanand Tripathi, in addition to being a very religious and respected man in his village in Devoria, Uttar Pradesh, had been quite active. When he was younger he had played soccer and field-hockey and up until the time of his stroke in 1987 he was still riding his old bicycle around the dirt tracks of the village. And that is why the stroke was such a surprise to his family and the rest of the village, even though he was well into his seventies. One day he was fine and the next he was in a coma. Word spread very quickly through the village that Tripathiji would soon be on his way to Kashi. He was a respected man from a respected family, so the whole village—in fact the whole locality—wanted to come and bid him farewell. Hundreds came and touched his feet. Some people who did not have a chance to see him even followed later to Kashi to see him off, especially the village women. A *gau dan* was quickly organized; a pandit was asked to make an offering of a cow in his name. Tripathi's youngest son, a judge in the high court at Allahabad, arrived in the village with a car to take his father to Kashi. After several hot and dusty hours they arrived and went straight to the house of the eldest son, a surgeon, who lived near the Banaras Hindu University hospital. The surgeon, the man who told me this story three years later, found his father unconscious and lying tightly packed across the back seat of his brother's Ambassador car.

They took him down to Banaras Hindu University hospital, where he got very good treatment because the surgeon knew all the doctors there. They tried for three days to revive him but nothing worked. The doctors explained the situation and eventually the surgeon came to accept that it was true, nothing could be done. As a doctor himself, the surgeon felt it was a little wrong because, strictly speaking, in the legal sense, they should always continue their efforts to revive a patient. But this was his father, and as a son he decided to go with "his sentiments and morality" and made the decision to remove his father from the hospital and to put him on the bank of the river Ganga. When he started gasping for air—a surefire sign, the surgeon told me, that death is imminent—they made preparations to move him. They took him by rickshaw across the Asi River, the southern boundary of the city, and into Kashi. From Asi ghat they carried him through some narrow winding lanes following the bank of the river north, until they came to Tulsi ghat. There, on the huge stone steps leading fifty feet down to the river, is a stone structure with a roof and three walls. The missing wall provides a panorama of the river Ganga sweeping auspiciously south to north. They took him in and laid him on the stone floor with his head to the north. They expected that he would die very quickly but, to everybody's astonishment, he did not. He recovered slightly. He stopped gasping, though he never regained consciousness; it is doubtful he ever knew where he had ended up. He lived there on the edge of the river for two full days before the gasping returned and his life slipped away. Within hours his body had been wrapped in colorful cloth and carried through the lanes of Kashi, the bearers chanting *"Rama Nam Satya Hai"* (the name of Rama is truth), to Harischandra ghat where it was placed on a pile of wood and set ablaze.

Though this story is from the 1980s, in many ways it is a scene from earlier times. Nowadays, very few people die camped out in places on the edge of the river. Things have changed; even the pilgrimage to die has been changed by the times. In what follows I will discuss the phenomenon of traveling to Kashi to die, with the objective of sketching a cultural setting and constructing a history in which this old pattern, and the newer institutions, make sense.

Pilgrimage to Kashi

For a Hindu, Bharat (India) is a land covered with sacred mountains, flowing with sacred rivers, and dotted with sacred cities, all of which are tied together by sacred pilgrimage routes. Going on pilgrimage to see the sacred sights has long been an important part of Hinduism and it is a part whose import is increasing in the modern era as more and more pilgrims set off on journeys (Fuller 1992, 204–23). It used to be that pilgrimage was a dangerous enterprise; the roads were full of robbers or wild animals and outbreaks of cholera awaited in the crowds at the destination. As Srinivas (1976, 321) told us, in the early twentieth century "a pilgrimage to Banaras [Kashi] was regarded as a hazardous enterprise though much less so [than] in the nineteenth century when a pilgrim's successful return from it was a fortuitous accident." Trains, buses, and private vehicles have made pilgrimage significantly less demanding and the mass media has improved the knowledge of ordinary people about India's sacred centers, resulting in an increase in pilgrimage.

A pilgrimage, for many, is commonly combined with ordinary tourism; a clear distinction between sacred and secular journeying is difficult to make. However, at the heart of a pilgrimage is often a visit to a *tirtha,* a "crossing place." Often, *tirthas* are places, as the name suggests, where a river can be forded. This is true of Kashi, where like at many pilgrimage destinations, it is the river itself which is an object of pilgrimage. Kashi is always included in the list of seven holy cities, a list which is variably completed by six of Hardwar, Ayodhya (Rama's capital), Mathura (Krisna's birthplace), Dwarka (Krishna's capital), Kanchipuram, Ujjain, Brindavan, and Gokul (Fuller 1992, 206). These pilgrimage centers and many more, can be considered "all-Indian" to the extent that their importance would be attested to all over India, even though people far afield would be unlikely to visit them. These are differentiated from many other pilgrimage spots of mostly regional significance. Rajastani villagers, for instance, distinguish between *yatra* and *jatra;* the former indicating a pilgrimage to a *tirtha,* and the latter indicating a short trip to any of numerous local shrines (Gold 1988, 136).

Though *tirthas* are often places on rivers where a crossing is possible, they are more generally places where the gap is narrowed between divine and human worlds, between sacred and secular. Fuller (1992, 207) suggested that the term *tirtha* also contains a reference to the terrible Vaitarni River, a river flowing with urine, blood, and pus and inhabited by terrible monsters, which the dead must cross on their journey to Yama, the God of death. He went on to say that the crossing of this river is understood as liberation from rebirth *(moksha)* suggesting that the importance of a pilgrimage to a *tirtha* during life is that it will help you cross the river after death. What is certain is that these pilgrimage spots are associated with obtaining great boons, including the wiping out of all sins and the accumulation of great spiritual merit. The most precious spiritual goal of all, *moksha,* is said to be also attainable at some *tirthas,* especially Kashi. In fact, all the big pilgrimage centers claim to be vastly superior to all the others, but Kashi is probably the most widely accepted as preeminent, and so to many is *the* holy city of the Hindus.[1]

How long have people been coming to Kashi to die? The assumption of most people I talked to was that it has been going on for as long as Kashi has been there—which to them is forever. There is not much written history of coming to Kashi to die; it is mostly the stuff

FIGURE 3.1

A *rogi marnewala* (afflicted dying person) and his son at Kashi Labh Muktibhavan

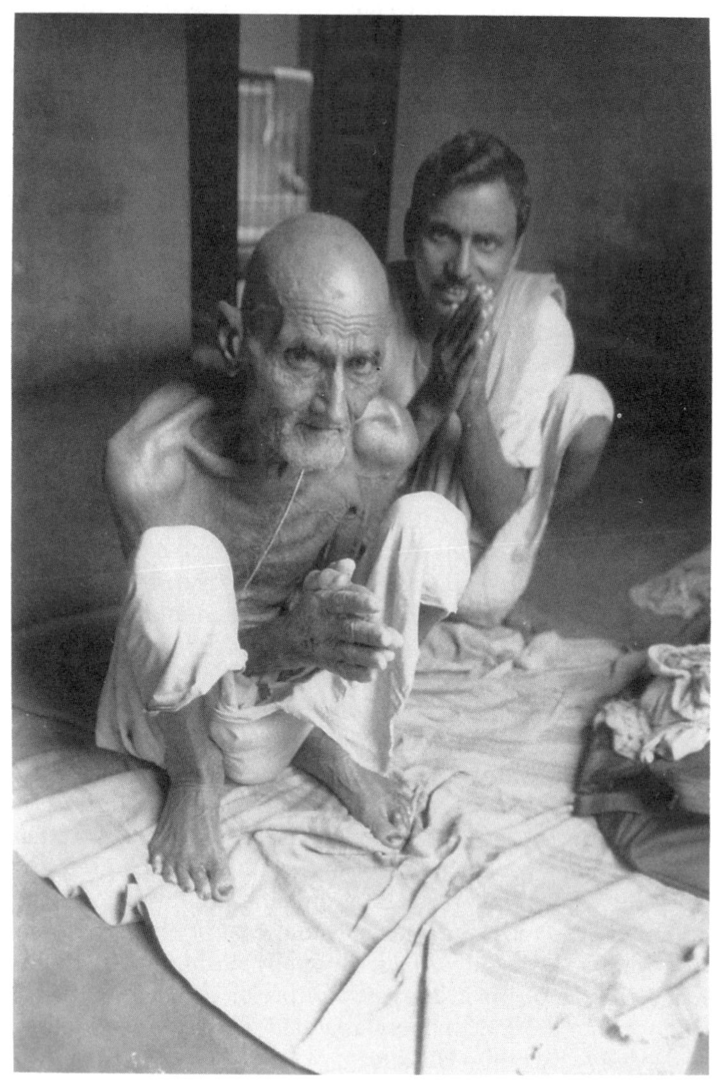

of myths and legends. Eck (1982, 5) argues that, "It is not the events of its long history that make it (Kashi) significant to Hindus, rather it has such a long history, and it has changed and flourished through the changing fortunes of the centuries *because* it is significant to the Hindus." It is tempting to accept this and dismiss the need to understand dying in Kashi in its historical development. But there is another perspective, the other half of a dialectic, which sees the religious significance of Kashi as a product of historical processes, rather than the driving force behind these processes.

Pilgrimage to Kashi can be seen in relationship to pilgrimage to other *tirthas.* In particular, the important triad of Kashi, Prayag (Allahbad), and Gaya all have a historic association with death which continues to the present day. The entrenchment of pilgrimage in Hindu society seems to have occurred well before the "Christian Era" and the compilation of the Puranas, a body of literature dated to between the third and eleventh centuries AD. The Puranas, according to Bhardwaj (1973, 71), seem to "have fixed the major lineaments" of the sacred geography of India. Bhardwaj argued that while people must have undertaken pilgrimage for a variety of reasons in these early times, one of the major reasons for undertaking a pilgrimage was to perform religious rites for the dead. Kashi, Prayag and Gaya, all cities on or near the River Ganges and in the heart of orthodox Hinduism, developed as important sites for death rituals (Bayly 1981, 161) and quickly developed classes of priests dedicated to pilgrims and death rites.

Gaya, where it is widely accepted that performing a *shraddha* ritual results immediately in one's dead relatives achieving *moksha,* was the most popular *tirtha* in the Puranas, as measured by the number of times it received mention and praise in these works. However, by the twelfth century, according to Bhardwaj, things had changed a little. The association of North Indian pilgrimage sites with flowing water and especially the Ganges had become well established, and it appears that Kashi had surpassed Gaya and other *tirthas* as the most popular pilgrimage spot. The text *Agastyasamhita,* composed in Kashi in the twelfth century, refers to Kashi as *Muktiksetra,* a place which bestows *moksha* on all who visit it (Bakker 1986, 69).

Bayly (1981) wrote that Kashi seems to have developed its present form since about 1600. The majority of the ghats, temples, and resthouses for pilgrims were constructed between 1730 and 1810, a transitionary period between Moghul and British rule. Gaya and Prayag seem to have also become elaborate pilgrimage cities in roughly the same time period. Bayly suggested that the surge in interest in pilgrimage cities reflects the unity conferred on India by the consolidation of the Moghul Empire, under which pilgrimage prospered as travel became safe and routes of communication opened.

Pilgrimage also seems to have prospered under the British. Bayly said that "between 1780 and 1820, the number of pilgrims who went to Allahabad (Prayag), Gaya and Benaras (Kashi) each year may have trebled." The people of the "new Hindu regimes" emerging in the eighteenth century and mostly in Western India, such as the Jats, Mahrattas, Rajputs, and Bhumihars, became great patrons of the pilgrimage cities. "By 1820," according to Bayly (1981, 165), "nearly eight per cent of the resident population [of Kashi] was Mahratta and the city was regularly visited by armed Mahratta pilgrimages of up to 200,000 men in the most auspicious years." The ritual centers benefited from the railways which came in around 1850. Bayly recounts a story told by Monier-Williams, a Sanskrit scholar, of the time in 1870 when he was told by a priest in Gaya that with the coming of the railway, he had noticed a sharp decrease in the number of ghosts, as people now were more easily and quickly arriving in Gaya to deliver their dead relatives from ghostdom (1981, 170).

The ritual specialists played an active role in spreading the fame of the holy places and the very need for conducting rituals in these places, according to Bayly. They had a near monopoly on the written word and were able to "embroider, and build up references to Benares (Kashi), Gaya, and other places in everyday devotional works, such as the Puranas which were subject to constant revision and recension" (1981, 165). Ledgers from *shraddha* priests, or *pandas,* show that *shraddha* at Gaya and Kashi had become "large-scale ritual industries" before 1800. The ledgers were necessary for a *panda* or familial line of *pandas* to maintain and enhance their clientele. *Pandas* used to make regular tours of the distant areas where their clients lived in order to remind them of their ancestors' needs. In Kashi several of the untouchable Dom families—the traditional operators of the burning ghats—amassed considerable fortunes.

It is difficult to assess the number of people who were coming to die in Kashi. Bayly (1981, 161) found figures in an old *District Gazetteer* which indicate that in Kashi between 1880 and 1908, there was an annual surplus of deaths over births of "about 24 per cent or 2–3,000 people out of a population of about 180,000." He interpreted this as meaning that there were a lot of elderly people coming to Kashi to die during this period. Qualitative evidence, he went on to say, suggests that this surplus of deaths over births has long been the case, though he did not say what that qualitative evidence is.

In the 1970s, L. P. Vidyarthi and his group (1979) went to Kashi to study the city as a "sacred complex" and pilgrimage destination. Among other things, they conducted interviews with 500 pilgrims who had come to Kashi. They reported that pilgrims come from every state in India, though generally more come from the closest states. Over 70 percent of the pilgrims they interviewed were on a repeat visit. Many of the pilgrimages, especially from the South, were "collective and commissioned" meaning that special buses or trains were organized in advance by pilgrimage organizers and pilgrims were gathered to fill the bus or train.

Vidyarthi's researchers also asked the pilgrims their main purpose for coming to Kashi. The authors do not make it clear, however, how they selected the pilgrims whom they interviewed and therefore it is hard to evaluate the significance of the following figures. Nevertheless, out of 500 pilgrims, they reported only one person whose stated purpose was to die in Kashi. Significantly, more had came for other death-related activities, such as 12 who had come to do a cremation, 14 who had come to consign relatives bones in the Ganga *(asthi pravaha)*, and 39 who had come to do rites for their dead ancestors *(pinda dan)*. From *panda*'s ledgers, they estimated that in 1972, about 40,000 pilgrims from all over India came to Kashi in the two-week period of *pitri paksh* (the fortnight of the ancestors) to do *pinda dan* for their ancestors (1979, 63).

The Kashi Karvat

Here I divert slightly to another aspect of the history of dying in Kashi and the possibility that in the past people came to Kashi in order to commit religious suicide. Kane (1973, 604) reported that although suicide is generally condemned by the *Dharmashastra* texts, there are some exceptions in the *Smritis*, epics, and *Puranas*. One exception prescribes religious suicide at either Prayag or Kashi. It is written in the *Padma Purana* that "A man who knowingly or unknowingly, willfully or unintentionally, dies in the Ganges secures on death heaven and *moksha*" and in the *Skanda Purana* it says, with reference to Kashi, "He who abandons his life in this holy place in some way or other does not incur the sin of suicide but secures his desired objects" (cited in Kane 1973, 607). The account of the Chinese traveler Yuan-Chwang, who was in India between AD 629 and AD 645, indicates that in addition to scriptural sanction, there actually was a tradition of traveling to pilgrimage centers and committing religious suicide in India. He wrote that people would arrive daily at the confluence of the Jamuna and Ganges rivers at Prayag to drown themselves in the sacred waters there (Chaudhari 1979, 55–57). In more recent times, according to Bayley (1981, 162), as per the instructions in the *Brahma Purana,* lepers' suicides were common near the great fort in Allahabad (Prayag) until the British authorities forbade them in the 1810s.

In Kashi, several people told me that they had heard it said that a long time ago people used to come to the city and commit suicide at the Kashi Karvat temple in order to get *moksha.* Parry (1981, 349) described suicide in this temple as if it were remote in the mythological past: "it is said that in a less corrupt age a karvat, or saw, was suspended from the roof of the shrine and would spontaneously fall on those on whom Shiva chose to bestow his blessing." The story which I was told by one of the Kashi Karvat Temple priests, however, located the custom in the more immediate past, just before the arrival of the British. As I will show, it is likely that the difference between Parry's story and the one I was told represents the evolution of a legend over the last couple of decades.

The Kashi Karvat Temple is located in the maze of choked alleyways in the vicinity of Vishvanath Mandir, the area most frequented by pilgrims to Kashi. Omji and I visited there one day. Winding our way through the heart of the city and up through a narrow *gali* we arrived at a small unostentatious entranceway. "Kashi Karvat" is written in Devanagari script on a tile sunk into the pavement, otherwise the temple entrance is unmarked. Inside, the temple is focused around a hole in the floor which opens into a large cavernous room below. On the floor of this room, about 30 feet down and directly below the opening, is a Shiva *linga*—the phallic, stone emblem of Shiva and main focus of his worship—which the *pujari* says sprang out of the ground on its own accord. He explained that the lower floor level was the original level of the city of Kashi, before a lot of people lived there and the level was gradually built up. The temple takes its name from the *karvat* (weapon or saw) which used to be down in this lower room, directly beneath the opening. Before British times, people used to come and obtain *moksha* by throwing themselves down the hole and onto the blade, thus killing themselves. They would go straight to heaven, as from the temple, below this room, there is a direct water connection with the Ganges.

The *karvat* apparently has its origins in a story from the *Skanda Purana.* Lord Krishna came one day, riding on his tiger, to test a certain king. He and his wife had only one son. Krishna demanded that they give their son up as meat for his hungry tiger. It was very important never to send a guest away hungry and, realizing it was a test, they agreed. Husband and wife, on either end of a saw, cut up their son and fed him to the tiger. Krishna was very pleased. The king was rewarded, the son was brought back to life, and the saw became famous as being a direct link to Krishna. It is this very saw which ended up in the Kashi Karvat temple.

The temple priest told me the British outlawed this institutionalized practice of suicide. Furthermore, they took the saw, the Kashi Karvat, off to some museum in Britain. Omji thought this likely, likening the situation to the banning, by the British, of *sati*—the burning of widows with their dead husbands—and sacrifice (though, he added, these things still go on). In any case, there seems to be no evidence that religious suicide occurs these days in Kashi and my research is consistent with that of Parry (1981, 350), whose informants regard suicide either equivocally or as sanctioned by stiff spiritual penalties. It is unlikely, too, that religious suicide was important in the immediate past.

It is likely that the legend of Kashi Karvat is a relatively recent adaptation of some old stories. The temple is on the figurative edge of the pilgrimage circuit and it is to the advantage of its owners and *pujaris* to more firmly entrench it there. The connection to Krishna by the saw, to *moksha* by the Ganges, and to Shiva who ultimately is the giver of *moksha,* accomplishes just this. Whether recent legend or ancient history, the pilgrims coming to Kashi hear the stories I heard and in this way, either recently or a longer time ago, they have become a part of the lore of Kashi and are contributing to its fame as a place for dying. This is an example of the ongoing process by which Kashi has become the holiest of holy cities for many Hindus.

Kashi-vasa and *Kashi-labh*

While people do not seem to come to Kashi to commit religious suicide, they definitely do come to die by "natural" means. There are two obvious categories of people coming for this purpose. As Parry (1981, 350) noted, there are "those who come for *Kashi-vasa* and those who come for *Kashi-labh*" (diacritics omitted). *Kashi-vasis* are those who have come to Kashi in their declining years to live a religious life and to await death while those brought for *Kashi-labh* are those who come "at the eleventh hour"—just in time to die (Eck 1983, 329).

The many widows who live in Kashi are, for instance, described by Saraswati as *Kashi-vasis.* They are there he said, "with a view to obtaining *punya* (merit), and reaching *mukti* at the moment of death"

(1985, 107). However, there are also deep sociological reasons why there are so many widows in Kashi. According to an earlier account by Saraswati (1975, 60):

> It has been the practice of Brahmin families in most parts of India to send their widows to Kashi where they have to live all their life. Although a cruel method, the Brahmanic society unburdens itself from the problems of widows by creating a sacred retreat for them.

It is interesting that many of the "*Kashi-vasi* widows" are from Bengal, where the custom of *sati* was most prevalent in pre-British times. The abolishment of this practice may be related to the practice of sending widows to Kashi.

The categories of *Kashi-vasa* and *Kashi-labh* are a bit problematic. *Kashi-labh* is the reward for dying in Kashi and *Kashi-vasa* is the condition of living in Kashi. They are not fully comparable categories. Someone who has come for *Kashi-labh* is in fact experiencing *Kashi-vasa* up to his or her death. On the other hand, people who come to Kashi for *Kashi-vasa* may be motivated to do so by the promise of eventually getting *Kashi-labh.* The problem is that the term *Kashi-vasa,* as it has been used, refers to a number of things. For some, it is living in Kashi for the last part of their lives which is important. For others, the reason to be in Kashi is to ensure that you die in Kashi.

Kashi-vasa is also the reason for the settlement of many ethnic areas of the city such as Bengali Thola and Dudh Vinainik where the Nepalis live. These people came for *Kashi-vasa;* they would come and live for three or four months a year and for major holidays. Only when they were old did they move permanently to Kashi and lived the holy life until their deaths. For these people, the importance of being in Kashi was both living in the holy city of Lord Shiva and, eventually, dying there.

Saraswati (1983, 99) mentioned three types of *Kashi-vasa* recommended in the Puranic scriptures, though the exact source is not given. *Kartika-vasa* refers to staying in Kashi for the one month of Kartika. *Garba-vasa* refers to staying in Kashi for nine months, as in the mother's womb, without once crossing the border. There is also *Kshetra sannyasa* in which the idea is to stay in Kashi forever. In fact, pilgrims are recommended to break their legs on a stone so that they will not be able to carry them out of the city.

In my experience, these textual prescriptions were far from reality. I never heard mention of one or nine month pilgrimages. I met a few and heard of a lot of people who had taken a vow of not leaving Kashi, but none had broken their legs. *Kshetra sannyasa* refers to people who have "renounced" the world and there are many experiencing *Kashi-vasa* in Kashi. But there are a lot of non-*sannyasa* people who have come for *Kashi-vasa* and plan to live the rest of their lives in Kashi. Some of the ones I met would leave the city occasionally for one reason or another.

A more adequate, though an outside or *etic* classification of those who have come to Kashi to die (however far off in time death might be) is in terms of the four *ashramas* (life stages). According to textual prescription, lives should be lived in four distinct stages each with different goals. The reality is far more complex. Some local traditions prescribe different numbers of stages and probably most people, especially non-Brahmins, do not follow the prescription fully or at all. Nevertheless, ideally the first stage is studenthood *(brahmacharya)*, in which the goals are to become ritually functional and to prepare for future life. At marriage the Brahmin enters the householder stage *(grihastya)*, the goals of which are the raising of a family, enjoyment and the acquisition of material wealth. When children are grown up and themselves beginning to marry, one should hand over one's business, wealth, and material possessions to one's offspring and begin to concentrate on spiritual goals *(vanprasthya)*. The final stage is a radical renunciation *(sannyasa)* of all material possessions, home, and even husband or wife.

People from all four life stages are supposed to be attracted to Kashi where it is said they will more easily accomplish all four of the prescribed life goals *(purusharthas)*. However, people from the final three life stages definitely do come specifically for the fourth and ultimate goal—*moksha. Sannyasis* are said to be bound for moksha no matter where they die but nevertheless Kashi is a major center for them and many have taken vows to never leave the city. *Vanprastis* retire to Kashi to live out the rest of their days and eventually to die. The move to Kashi is essentially a move into this third life stage from the householder stage. Finally, householders *(grihastyas)*, go simply for the reward of dying in Kashi. Their period of residence in Kashi is only a matter of days and is not really part of the objective. Householders go at the very last moment, having formally never left the material world of the family. Symbolically, perhaps, the last minute dash to die in Kashi could be considered a last minute transformation of life stage level to *vanprasti* or *sannyasi*, but it was not seen that way by the people who are doing it. Unlike the *vanprasti* and *sannyasi*, they were not aware or concerned about their stage in life. They simply came for *moksha.* As I will show, householders do not come alone, as do *sannyasis* or *vanprastis*[2] but are brought by their families who stay with them through their dying. It is householders *(grihastyas)* coming for *Kashi-labh,* the benefit of simply dying in Kashi, who are the subject of this book.

The Bhavan at Tulsi Ghat

The surgeon's father from the narrative at the beginning of this chapter was a householder who was brought into the city of Kashi to die so he would obtain the reward of *Kashi-labh.* He was brought only when it seemed death might be imminent. He was taken first to the hospital and only when there was no chance to save him was he brought in to Kashi. But it was more than just chance that he was at the Banaras Hindu University hospital, just at the edge of the zone of *moksha.* It was well planned, for the surgeon's father's death was just one of a family tradition of dying in Kashi on the bank of the Ganga.

The surgeon's grandfather, years before, at the age of 82 fell down and fractured his femur. He came to Kashi and stayed in a little house in Shivala, a neighborhood near the little place for the dying at Tulsi ghat, for two months. A doctor was looking after him at this time. When he became terminal he was taken to the bank of the Ganga at Tulsi ghat. He died that very same day. More recently there had been a spate of family deaths: the surgeon's father's had been the third of three deaths in his family just months apart. His uncle died first and quite suddenly in the village. They had had no time to bring him to die but they brought his body to Kashi and cremated it on the steps at Harischandra ghat. His "cousin-grandfather" was next. He was about ninety. He had many "geriatric problems" and was an invalid. "The people in the village thought that probably he is not going to survive. People can anticipate this," the surgeon told me. So he was brought and put on the bank of the Ganga. He lived there on the river bank for a full week, fully conscious, before dying.

The surgeon said that it was a family tradition to die on the bank of the Ganga at Tulsi ghat. He knew for sure that his great-grandfather died there as did his grandfather and father, and he thought it went back even much farther than that. Several women in the family had also died there including his "cousin-grandmother." They try to bring everybody. At least this was true in the past, "but in this period, people are forgetting," he said referring to tradition.

The surgeon maintained that everybody from the village would like to come and die in Kashi but only the well-off people can manage it. He reckoned that the desire to die in Kashi comes from exposure to religious books and that his father was largely responsible for the villagers' desire to go to Kashi. "People from all castes used to come to my father's house every evening. Harijan, non-Harijan—everyone. And they would listen to the *Gita, Ramayana, Mahabharata.* From this they got the desire." His grandfather did much the same thing, and he and his father learned this from him. "All the surrounding villages have the same desire. It is the culture of eastern Uttar Pradesh and Bihar. It is these people who are brought to Kashi to die or be burned. It is not just my family, it is a tradition." Only about one or two people a year actually come from his village to die on the bank of the Ganga, however. More would come but it is too expensive. Even though they can stay for free, there is the matter of transportation, food, and other items. And, also, the dying do not come alone but with several family members. In addition to being expensive, "it's not very practical."

As the surgeon saw it, the point of the pilgrimage to die in Kashi is to put an end to the cycle of birth, death, and rebirth:

> At death the soul leaves the body and step by step moves up toward heaven. At each step the soul is tortured by the gods working for Yama Raj (Lord of Death). If the soul doesn't make it (to heaven), it must descend down to hell from where it will eventually take rebirth. We don't believe that rebirth is a good thing. We don't want to come on this world again and again. That is why we want *moksha;* to have a place in heaven and not be reborn.

The chosen spot, the bank of the Ganga at Tulsi ghat, has some properties which make it the best place to die in Kashi though the surgeon didn't remember what they were. He said, "it is written in some *slokas* [verses], somewhere," though he acknowledged that generally the riverbank is preferred for dying over places away from the river. Now, however, the people from his village may specifically go to Tulsi ghat not so much for traditional reasons as for pragmatic reasons. The one room for the dying at Tulsi ghat is the last of its kind. On the other ghats there are no such places to stay. Also, being at the boundary of the city, Tulsi ghat is very convenient for bathing and from nearby Asi one can take a boat over to the other side of the Ganges for toilet facilities. The village people also like the fresh air and open space of Tulsi ghat, as opposed to the very crowded and hectic conditions at other ghats.

The surgeon was in the position of semi-outsider to what is going on in the village and how people think about dying. He grew up in the village in a pious household and heard many of the scriptural texts being read regularly. He had heard about, witnessed, and participated in many enactments of his family tradition of dying in Kashi on the bank of the Ganga. On the other hand, he had not lived in the village for most of his adult life but instead, lived in an enclave of academics on the Banaras Hindu University campus. In conversation he subtly distanced himself from the beliefs which are behind the family tradition, though he maintained that they are also his beliefs. This was evident in his use of words when, in answer to my query, he told me that when somebody is dying a pandit is asked "to put a *gau dan* on the name of the dying person." The gift of the cow, he said, will help him across the Vaitarni River:

> Now the belief is that he will go to heaven if he dies in Kashi, but if *I* have given a *gau dan* at his time of departure, probably his cow will pull *me* across the river even if I don't die in Kashi. If the person is dying quickly, gasping for air, people will act very quickly. Sometimes I laugh about this but it is always done. Other people are very serious about it.

It may be that as the surgeon ages and approaches death, he will take these traditions more seriously. On the other hand, it may be that the family tradition will end with the surgeon and his brother the judge.

In fact, there is change afoot more generally. The little place at Tulsi ghat which the surgeon's family uses is the last of its kind and the number of people coming to die there seems to be decreasing by the year. The person who owns the room for the dying on Tulsi ghat, a man named Mahantji, lives in a large mansion directly behind the ghat. The house occupies most of the river bank above the steps. Mahantji also owns the Sanskrit school next door, and is the owner and *mahant* (monastic head) of one of the largest and most popular temples in Kashi. He is a scientist at Banaras Hindu University and speaks internationally on water clean-up projects such as that being attempted on the Ganga, a project of which he is in charge.

Mahantji's family has lived at Tulsi ghat for eighty years or so. He believes that people were coming to Tulsi ghat to die when his family moved there. In his opinion, people have been coming to die there for hundreds of years. Now it is a simple operation; he merely keeps the room available. There are no records kept, there is no rent to pay. People can just arrive and there is a room to die in. Sometimes, Mahantji says, they stay for one or two months. More often they die within fifteen days. In general, he says, very poor people come. (But this is the statement of a very rich man and must be put in perspective; the surgeon's family, at least, is not poor from most perspectives.) Mahantji thinks that the people using his room mostly come from eastern Uttar Pradesh and northern Bihar, districts like Gorakpur, Devoria, and Chapra.

Mahantji has maintained the place for the dying because he does not want to "break the tradition." In his opinion, Tulsi ghat is located in an important part of Kashi known as *Kedar khand,* dying in which one does not get the *Bairavi yatna* (torture administered after death and before *moksha* by Lord Bairav). Tulsi ghat is also where Tulsidas, the man who wrote the *Ramcharitmanas,* lived and died. For these reasons it is important to Mahantji that people continue to have the opportunity to die at Tulsi ghat.

When Mahantji was in high school—roughly thirty-five years ago—he remembers that there were about eight or ten people coming there to die every month. Now the number has fallen to no more than five people per year. He sees this as part of a more general trend: "There were many more people coming in the past, there is no doubt about it. If today one hundred people were coming, then in 1950 perhaps one thousand people were coming, minimum." Most of those people were staying along the river on the *ghats. Ghats* like Manikarnika and Panchganga were used in great number, he says.

According to Mahantji, many years ago, perhaps up to about seventy years ago, people used to go to all the famous ghats in Kashi and just camp out there and wait to die. There were many structures like the one at Tulsi ghat; simple buildings in which people could sleep and cook their food. Some may have been reserved for this purpose but probably most of them were just empty and unused buildings. But as time went by the ghats became more and more used for specific purposes and more and more crowded. The facilities disappeared. When a room or building started to be used for something else then the people could no longer stay there. In addition to the loss of facilities, the police nowadays do not allow people to just sleep down on the ghats near the river.

This very thing happened at Tulsi ghat, though it was a conscious decision rather than simply the result of crowding and competition for space. Originally, the building which now contains the Sanskrit school just behind the little room on the steps, was used for the *mokshartis* (those coming for *moksha*). But they decided to turn it into a Sanskrit school between 1970 and 1975, and so it, like the other places, is no longer available for dying.

Another change also occurred. Mahantji feels that nowadays,

FIGURE 3.2

Dying pilgrim and family waiting for a room

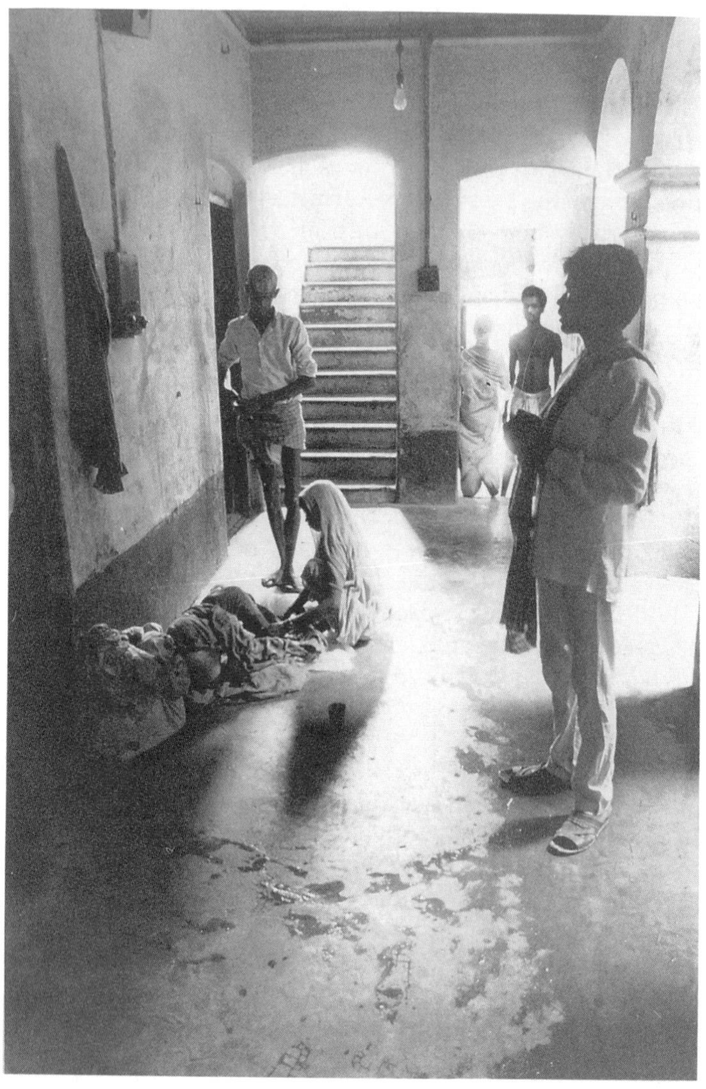

people want more than just the simple shelter to die in. The one at Tulsi ghat is very simple and open, facing on to the river. In fact it is flooded every year for three months when the monsoon rains raise the river to the top of its banks. He feels that people now want toilets and other things and a couple of times a year he gets requests for such things from people who have come there. He thinks that if he makes such facilities available then more people will come again, but he probably will not do it. The demand is related to the increased population of Kashi: along with more buildings has gone a loss of open spaces. Before, at Tulsi ghat, people could just walk down to Asi and use the open space for a toilet. There are now buildings where the open spaces were.

I searched the bank of the Ganga and talked to many people but I never heard of another such place as the room for the dying at Tulsi ghat. If it is true that years ago they were dotted along the riverbank, then the room at Tulsi ghat is the remnant of an old tradition. The loss of facilities along the river did not, however, result in the end of the tradition of coming to Kashi to die. It simply resulted in an increase in dying people with no place to die. This is a scenario that fits with the story told to me of the origins of the Rama Krishna Mission Hospital.

Ramakrishna Mission Hospital

The Ramakrishna Mission Hospital is now a medical hospital of roughly 200 beds which is run by the charity of the Ramakrishna Mission and is based on the philosophy of Vivekanand where, according to their brochure, "spiritual people do charitable work for the poor." It is an eye-catching place as the staff generally prefers saffron robes to white lab coats. Many of the medical doctors are also *sadhus;* they are religious men who have "renounced" the material world and do their medical work as a type of religious discipline.

The hospital grounds are tranquil and park-like; a contrast to the bustling city just outside the walls. Off one of the busiest streets, a large, ornate gate heralds the driveway and small administration building. Inside the compound, an unpaved ring road encircles an inner area of grass, bougainvillea, and palm trees. Perhaps ten buildings form the various departments and concerns of the hospital. I met Swami Shivishvaranand, a tall, bespectacled man dressed in flowing saffron robes with a shaved head and a stethoscope around his neck. He told this history of the Ramakrishna Mission hospital.

Before the turn of the century, about 100 years ago, dying people had no place to stay in Kashi and were dying on the streets. In 1898 some of Ramakrishna's followers in Kashi started going around the city and picking up the dying as a social service. They had hired a couple of rooms where they could keep and look after four or five dying people. After about ten years they needed more space and they decided to make it a permanent operation.

This is the official story of the hospital's early days. It makes good political sense for such an institution to have such a history, especially in Kashi, and it is difficult to evaluate its truth value. Nevertheless, the situation it portrays at about one hundred years ago is consistent with what I heard elsewhere. It seems that there were enough dying people in Kashi without places to stay that people felt the need to act on the situation. It is unlikely that the dying people were from Kashi as they would have had places to stay and people to care for them. It is likely they were pilgrims who had come to Kashi to die but had found that the traditional places along the river were no longer available.

The Ramakrishna Mission Hospital changed over the years from a place dedicated to the dying to something more and more "like a normal hospital." The hospital, like others, is now oriented to saving lives. There are, however, certain restrictions as to the availability of the hospital to certain people which differentiate it from other hospitals. People who have attempted suicide, for instance, are not allowed admission to the hospital. Also people with infectious diseases, such as smallpox—a disease thought by many to still exist—and chickenpox, and people who have had accidents, including being burned, are not admitted. "Medico-legal cases are not treated here. There are certain technical restrictions," is the explanation Shivishvaranand offered me. But there is another possibility: such cases also fit into the category of immoral sicknesses—sicknesses which would result in a morally bad death.

Another way that the Ramakrishna Mission Hospital differs from a "normal" hospital is that even now there are homes on the grounds for old people who want to spend their last days in Kashi but have no place to stay there or anybody to look after them. There are three homes in total where *mumukshus* (seekers of *moksha*) can stay: "one for old women, one for old men, and one for old monks." These homes usually take in those people who have worked for the Mission in their younger years. The homes are not homes for the dying *per se* but are where people live who have come to spend their last days in Kashi and eventually to die there. The mission also has such homes in other places because "some, but not all, are interested in dying in Kashi."

Hospital policy seems to be an uncomfortable compromise between traditional Hindu attitudes toward death and modern medico-legal concerns. If a person who is dying arrives at the hospital they will not be admitted. Swami feels that this would be the policy of all medical institutions as it would be unethical to accept such a dying person; it would be taking their money for nothing and it would be offering them and their families false hope. In such cases the doctors sometimes recommend that the family take the dying person to one of the institutions for the dying in Kashi like the Kashi Labh Muktibhavan.

On the other hand, if a patient is on life support, said Shivishvaranand, the doctors will never turn it off. If somebody asked them to let their father die the doctors would not do it; they would not completely cut off the medicine needed to keep the patient's vital functions going. However, the family can, if they want, take the patient home (and thus off the life support system).

> In our hospital we are in a sense more liberal, or you may use the word careless also. We will say "Oh, let him die." We don't really treat much. We have this invalids home for old men, other than the monks. When we find someone there in such a state that he cannot get up, take food or is losing his mental functions, then we try to serve him as much as is practical but don't become heroic, you know, with trying to save him.

There is another institution which houses dying people in Kashi which should be mentioned: the Mother Theresa charity home for the dying which was previously the Nirmal Hirdy Ashram and before that, the Din Sin Sadguti Nivas. Like the Ramakrishna Mission ninety years ago, Mother Theresa's workers still go around to places like the train station and pick up the destitute dying. I interviewed the nun who was temporarily in charge of the institute which is located in a large and grand building near Kedar ghat. She told me that mostly the people who are dying there are Hindus who have arrived in Kashi with no money and without family to look after them. Some die very quickly, within a week, and others live there for a decade or so. The home provides food and medicine and though their stated objective is to treat and cure people, they acknowledge that mostly everybody dies. There was a total of seventy-four patients there when I visited in 1990 and I was told about fifty people die there each year.

Summary of History and the Present Situation

Kashi seems to have a long history of attracting people to die. One type are those in the *grihastha* stage of life—people who have not moved beyond the householding stage—who are brought by their families to Kashi more or less on their death beds. In the distant past, according to the glowing descriptions of the ancient texts, Kashi was a beautiful forest in which people could pleasantly camp. In the more recent past, according to some people's memory, those coming to die in Kashi could go to one of the ghats along the riverbank, where there were buildings or rooms in which they could take shelter and await death.[3] Growth and modernization over the last two or three generations has resulted in fewer and fewer such facilities being available. After independence all the religious schools and institutions which previously were private, were put by the government under the auspices of one or another university and before independence, according to Omji, the majority of the *mathas* and *ashramas*[4] in Kashi had come under the control of organized sects. At any rate, many of the places for the dying along the river seem to have been absorbed by other interests and began to be used for different purposes. It is also no longer possible to just sleep on the bank of the river. Not only will the police not let people camp out along the river in the city, but also there is a danger now of being harassed and robbed that did not exist before. Omji says that even ten years ago people used to come and sleep on the ghat, but these days the river banks are deserted at night.

Despite the new difficulties and lack of facilities, people did not stop coming to Kashi for *Kashi-labh.* Rather they kept on coming and a need arose for places to house the dying. One hundred years ago the founders of the Ramakrishna Mission hospital recognized this need, as probably did the founders of the institution which is presently the Mother Theresa home for the dying and destitute.

The need was also recognized by a few big industrialist families a little more recently. They responded by independently setting up charitable organizations which began to run large institutions specifically for housing people coming to Kashi to die. Parry (1981) mentions the existence of three such institutions when he did fieldwork in Kashi in the late 1970s. When I went to Kashi in 1990, there were only two.

Kashi Ganga-Labh Bhavan at Manikarnika Ghat

Mr. Upadhya can often be found in his usual place, a cubby-hole in the side of a building in Manikarnika ghat, an area surrounded and cut off from the world by the river Ganga and a labyrinth of narrow alleys. Across the alley, Upadhya faces out onto a mammoth pile of wood, wood that is destined to be stacked into pyres and to carry souls toward heaven. Upadhya's cubby-hole is the office of the Kashi Ganga-labh Bhavan, and Upadhya is the manager. The Ganga-labh Bhavan is in a rather auspicious place—right in the heart of Manikarnika, the center of the Hindu universe, where it is said bodies have been burning continuously since time immemorial. Often gusts of cremation smoke, with the unforgettable smell of burning flesh that has been basted with ghee, fill up Upadhya's office and the rooms of the Ganga-labh Bhavan.

Manikarnika is clearly a place of death and in addition to the burning ghat and the Ganga-labh Bhavan there are a couple of other significant features. Above where the bodies are burned is a yellow building which separates the Ganga-labh Bhavan from the river. A "very big capitalist" named Birla, Upadhya said, originally set this place up as a resthouse for people who came to the city with dead bodies for burning. After some years, however, it seems the building was "grabbed by beggars and that sort of people." Now, the "beggars," and usually some water buffaloes, are its main occupants: pilgrims with a dead body sometimes stay there for an hour or two, but not much longer.

On the right side of the ghat facing the river is a large building which used to be known as Vishvanath Seva Ashram, a place also started by Mr. Birla. According to Parry (1981) people were going there to die in the late 1970s. However, in 1990 they were not. Upadhya and Shuklaji, the manager of the other *bhavan,* told different stories about this place. Shuklaji says that people used to go there to die but that the place had some serious problems. Though it was supposed to be a religious trust (and therefore free) the employees had been extracting money from the dying people. It had become very corrupt, Shuklaji thought, and so had been shut down. Upadhya, on the other hand, claims it was never a place for the dying at all but was primarily aimed at curing people. The Vishvanath Seva Ashram was shut down about 1988, and the building now functions as a school and a medical dispensary. Once in a while, too, it is occupied by pilgrims doing the famous five-day *panchkroshi* pilgrimage around Kashi. At any rate, the Ganga-labh Bhavan is now the only place to die in Manikarnika ghat.

The Ganga-labh Bhavan is a three-story building which, Upadhya says, was at one time the Manikarnika police station. It is painted a light blue color but, like most buildings in Kashi, is mostly grey where the paint has been worn off by heat and monsoon rains. From the alley beside the cubby-hole, a narrow, dark tunnel runs up a flight of stairs and along a passage into the heart of the building, an open-air inner courtyard. Enough light streams down from the sky above that the weeds growing in the cracks along the end of the passage are thriving. About halfway along the passage is a pile of plaster and cement that long ago fell out of the wall but has been unattended to. Inside, the walls and pillars of the courtyard were, years ago, mustard yellow. Off the courtyard, four to a floor, are twelve dark, cavernous rooms in which the *rogi marnewalas,* the afflicted dying people, and their families make temporary homes. The rooms, also mustard yellow, are empty of furniture. Only bare light bulbs hang from the ceilings.

Graffiti are scrawled in charcoal all over the staircase and the walls of the rooms. But this is no ordinary graffiti; it is death graffiti, memorials of a kind to those who have died there.

Though there are dozens of these memorials on the inner walls of the Ganga-labh Bhavan, their number pales in comparison to the number of people who have died within these walls. According to Mr. Upadhya and the record book, about twenty-one thousand people have died here over the last sixty years or so. Having looked over the available records, however, I estimate the number to be closer to a still impressive ten thousand.

FIGURE 3.3

Death graffiti scrawled in charcoal on the interior walls of Ganga-labh Bhavan

Mother of
Dethendra Pd
Came here 19/9/86
Village: Nathanpur
Birlapur (Bihar)
She Dead 30/9/86
7:50 pm

Jagernath Shukla
Reached 6/9/89 AND
Daid on 15/10/89 Village Bhagalipur
P.O. Jangigang
Dist. Varanasi

Upadhya claimed that the Ganga-labh Bhavan was the first of its kind. He, himself, has been there since 1965 and another manager was there before him. The Ganga-labh Bhavan was apparently started by two "rich capitalist" families. They were Marvaris by caste, and Marvaris, I was told, typically do a lot of religious charity work. In the Indian calendric year 1990[5]—which was fifty-eight years before the 1990 when Upadhya was telling me this history—one of the "capitalist families" came and brought their grandmother for *Kashi-labh.* It seems that they had some difficulty in finding a place to stay with a dying person. After she died, they thought to themselves, "if *we* can't find a place to stay, then how will the poor people find a place?" They thought that it would be good if they could do something about it. So they leased the building from the municipality and started running it as a hostel for very old people coming to Kashi to die.

Another element of this story was added by a man named Mishra, the overseeing representative of the *bhavan's* trustees. Manikarnika ghat was selected as the site, he said, because there was an existing need—people came to Manikarnika ghat to die long before there was such a place—and because people like to die at Manikarnika ghat. For some it is a special place for dying, even within Kashi, and dying there results in *Ganga-labh,* the extra benefit of dying next to the river.

Nowadays, the place is run by a Charitable Trust, part of a large set of holdings of an industrialist family based in Calcutta. They have several business concerns in Kashi and several managers. Mishra, whose main responsibilities lie elsewhere, oversees the running of the Ganga-labh Bhavan. Actually he doesn't do much; he only sees the place once a month or so and he really only has to sign a few papers and distribute the small amount of money on which the place is run. Upadhya pretty well runs the place single-handedly, with only the help of a couple of sweepers.

Inside Upadhya's cubby-hole is a rickety wood-bladed fan and a small wooden bench. Behind the bench is a large black sign with all the rules of the *bhavan* written in small worn-out white letters. A translation of these rules can be found in Figure 3.4. Upadhya told me that the rules have been in existence from the very beginning (implying that they are older than the rules at the 'newer' bhavan which therefore copied theirs from his), though they were only written down twenty years ago.

The rules state that the Ganga-labh Bhavan is for very old people who are there to die, not to be saved, and who are essentially on the verge of death. The rules say nothing about age, but the manager says sixty years is the minimum. Could a thirty-year-old dying of cancer stay there? "No," says the manager "because if I allowed that how

FIGURE 3.4

Translation of the signboard in the office of the Kashi Ganga-labh Bhavan

Sri Kashi-labh Bhavan Manikarnika Ghat of Varanshi
—Rules—

This Bhavan has been made for twice-born Hindus who come to stay in Sri Kashi with the purpose of obtaining moksha. Those noble people staying here will abide by the rules written below.

1. Those *rogis* [sick people] for whom there is no hope of being saved and who will die in 5 or 7 days can stay in Bhavan.

2. A *rogi* can stay at the most 15 days. After this, they will have to free up the Bhavan, having found another place by themselves.

3. *Rogis* with smallpox, plague, and cholera, and other untouchables, can absolutely not stay in this Bhavan.

4. At the most four extra people can remain with someone staying here. More people than this cannot stay.

5. Do not associate with those noble people staying at the resthouse next door (which was built for people who have come with a corpse) nor sit around there.

6. Within twenty-four hours of the *rogi* becoming *Kashi-labh (moksha),* the accompanying people must free up the Bhavan.

7. The people staying in the Bhavan shall have the duty of keeping their own places absolutely clean and tidy and should not mess up other areas of the Bhavan nor allow others to do so. Otherwise, cost of cleaning must be given.

8. People must pay 60 *praise* a day per bulb for electricity expenses.

9. Those people who come with the *rogi* are not allowed to use eggs, meat, garlic, onion, marijuana, *bhang* (edible cannabis), liquor, etc. No intoxicants may be used.

10. Those people staying here must watch their own things. If they lose anything, neither manager nor any worker will be responsible.

11. Each person staying here should pay special attention that they do not do things which may trouble or inconvenience other people.

12. Serious action can be taken against people found using the Bhavan's toilets, etc., other than those people having come with a *rogi.*

13. It is strictly forbidden to spit or write anything on the *Ganga Labh Bhavan's* walls, stairs, courtyard or verandah.

14. In addition to these rules, if anything reprehensible is seen being done by the people staying here, the manager has the authority to remove them.

15. No manner of reward or *bakesheesh* should be given to the manager.

16. Any complaint related to the *Bhavan* should be related to the manager. If he doesn't listen or if the complaint relates to the manager, it should be written to the below written address.

Time of opening from 5:00 in the morning until 9:00 at night

could I show the records to Mr. Mishra." "No," says Mr. Mishra, "because such a person could live any length of time. We accept people who will certainly die very quickly." This seems to be the main criteria for acceptance; although the rules say that people with infectious diseases are not allowed, Mishra says, if somebody comes who is just about to die nobody will bother about what kind of a sickness he has.

The rules say that you can't stay for more than fifteen days. Upadhya explained that there are two types of people coming to Kashi to die; people who come and stay for years before dying, and people who come just for dying. They cannot cater to the former type, he says. However, the categories aren't as clear-cut in practice as they are in Upadhya's theory and people sometimes stay more than fifteen days. In these cases Upadhya records the person as "returned home" on the fifteenth day and then registers them anew, as if they had just arrived. This has the effect of creating the illusion in the records that more people have come there to die than is actually the case.

According to the rules the place is for the twice-born people, which normally means the top three *varnas*, but which Upadhya said means only Brahmins. However, he also said, "when the other castes come what can we do? Mostly the low castes do not come anyway." This, in fact, is far from the truth; the records show that Brahmins account for less than one-third of the total. Mr. Mishra, on the other hand, perhaps acting his role as public spokesman, claimed that even in principle there is no discrimination by caste. "Anybody can use it," he said, "except gamblers, drug addicts, people who use alcohol, and others like that."

Upadhya has seen thousands of people come to die in the *bhavan* during his time there as manager. He said all sorts of people come: farmers and businessmen, educated and noneducated. Rich people do not come—it seems they only bring dead bodies for burning—and also very poor people do not come because they cannot afford it. Mostly people are from the state of Bihar, either Bhojpur or Rohtas districts. He remembered one person coming from Nepal and one or two people from Calcutta. Some people come after having been in a hospital, but most come straight from their homes. Most people are from small villages as opposed to cities. Upadhya estimated that about half the people come knowing that the Ganga-labh Bhavan is there for them and the other half just arrive in Kashi and find it once they are there.

My overall impression of the Ganga-labh Bhavan is that it has seen better times. Upadhya admitted that there are fewer people coming these days than before. He thought this is a general trend and blamed it on the rising cost of everything and the rising abusiveness of the burning ghat Doms and the other people who deal with the pilgrims. He told me that between six and seven hundred people (still) come to die there a year, even now. I was astounded when he told me this, as virtually every time I visited the Ganga-labh Bhavan it was completely empty. The records of the place show that there are, in fact, about one-eighth the number of people coming as Upadhya estimated.

Upadhya said, and the record book indicates, that since the place opened almost 21,000 people have died there. This would be around 350 per year if it were true. However, I found a huge gap in the registration numbers; in 1984 the registration number skipped from 10,983 to 20,000. If there is no similar jump in the pre-1975 records, which I could not examine, then at the most 12,000 people may have registered there. As previously mentioned, the numbers are apparently increased by registering the same person several times after each fifteen-day period; according to the records I examined this double-registering accounts for about five percent of all records.

In addition to the evidence from the records, several people told me stories about the Ganga-labh Bhavan and the troubles it is facing. Mishra, the trust representative, told me that from time to time "people who are not welcome" come and forcefully stay there. Also some people try to "grab" the building, probably the same type of people who took over the Birla resthouse. Shuklaji, manager of the Kashi Labh Muktibhavan, explained that it is the "*ganja* people"—by which he means drug-users—who are trying to "grab" the building. Ganga-labh Bhavan, in his view, is now a place which is "just like nothing." It is a place where (he said) he sends the people he will not accept at the Muktibhavan, like cancer patients and Harijans (Untouchables), or where he sends other people when the Muktibhavan is full.

Kashi Labh Muktibhavan

The Kashi Labh Muktibhavan was started, and continues to be operated, by a charity organization called the Dalmia Charitable Trust. This trust is one part of a large industrial organization run by the well-known Dalmia family. I met with them at their office complex, which occupies two floors of one of the tallest buildings in New Delhi. Jaydal Dalmia, then a man of 85, now dead, started both the industrial empire and the Kashi Labh Muktibhavan. My interview with him occurred in the presence of four of his son's cronies, who continually tried to answer for him. As his influence around the office was obviously diminishing, so too seemed to be the interest the head office took in the Muktibhavan.

Here is what they said about the Muktibhavan's origins: Before her death in Kashi, Jaydal Dalmia's mother refused to leave Kashi for fear of dying outside its boundaries. As her mother was dying, Dalmia became aware that there was no place to stay in Kashi for the poor people who come to die. He learned that *dharmsalas* and even hotels refused admission to those coming with a very sick person. Eventually he decided to buy a building where the poor and dying could stay.

This epiphany story is intriguingly similar to that of the origin of the Ganga-labh Bhavan. However, Shuklaji, the manager of the Muktibhavan, told me a more elaborate version. Dalmia's mother, he said, came to Kashi in her last days for *Kashi-labh.* She was staying at the Dalmia property at Ghai ghat, and she died there after some time. Dalmia and his brother had quite a bit of money for conducting the cremation and various ceremonies celebrating death. At the end they had some sixty thousand rupees left. They thought that because the money was connected to their mother's death that it must be used in some religious way. They went to the Mumukshu Bhavan and discussed the matter with the Swami who ran that place, whom they knew quite well. The Swami gave them one of his workers, a man named Chaubey, who became their manager (whom Shuklaji later replaced). Then they purchased a building with the money left from the funeral. At first they had no intention of starting a home for the dying. Their idea was to provide a place for *satsang* (association with good and pious men) where all the time there would be *bhajans* and *kirtans* (religious music and chanting) and recitation of the *Bhagavad Gita* going on. That was about 1955. It existed like that for a full year. Only after it was set up and running like that did they think "these people coming to die in Kashi have no support" and so they decided to invite dying people to stay there.

Chaubey spent the early days "advertising" the place. He mostly did this by going to villages, mostly in his home district of Rohtas, and telling people what types of things were available at the Muktibhavan. There was also a flyer (in Hindi) produced, though it is hard to know the extent to which it was distributed. Also, they initially advertised in Hindi newspapers. It seems as though they decided consciously to restrict it to Hindi language: Dalmia said that people from other areas, like the South, would have their own religious cities *(puris)* in which to die. The flyer, which can be seen in Figure 3.5, promises people a beautiful building with a range of conveniences they themselves probably do not have at home, as well as describing a religious atmosphere, dying in which would result in eternal peace for the soul, "of this

FIGURE 3.5

Flyer distributed in early days of the Kashi Labh Muktibhavan
(translated from Hindi)

In Kashi Labh-Mukti Bhavan
(for those sick people on the verge of death
coming for the benefit of Kashi)
A Free Place

It is very difficult for those sick people *(rogi)* on the verge of death who are coming from outside of Kashi to find a temporary place for a few days or a week or two. Addressing this limitation, the Dalmia-Jain trust has made available, as charity to the common man, a beautiful mansion by the name of "Kashi Labh Mukti-bhavan." In this place a whole room will be given to sick people and even a second room for accompanying family members or servants. Seats, string beds, stools, etc. will be arranged. Latrines, electric lights and other conveniences are available. Here, twenty-four hours per day, there is religious singing *(Hari-kirtan)* and from time to time the adoration of God *(Bhagavan ki arti)* is performed near the sick person who is given *tulsi* and water from the Ganga. There is the benefit *(satsang)* of hearing Gita and Ramayana and in this type of religious atmosphere *(dharmik vatavaran)* the sick person will get the benefit of Kashi *(Kashi labh)* and, according to the scriptures *(shastra)*, their soul *(atman)* will get absolute peace and salvation *(sadgati)*, of this there is no doubt.

You should profit from this charitable arrangement. You should correspond by letter for more of above information. You should bring the sick person only after getting information that rooms are free.

Manager
Muktibhavan

there is no doubt." After a year or so people started arriving at the Muktibhavan to die.

Some Trends in Use

Trends in the post-1975 records from the Ganga-labh Bhavan, when compared to those for the Muktibhavan, indicates that the Muktibhavan is the newer of the two presently operating bhavans. Figure 3.6 illustrates this point clearly. It shows that in 1975, the first year for which records[6] are available for the Ganga-labh Bhavan, there were more people going there than to the Muktibhavan. It also shows that, at least since 1975, there is a general trend of fewer and fewer people showing up at the Ganga-labh Bhavan every year. On the other hand, more and more people have been arriving at the Muktibhavan each

Figure 3.6

Trends in Dying: Graph showing the trends in numbers of people registering at the Muktibhavan, the Ganga-labh Bhavan, and the two combined, over time.

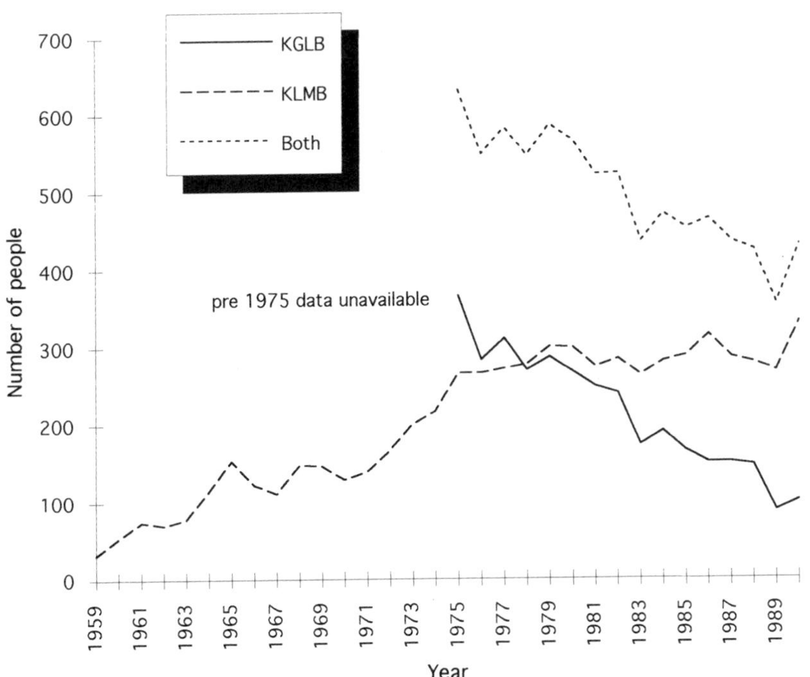

year from the time it was opened in the late fifties. The Ganga-labh Bhavan in 1975 registered 366 people but only 93 in 1990, an average decrease of about twenty people a year. At the Muktibhavan, in contrast, the number of people coming to die each year has been increasing by about ten and in 1990, 365 people were registered in the Muktibhavan. Extrapolation of these trends backward suggests that the Ganga-labh Bhavan was well established and busy at the time when the Muktibhavan was founded.

The difference between the increase at the Muktibhavan and the decrease at the Ganga-labh Bhavan is represented in the downward slope of the uppermost line on the graph in Figure 3.6; the overall trend for both institutions is a steady decrease in the numbers of people coming for *Kashi-labh.* Every year about thirteen fewer people have been arriving in Kashi to die, according to these figures. To the best of my knowledge, this represents a real trend in the numbers of such people coming to die in Kashi (that is to say, there are no other such institutions which are unaccounted for). This has some interesting implications depending on how far backward and forward one is willing to extrapolate this trend. The trend extended backward suggests that in the not too distant past many more people might have been coming for *Kashi-labh;* extended forward it suggests that the phenomena of coming to Kashi for *Kashi-labh* may be coming to an end.

I will focus on the above possibilities in Chapter 5 which examines the tradition of coming to Kashi for *Kashi-labh.* But first, in the following chapter, I present an account of the Kashi Labh Muktibhavan, the newer of the two *bhavans* and the one gaining in popularity. It was there that most of my fieldwork was conducted and where all but one of the families whom I got to know and interviewed were staying.

4

The Kashi Labh Muktibhavan

The Muktibhavan

Church Godowlia is the busiest intersection in Kashi. It is where two major roads from different areas of the city raucously converge into one. During most daylight hours it is completely jammed with bell-ringing bicycles and cycle-rickshaws, screeching auto-rickshaws and big, rumbling Ambassador cars. The tradition in Kashi, when your lane is jammed, is to slip down the inside of the opposing lane, and this continues often to the logical conclusion that the entire two-way street is clogged from both sides with vehicles going in one direction. Lane barriers erected on the roads at Church Gowdolia have only partially solved this problem and not at all in the roundabout itself. So the incredible din is added to by policemen yelling at violators and by the crack of their long cane *lathis* over the backs of the poor, low-caste rickshawwalas who have dared to stop in the confusion to try and pick up a fare.

Perhaps no more than one hundred meters from this intersection as the crow flies, and nestled into the labyrinth of small, timeless alleys and houses which fit each other like pieces of a jigsaw puzzle, is Kashi Labh Muktibhavan. Here the noise of the large streets is lost to that of the residential city. The first time I went to the Muktibhavan, I was immediately struck by the building and its property in comparison to not just its immediate surroundings but to virtually anything in the heart of the city. It is an imposing mansion with such unusual features (for the heart of Kashi) as a driveway to the front entrance and extra property out front that is used as a garden. The property is surrounded by a high wall which the surrounding city has built up against to such an extent that it seems almost about to flow over into the Muktibhavan courtyard.

A large iron gate is kept chained so that only people and bicycles can slip through—and not the many cows that wander freely in the alleys. The gate is opened only when a dying person arrives by rickshaw or when a body is carried out to the burning ghat. From the gate, a cement driveway leads up to the main entrance of the building which is protected from the elements by a pillared portico like that of an English manor. Up the left side of the driveway a wall runs down the length of the property—a wall on which monkeys like to sit, but it is a boundary heavily guarded by the priest-workers who chase the monkeys away with big sticks. Against the wall is a thin flower garden in which grow a couple of small shade trees and some holy *tulsi* plants. To the right is a multitiered cement structure—a well—on which the priest-workers nap in the sunshine in the colder months, or in the evening during the hot months. Between the well and the house is a small tract of land used as a vegetable garden during the appropriate season, but most of the time simply as unused, open space; a type of space quite unusual in the heart of Kashi. The back and sides of the main building are separated from the huge walls at the property's edge by a thin alley-way, but in this space there is a series of small sheds where the priest-workers sleep and cook and eat their food. The manager and his family occupy a rather larger series of rooms behind the garden.

I did not really notice the building the first time I went there, however, as having squeezed through the gate I was preoccupied by a courtyard full of faces, turned and staring at me. There are always a lot of people at the Muktibhavan; some live there and some just while away the hours in the pleasant surroundings. When the weather is appropriate, there will certainly be one or a few of the eight *karmacharya*—the live-in priest-workers—relaxing somewhere in the courtyard. They are recognizable by the tattered *dhotis* they wear, the elaborate *tikka* marks on their foreheads and by the slowness with which they seem to move. Perhaps someone who used to work at the Muktibhavan has come back for a visit and is recounting tales of the outside world. During the school season, there are children living and playing at the Muktibhavan; the large family of the manager, cousins and friends' children who have come to get their education in the city. Often neighbors, like the betel seller from across the alley, who have made friends with the manager, come to visit and to take in the religious atmosphere. Also sitting in the courtyard will be some of the men of families who have come with a dying person. They are probably sitting by themselves or with men from another visiting family. They can often be distinguished by their relatively unsophisticated appearance and often their wide-open eyes and wonder-struck expressions, for they are likely fresh from the villages and in awe of their surroundings.

The social atmosphere of the garden and courtyard of the Muktibhavan belies, to Western sensibilities at least, the fact that inside the building up to ten pilgrims lie dying. At first it struck me as strange that the workers, inhabitants, and visitors to the Muktibhavan do not seem at all somber. However, I learned that in India, or perhaps more specifically in Kashi, it would be a somber attitude that would be strange. Down at the burning ghats, local children swim and play around the corpses; it is neither disturbing to them nor to the relatives of the dead people. At the Muktibhavan, and in much of Kashi, life goes on around death without skipping a beat.

Just above a very popular bench—shaded and commanding a view of the entire Muktibhavan courtyard—hang two signs handwritten in Hindi on pieces of cardboard. The first simply reads *"Kamre Kali Hai"*—unoccupied rooms. Flipped over the sign indicates the opposite, for those times of the year when all the rooms are full. A more permanent sign below the first reads that in the case that there are no rooms available, dying people are not to be kept on the verandahs and that this is in the interest of the cleanliness and security of the institution.

Behind the wall on which these signs hang, is the Muktibhavan's administrative office. When the manager is not there, a big iron padlock hangs from the dead-bolt which holds the office's two dark green half-doors together. But visible through one of the barred windows, an old table surrounded by four mismatched chairs—essentially the only furniture in the building—indicate that this is where the business is done. When the manager is there, he is not at the table, but is sitting cross-legged on the thin white-covered mattress at the far side of the room and underneath the window. The walls here are painted a shocking lime-green, and on them, near the high ceiling, are a series of colorful gods, captured in posters, carefully framed and glassed and attached so that they are looking down from all around the room. Recessed into the walls are shelves crammed with religious books, pamphlets, old yellowing stacks of papers, and other things seemingly from decades ago. In this office, the Muktibhavan finances are done and records of the dying pilgrims are kept. A wooden cupboard holds the record books and a huge iron safe that is opened with a skeleton key keeps the small amount of money that comes in to pay wages and expenses. The office is really alive only on payday, when, one by one, the priest-workers and other staff are called in for the monthly reckoning. On this day there is usually some lively debate about how many days off the individual had and how much he is due. On other days the office is not really used.

The main door opens onto a short hall—a passage from the apparently mundane to the seemingly sacred. This hall moves from the realm of the living to the realm of the dying. Most of the time it is a sea of shoes and sandals which are allowed no further into the building. To the right is the office and its pantheon and to the left a room used for religious sermons and napping priest-workers. But just ahead the hall opens out into a dark chamber where several of the priest-workers are sitting in a circle on the floor rhythmically chanting, and tapping drums and chimes. This is the *puja* room, where the worship is done and where the priest-workers perform their ongoing music and singing *(kirtan)*. Through the door across the *puja* room is the true inner sanctum of the Muktibhavan, the inner courtyard and the rooms for the dying.

Like many of the old stately homes in Kashi, the Muktibhavan has two tall stories built around and focusing on this central open courtyard. The courtyard space is deeper than it is wide or long and so, despite being open to the sky, it is dark and dungeon-like inside, except for the couple of hours when the noon sun is directly overhead. It is a space that plays with the boundaries between inside and outside. And it is a space always filled with the sounds of the *kirtan* which enter through the *puja* room door and hauntingly reverberate around and upwards, escaping eventually into the open sky. The cement floor of the courtyard is sunken about one foot and like a giant basin, it captures and drains the torrential downpours of the monsoon. It is also the area used by the families of the dying for washing and bathing. Around the courtyard is a walkway off which four rooms radiate. These, and four analogous rooms on the second floor, are where dying people with their families stay.

Visually, these rooms are overwhelming. The only light source during the day is from small barred windows through which the intense, crisp tropical light pours, lighting up the dusty air and highlighting the inhabitants against shadowy backgrounds. The painted surfaces of the cement or plaster walls, as in most of the buildings in Kashi, are deteriorating due to some combination of cheap paint and the omnivorous climate of the monsoon. Over each door and attached precariously by a nail driven into the cement are olive green metal speakers through which religious speeches occasionally crackle. The stone floors were beautiful at one time, inset in places with intricate tile designs. Generally, the only piece of furniture in any of these rooms is a small wooden cot. Sometimes the dying person will be lying on this cot separated from the wooden slats by only a blanket. Mostly, however, and almost always as death approaches, the dying person will be lying on his blanket on the floor. In one corner of the room, a cooking area will have been set up—perhaps a portable one-burner kerosene stove, a couple of banged-up pots, and a sack of rice or lentils. Elsewhere in the room there may be a few folded-up blankets and some old sacks containing whatever the family brought from the village. Somewhere in the room there will definitely be a shining brass *lothi,* a special pot filled with Ganga water brought up from the river by one of the family members after his daily morning bath.

The Muktibhavan—its grounds and its building—is quite luxurious, a fact that escaped me until I had been there for several months, and could begin to appreciate it through eyes other than my own. At first I could only see it against a backdrop of strange and deteriorating buildings and I missed its luxury in the apparent squalor of its peeling paint. But, for the families of those coming to stay in the Muktibhavan, as for the dying people themselves, it is a place of wonder—a place such as they have probably never seen before, let alone had the opportunity to make their temporary home. The Muktibhavan, in the eyes of the people who come there with somebody to die, is a wonderful mansion, one of the most luxurious buildings in one of the holiest and most beautiful cities in existence.

Shuklaji: The Manager

At some time in the past, a sound amplification system was installed in the Muktibhavan. It had been broken for several years before I arrived. Six months into my visit the manager had it fixed. From this point on the *kirtan* singing was amplified and broadcast to various rooms as well as out into the city. Amplification began a new event at the Muktibhavan: afternoon "sermons" from the manager.

The manager is a man named Bhairavnath Shukla, whom I always called Shuklaji (*ji* is an honorific suffix). His lectures took place in the front room normally used by napping priest-workers. Shuklaji would sit cross-legged in the corner of the room facing the windows, an oversized microphone and a huge copy of the *Bhagavat Mahapurana* in front of him. Like the office, the walls of this room are a bright lime-green but there are many worn patches revealing years of white and blue undercoats, water stains, and several dirty black patches about three feet off the ground where people's hair oil has rubbed off as they sat leaning against the walls. The walls too are hung with colorful framed pictures of Ganesha, Shiva, Vishnu, and Radha and Krishna, and here and there on hooks and window shutters are hung the *dhotis* and other paraphernalia belonging to the priest-workers. Hanging from the ceiling is an old, rickety fan and a single light bulb dangling on the end of its cord.

Through the windows comes the sounds of birds and nearby

traffic and perhaps the noise of a couple of priest-workers talking and washing their cooking utensils outside. Shuklaji starts lecturing to an empty room, but his voice crackles electronically through the Muktibhavan. By and by, family members of the dying people drift in and sit down on the floor facing Shuklaji. They become quite enraptured with the sermon which he is giving with some passion. Sometimes there are as many as twelve people in the room; the men are up front, the women behind. The men participate to a certain degree, laughing at the appropriate moments and nodding their heads in agreement, and occasionally blurting out "Yes! yes!". Shuklaji speaks spontaneously for the most part but is constantly waving a small white booklet around and occasionally reading a sentence out of it. He will speak without a break for almost two hours.

Shuklaji is from a small village several hundred kilometers north of Kashi in district Ghorakpur. He came to Kashi in 1972 to do an M.A. at Banaras Hindu University, but after that he felt some desire to stay. His *guru* also thought he should stay in Kashi and that settled it for him. He had a series of jobs, all of which were very unsatisfying to him because, he says, "when people come to Kashi it is to take God's name and to do worship" and not to work in the Punjab National Bank. He also had trouble with his father's desire that he should be back in the village, especially at the time of his brother's death (or, as he put it, his taking up of residence in heaven). He attributes these early difficulties remaining in Kashi to Lord Bhairav, the gatekeeper of Kashi, who keeps some people from entering the city and others from leaving. Shuklaji had to appease Lord Bhairav in order to stay:

> At that time [a friend] used to bring me very nice leaves from the wood-apple trees in Chapra on which I would write "Rama, Rama, Rama." I used to offer these leaves to Hanumanji. . . . For six months I used to offer these writings on the leaves to God, and sing the praises of Lord Bhairav.

During this period Shuklaji's father died and he had to return to his village in Ghorakpur district. However, later he came back to Kashi to perform the special death rites for his father that would establish him in the realm of the ancestors. Things started going much better then. His health improved and he started a job that allowed him to both do work and praise God. He felt that finally he had won the permission of Lord Bhairav to live in Kashi.

Shuklaji played a big part in my research. Though he has been at the Muktibhavan for only a few years, he seemed to know a lot even

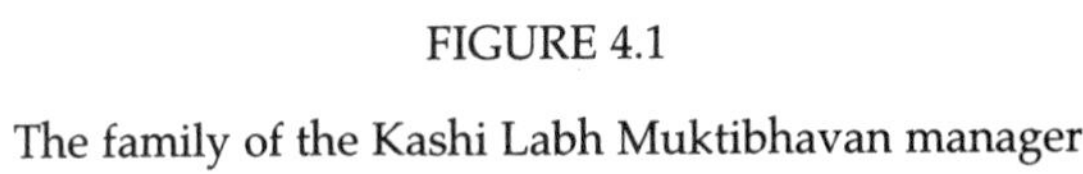

FIGURE 4.1

The family of the Kashi Labh Muktibhavan manager

about earlier times. He is quite highly educated and was very willing to share his time and knowledge with me. He took me on several trips. One time we went to stay with his extended family in his village. Another time I went on a pilgrimage with him to bathe in the auspicious waters of Prayag in order to help his son who had been struck down by "Durga," a disease caused by the Goddess of the same name. A friendship developed between us, though it was a strained one. I always felt that I had to hide from him my moral flaws. He wanted to teach me to be a better person. In trying to do that, he taught me a lot about the Muktibhavan, the priest-workers, and the people who came there to die.

Shuklaji is an honest man, but he might lie rather than talk badly of someone. He also had a remarkable power of not seeing things which he did not want to: he would tell me how unusually pure and good I was, because I did not smoke—which he had seen me do—and because I did not drink or eat meat—which I had told him I did. I believe that he did this for a couple of reasons: he thought this "positive reinforcement" might change me, but more importantly, he had to pretend, to himself and others, that I was fully virtuous because he could not tolerate the company of somebody with such moral flaws. I raise this because Shuklaji does much the same thing with the running of the Muktibhavan. As I will discuss later on, those things which happen at the Muktibhavan which do not conform to his moral sense, are in some cases dealt with, but in other cases "disappeared" from thought.

Other than his sermons, Shuklaji's duties include all the administrative work, keeping the priest-workers doing what they are supposed to be doing, and basically troubleshooting. Administrative work includes mundane paper work, accounts, and bookkeeping. He must also give a report to the administrators in Delhi every month so they can check everything out. He must even give some names and addresses so they can check from the people who came whether or not any bribery was given and to which priest-workers. From my own experience I know that most of the priest-workers would gladly accept a few rupees "gift." The difficulty for them is that people like to give gifts at the time of a relative's death. The employees of the Muktibhavan, being Brahmins, could normally be the ideal recipients of such gifts. But because of the way the Muktibhavan is registered as a charitable trust (and presumably a tax shelter), the order came down from Delhi that money should not change hands. Shuklaji says that, regardless, he would never take a gift because of his desire to maintain his high status and his position at the Muktibhavan.

One of Shuklaji's functions at the Muktibhavan is to fill out death "receipts" for which he has a kind of special government authorization. The family members of a dead person require these in order to have a body burned at the burning ghat. They take the "receipt" down to the little death registration office near the ghat. There it is checked and exchanged for the official death certificate, which is needed for inheritance and other legal matters, and permission to have the body burned. Before the Muktibhavan started issuing receipts, the families were getting a hard time when they arrived at the registration office with a dead body. Somebody who dies at home must get a similar certificate from the village *panchayat* (authority) or an elder of the village. In the city now, a doctor's certificate is required or a statement *(panchnama)* signed by four or five people from the neighborhood. Sometimes people from the village will arrive with a dead body but will not have a *panchnama* from the village *panchayat*. In such a case, the *murdu-muni,* the officer who registers the dead body, will not give them permission to cremate the body. If there are four or five of them from the village, however, they can act as witnesses, and will receive a certificate. The receipts that Shuklaji fills out do not require him to identify the cause of death, but only that the death took place at the Muktibhavan.

Shuklaji seems quite committed to the Muktibhavan and proud of the service that it provides. He feels that part of his duties are to improve the place as he sees fit. There are two types of changes he is working on, both of which concern the priest-workers. He wants to get them better facilities as their little rooms around the back are very cramped and leak when it rains. However, he also wants to improve the way in which the priest-workers perform their spiritual duties. Now, some of the priest-workers are not doing their duties properly, "not from their hearts." Shuklaji felt that when he is not there, they are careless. For instance, they might not come five minutes early or stay five minutes longer to ensure uninterrupted chanting. Sometimes too, Shuklaji felt, when the priest-workers were chanting they were not giving their full attention to God, but were thinking of other things. He believed these sorts of improvements must come from the priest-workers themselves: "they must look to God, not to Dalmia [their employer] for help."

The Priest-Workers *(Kirtan Karmacharya)*

> Lord Rama was in the forest looking for his wife Sita. He met Sugriv, the king of the monkeys, whose wife had been stolen by his own brother Bali. Rama helped Sugriv by killing his brother Bali with an arrow. After being killed Bali was standing in front of Rama and Rama offered to restore his life and make him immortal. But Bali turned him down. He said "Who can be as lucky as me, that God has come in front of me. Through your name alone, in Kashi, Shivaji gives *moksha.* Everybody who dies in Kashi will get *moksha* because Shivaji chants your name there."

In this manner, with an excerpt from a story, Tikka Baba, one of the priest-workers, explained to me the importance of Lord Rama to people obtaining *moksha* by dying in Kashi. I had wondered why, in the city of Lord Shiva, where it is said that Shiva himself grants *moksha* to all who die, there is so much focus on Lord Rama. In this story it is explained, and it is a question of mechanism; Shiva grants people *moksha* by chanting Rama's name to them. Tikka Baba often answered the questions I asked by telling stories. The story cited above is actually a version of one at the beginning of the Kishkindhakanda section of Tulsidas's *Ramcharitmanas,* the famous Hindi (Avadi) version of the renowned epic poem, the *Ramayana.* Tikka Baba knows by heart all the verses of the *Ramcharitmanas* which tell about the importance of Kashi. He sung them to me beautifully, the way, he said, they are supposed to be read. Tikka Baba claims that from the *Ramcharitmanas* he first learned about dying in Kashi and obtaining *moksha.* He believes that "anybody who has read or heard either Valmiki's *Ramayana* or Tulsidas's *Ramcharitmanas* would know about the benefits of Kashi."

Tikka Baba is a small, delightful man with an infectious toothy grin. His grey hair is very short, almost shaved, except for a longer tuft at the back tied into a pony tail and dyed dark orange. His face is skull-like due to his leanness, and he covers his skinny body only in a *dhoti* or, on more formal occasions, in a bright yellow *Rama Nami* scarf. Tikka Baba is a nickname. The old manager started calling him Tikka Baba when he came to the Muktibhavan because of the elaborate *tilak,* or *tikka,* he paints in sandalwood on his forehead every morning. He said that it signifies that he is a Vaishnava (a worshiper of Vishnu), that he does not eat meat or fish, and that he would not harm any creature. In its detail it is specifically modeled after the *tikka* that Lord Rama wore when he was incarnate on this earth. He wears it because he is a devotee of Lord Rama, as he wears the *tulsi*-wood necklace around his neck.

Tikka Baba is "fifty-five or sixty" years old. He comes from a small village in Darbhanga district in Bihar, about four hundred miles to the northeast of Kashi. He has been working at the Muktibhavan for twenty years—longer than anybody else. He is a *karmacharya* (worker) to the manager and a *pujari* (priest) to most of the people who come to die. He calls himself, as do the others, *kirtan karmacharya* (devotional singing worker), which stresses the job they do the most.

This is how Tikka Baba came to be a priest-worker at the Muktibhavan: Over twenty years ago Tikka Baba left his village and came to Kashi in search of a job. One day, he was down somewhere in Safarkanj *gali* (alley), near Mir ghat. There he found work in the temple of Nil Kanth Mahadev. His job was to make offerings of leaves from the wood-apple tree, one by one, each with the recitation of a mantra. Many people come there to offer leaves and he would have to stay until they were all finished. The arrangement was that he would do this everyday until about two o'clock and then they would give him some food. Every month he would get twenty-three rupees (now less than a dollar). Tikka Baba, who had worked the fields all his life, found that the work was very difficult and dull. And it generally never finished when they had said it would. He was frustrated and thought of a way to speed up the work. He started saying "Aum Nama Shivaya" and offering whole stacks of leaves at the same time. He sat there day after day, he said, and wished that he could find a different job and be able to move out of there.

Then his wish came true: A man from his village came by, a man named Amod Nath who at that time was working at the Muktibhavan. His son had disappeared and so Amod Nath had become preoccupied with searching for him. He would spend days away searching. Because he was away so much, there was need at the Muktibhavan for another worker. Tikka Baba said:

> He asked me if I knew how to sing devotional songs. I said no. But he asked me to try. So I started singing a devotional song. Then he told me to do some reading. My voice was very beautiful, so he said. He said that I should bring whatever belongings I had and come right away. All I had was a *dhoti* and a *lotha*. So I brought them here and I have been living here since that very day.

He considered himself very lucky. He started out getting 60 rupees, almost three times what he had been getting for offering leaves. He has been astounded to watch his pay go from 60 to 80 to 130 to 215 to 315 and recently to 425 rupees over the last twenty years. This money has allowed him to fulfill all his worldly obligations of raising a family. For Tikka Baba, as probably for most men in India, it was a struggle.

Tikka Baba had about five *bighas* (about three acres) of land in his village. He lived there in a mud-brick house. He had a wife, three daughters, and four sons. He left for Kashi by himself when his eldest son was about eighteen. He left because he had to somehow make enough money that he could pay for his daughters' weddings. As it turned out, in order to get his three daughters married into good families—in order to raise enough money for dowry—he had to sell most of his land, and mortgage the rest. He got all three of his daughters married, and his dowries were even generous. He is considered to be a very great man for having done this. His reputation in the village is now very good.

Marriage problems have not stopped with Tikka Baba's daughters, however. His eldest son is not marriageable and his second eldest was too marriageable;

> He was very intelligent and always got first division grades. He was also very handsome, and I have a good reputation. He was considered to be so full of potential that he was kidnapped on two separate occasions by village men who were trying to force him to marry their daughters. The first time he came back. He married the second kidnapper's daughter but they had to pay me a dowry of 10,000 rupees, which was enough to pay the mortgage on the two *bighas* of land I have left.

This second son has now done a Ph.D. at Banaras Hindu University. Tikka Baba's eldest son is not so lucky. He will not be getting married because he has only one (working) arm, and because he is not handsome.

> When he was young he fell and tore his arm very badly. A doctor told us to take him to the hospital and that they could operate and rejoin the ligaments. But my wife said "His ligaments are torn but if we send him to the hospital something else could happen and we will be blamed. So let him remain like this." His arm was not fixed and now the blood does not flow through it.

The eldest son, "that man with one arm," as Tikka Baba said trying to make me understand who he was talking about, is also a priest-worker at the Muktibhavan. With their two salaries, the one highly educated son, and two more dowries to look forward to, their future is financially secure. He made the right decision coming to Kashi and was lucky to get his job at the Muktibhavan. He brought all his sons to study in Kashi and they were thus able to keep "good company" as opposed to that of the "cowherds and farmers" back in the village.

During a lull in our conversation Tikka Baba volunteered:

> Kashi is a great place *(buri mahatma)*. People from many countries come here for dying in this Kashi Labh Muktibhavan. If I stay here in Kashi I will be secure. I will spend my whole life here.

Tikka Baba's wife still lives back in the village in the little house. Tikka Baba and his sons travel back to the village every once in a while to visit her and the extended family; it is only a few hours by train. But Tikka Baba will never move back there. He will never leave Kashi or the Kashi Labh Muktibhavan. Shuklaji told me that as Tikka Baba gets old, his duties will be lessened while he will continue to get his pay. Eventually, he will only have to sit and meditate. Tikka Baba will die where he has lived and worked and will achieve *moksha* chanting and hearing the name of his beloved Rama.

Tikka Baba is just one of the eight full-time priest-workers at the Muktibhavan. Though apparently quite different, the priest-workers have several features in common. All of them, for instance, are from small farming villages, mostly from the neighboring state of Bihar. They are all married and they are all sending the money they make back to their extended families. And, of course, they are all Brahmins by caste. Tikka Baba is the oldest of the priest-workers, and is the only one in fact who *is* "old." Five of the priest-workers are more or less middle-aged, and two are just in their twenties.

The priest-workers do not come to the Muktibhavan as trained priests, but rather as workers who for the most part have done nothing but farming work. The young ones, in fact, are still a little too young and seem naive about what is going on at the Muktibhavan. They learn their priestly work from the other priest-workers—sometimes the hard way. One of the younger ones admitted to me that he is very frightened when he has to do *kirtan* (singing) duty in the middle of the night. One of the older priest-workers—no doubt to keep the young man doing his duty—told him that the *kirtan* is done in order to keep the ghosts away, and that if he falls asleep and the music stops, the ghosts of the thousands of people who have died in the building will start creeping toward him.

The younger ones do not see their jobs at the Muktibhavan as a lifetime work. They say they will not stay on as has Tikka Baba. Though I never saw anybody come or go in the year I was there, I gather that the jobs change hands fairly regularly; many times someone who was a priest-worker in the past comes and stays for a few days, meets with his old friends and shares stories of pilgrimages or of life back in the village. The middle-aged priest-workers seem delighted that they could be paid for sitting around and singing the praises of God. Several of them hold that the spiritual benefits of the work are as significant as the pay. One such priest-worker is Hridyanand Pandey, who played a big part in this study as he taught me a lot about the dying people and the institution.

Like many of the priest-workers Pandey has a wife and children back in his village in Rohtas district of Bihar. Pandey's family has some agricultural land which is being worked by his brothers. During my time with him one of his daughters was preparing for her wedding. This wedding would cost him several years of his Muktibhavan pay so he was a little anxious at that time. He goes home once every six

FIGURE 4.2

Kirtan karmacharya: The Kashi Labh Muktibhavan's priest-workers

months or a year, for only four or five days. He cannot be gone long as he loses pay for each day he is away from the Muktibhavan.

Pandey went to school until the eleventh standard. After his studies, he worked at home in the fields for a while. Then he left and went to work for a year in a brick factory. The work was fine but he decided to leave because there were so many lower caste people working there. He complained: "The laborers there did not have clean habits, and they all used to eat together. I must have clean habits in eating. I cooked my own food but I could not maintain my cleanliness there."

He came to Kashi and for one year he worked in a plastic factory. Again, however, he was not satisfied. He eventually took a cut in pay to come and work at the Muktibhavan. He apparently found what he was looking for. As he says, he will stay there until he is finished with working. His job, as he describes it, is to do just what he would like to do anyway: singing the praises of God and doing His worship *(Bhagavan ka bhajan* and *arti* and *puja).*

As Pandey said, "here there is *bhajan* and *bhojan"* (song and food), meaning he can sing religious hymns to God and reap benefits from doing so. But it is the spiritual benefits which tie Pandey to his job. And he must value them highly because there are not many material ones. His salary is quite low and the job is seven days a week and virtually twenty-four hours a day. In any spare time he pursues spiritual goals. He reads the *Ramayana* or some other religious book. "In this way my time passes and I gain a little knowledge," he said. Sometimes he asks for leave to go to one of the temples like Sankat Mochan, Tulsi Manas Mandir, or Vishvanath to have *darshan.* Nowadays, however, he does not get much opportunity. A couple of times he has gone on a short pilgrimage to some religious place like Allahabad, Badrinath, Haridwar, and Rishikesh. This is how he would like to spend more of his time. But for now, Pandey is a householder and he must spend his time and money on his family at home and attending weddings of his relatives. For a householder, Pandey, in fact, has an unusual opportunity for spiritual pursuits through the work that he does.

The priest-workers are not directly responsible for the care of the dying; the family is expected to do all the care. Their primary responsibility is, rather, to create the desired atmosphere *(vatavaran)* in which people should die. The priest-workers participate in caring for the dying only to the extent that they might offer advice or insist that the dying person be regularly bathed. Their concern in this case, is that the dying person be kept ritually pure at all times. The only other time a priest-worker would be involved in the physical care of a dying person is in the very rare case when there are insufficient relatives to do the job.

There was a tradition on Tuesday afternoons, for the first half year that I spent visiting the Muktibhavan, for the priest-workers to have what one of them described as a *"Ramayana* party"; an afternoon of fast-paced, mood-altering chanting of the *Ramcharitmanas.* At about four o'clock all the priest-workers and a few neighbors would gather in the *puja* room. Shuklaji's son, and soon-to-be priest, Ajay Hari, would instruct people how and where to sit and he himself would sit in front of the largest of the many copies of the famous epic poem. Drums and chimes would establish a slow rhythm. Chanting of the *Ramcharitmanas* verses would begin. Over time, the speed, intensity, and loudness would increase until the playing of the instruments became a frenzy of activity. These were times of intense joy for the priest-workers; their eyes were filled with the smiles and laughter of the believer immersed in the believed. The sound and the emotion coming from the *puja* room during these times would drift up and into the rooms of the dying. The sound would be of an intensity that would certainly not be conducive to sleep. It would disturb the dying but they would also take great pleasure from it, knowing the benefit it was doing them to hear it.

The *Ramcharitmanas* is the most important of all scriptural texts at the Muktibhavan and for the priest-workers. As Tikka Baba has said, it is where he had learned of the importance of Kashi for dying and when teaching somebody about dying in Kashi he tells stories from out of *Ramcharitmanas* and sings its verses. Pandey advises and even forces people to die according to the *Ramcharitmanas* and himself takes great pleasure in "spending his life" chanting the name of Rama, as the *Ramcharitmanas* advises. The Ramayana parties stopped occurring temporarily when Ajay Hari became very sick with "Durga." In celebration and in thanks for Ajay Hari's recovery from Durga several months later, the priest-workers performed a twenty-four hour nonstop chanting of the entire *Ramcharitmanas,* something that they had promised God they would do if he got better.

The Afflicted Dying *(Rogi Marnewalas)*

Jaganath Mishra was perhaps the most miserable looking *rogi marnewala* I had seen. He was so skinny that virtually every bone in his body was visible. He was a skeleton in a tight wrapping of thin brown leather. He was lying semi-prone on the floor, naked except for a loincloth wrapped loosely around his waist and draped over his hips. At his feet was a puddle of water, or urine. I thought he must be in an awful lot of pain as his bare bones were pressing directly against the hard cement floor. His hair was only partially grey and he had several days growth of a full peppery beard through which a couple of yellow bucked teeth were visible. His eyes fixed on me clearly and deeply; he was very much alive still. He waved an arm about and made a groaning sound which I took to be a sign that he wanted me to go away. His family told him that I was a photographer—which they knew I was not—and that I would take his picture for free. The family told me he had just wanted to know who I was, and now that he knew, it was okay. My sense was that he did not want me to take his picture. But his family wanted a photograph of him very much and insisted that he also wanted to be photographed. Feeling mildly uncomfortable, I took his picture.

I came back often to see them after that and both the initial shock of Mishra's condition and my perception of his discomfort faded. I became friends, of a sort, with his daughter. Most of what I learned about the old man's life came from a long interview with her and Mishra's sister. They said Mishra was eighty years old, but (as in most cases) I doubted it. In this case, it was because of his only partially grey hair, and his daughters' ages of between 19 and 30. They said that his wife was 60 or 65 years old. She had not accompanied her husband to where he would die because, they said, she was too old and weak to travel. Mishra was brought by two of his five daughters, his sister, and his brother-in-law of a different sister.

Mishra was born and lived all his life in a small mud house in a village in eastern Bihar. He had reached the eighth standard of school and could read and write. He worked for the railroad and toward the end of his career had reached the rank of inspector. He had retired three years earlier. Because of his position in the railway department he had had the opportunity to do many pilgrimages in India (always by first-class compartment, they stressed). He went to Ayodhya, Brindhavan, and many other places. He went to Gaya and gave the gold donation. He gave the cloth donation where they establish the ancestors and having done the *pinda dan* ceremony at Gaya, had made himself free from his debt to the ancestors.

He became sick in January, just three months before, and his family took him to a nearby hospital. The hospital did not manage to cure him. He was also trying to cure himself with Ayurvedic medicine. He used to prescribe Ayurvedic medicine for the people in the village, so it was assumed that he knew what he was doing. But he became weaker, and after a while the family took him to another hospital. The medicine from there also did not cure him. The doctor told them they should take him to a big hospital where they might be able to cure him. But, his daughter told me, it would have been too difficult a journey because he had only daughters and no sons. So then Mishra declared: "I will not go anywhere. I will die here, at home." He started to take Ayurvedic herbs which would help him to die as soon as possible. Nobody knows what he was taking. He then arranged to do *gau dan*—the gift of a cow to a Brahmin done when death is approaching. He believed that if he gave a cow it would help him cross the terrible Vaitarni River on his post-death journey to Yama-lok.

When he became very weak, he declared: "Take me to Kashi, I want to die in the *tirtha.*" Word got out that he would be making the final pilgrimage, and kith and kin gathered at the house to touch his feet and to receive his blessings. They left for Kashi by train, first-class compartment, the very next day. Dying in Kashi would, he believed, secure *moksha* for himself. However, for Mishra, as with others, *moksha* meant something different than the religious and philosophical treatises would have one believe. His goal was not escape from the eternal cycle of birth, death, and rebirth. What he wanted was a *decent* next birth. He would be a Brahmin, perhaps a saint. By living the religious life and by dying in Kashi, he would be avoiding the common fate of taking rebirth in the form of an animal, ghost or devil.

Arriving in Kashi, they sought out the place that they had heard about way back on the other side of Bihar, the Kashi Labh Muktibhavan. The manager gave them a room on the upper floor with two barred windows and a wooden cot. In his case the cot would not be used as he believed it to be far better to die on the floor than raised up in the air.

Mishra stayed in this room for fourteen days. He gradually stopped talking and became unconscious for longer and longer periods. At other times he was probably kept conscious by the pain he was experiencing from his bedsores. His family all agreed, however, that he was overjoyed to be in Kashi, and considered himself to be blessed and lucky to have reached the city. They put no extra padding under his sores, but waited by his side day and night and rolled him when he moaned.

One night at about three in the morning he became quite lucid and the family helped him into a sitting position. He drank a glass of milk, the first food that he had taken in weeks. He lay down and, with "eyes open and listening to the name of God, abandoned his body." His daughter thought it was a very good death.

I caught up with them at the burning ghat that morning. Mishra's body was about half burned and the pyre was getting low. It was very hot and the wind was blowing sand into our mouths and eyes. We were huddled in a small piece of shade; their expressions were glazed. Nobody had shoes and they had, one at a time, to borrow my sandals to go on to the scorching sand and look at their burning father. It was over when the ghat attendant started breaking up the fire and tossing the unburned logs and pieces of flesh into the river. Children were splashing and swimming just a few feet downstream, unconcerned with anything else in the holy river. Likewise, the last thing Mishra's family would do before leaving the city was go downstream and have a swim in the Ganga and scrub away the impurities of death.

Who are these people who come to die in Kashi? The priest-workers most often refer to them as *rogis* (diseased or afflicted) or as *marnewalas* (people who are just about to die). More formally—often in writing—they are referred to as *rogi marnewalas,* which translates as something like "afflicted dying people." In the context of describing a new arrival they sometimes called them *yatris* (pilgrims), though this status seems to end with their ensconcement in the Muktibhavan.

What I know about the *rogi marnewalas* comes from several

FIGURE 4.3

Rogi marnewala and his family at Kashi Labh Muktibhavan

sources. The Muktibhavan records contain some information about the people who are registered and I learned more about a sample of the people who came to die in the year 1990 from the questionnaire I administered. From my interaction with the families of dying people and the interviews I conducted with them, I began to get a feel for them as individuals. As importantly, because of the priest-workers breadth of experience with these dying pilgrims, I also learned how some of them understand and classify the *rogi marnewalas*. I will begin my discussion of the *rogi marnewalas* with the understandings of one priest-worker but I should first briefly discuss the questionnaire.

I designed the questionnaire to get at some basic demographic details of the user population, apart from what is available in the Muktibhavan records, and to get an idea about how widespread were some of the things I had learned in interviews (see appendix). It was part of the arrangement I was obliged to make that the questionnaire would be administered not by me but by Hridyanand Pandey, the priest-worker who registered people at the time of their arrival.

The questionnaire was administered to eighty-six people who were taken to be acting as guardians for the dying people. It was not administered in a predetermined pattern, but according to Pandey's whim; it turned out that about twenty percent of arrivals were questioned. I am satisfied that the sample represents the population based on concurrence between sample and population in all categories I was able to assess. For example, the same proportion of people dying (as opposed to returning home alive) occurred in the sample as well as in the population. This is also true for average reported age, sex ratio, and distributions of caste and home district, which were all proportionately similar between sample and population.

On the other hand, there were some problems with both the design and the administration of the questionnaire. Perhaps most serious is that it is, by necessity, a proxy questionnaire. In designing it, I had to make assumptions about how well a guardian might be able to represent the dying person's opinion early on in my fieldwork, some of which have proven difficult to evaluate.[1] In terms of the administration of the questionnaire, I can see patterns in the responses when they are sorted in the order in which they were filled out, which strongly suggest that Pandey was helping people "fill in the blanks" at times and for certain questions. For the above reasons, I treat the survey data cautiously, and select from it on the basis of my assessment of its validity.

However, Pandey is probably the priest-worker who has the most interaction with the dying people and their families. He has been at the Muktibhavan for twelve years and has probably registered and talked to most of the roughly four thousand or so families who have brought dying people over this period. Here is how he described the type of people who come to die in the Muktibhavan:

> The people who come to this place are those whose final stage has come and who have stopped eating and drinking. They can no longer do anything by themselves. We let them stay here only if it appears they will last only three or four days. But some end up lasting up to a month. We do not let people stay more than a month. We do not keep people with contagious diseases like cancer, TB, etc. Often the people will have some affliction like diarrhea or not being able to urinate.

I had asked Pandey who they were, thinking he would describe them demographically, but the answer he gave me was a description of their condition. The most obvious feature of these people, and the feature that they share most commonly as a group, is that they are, as a rule, quite far advanced through the dying process. Furthermore, they are resigned to dying; they are not trying to recover. That the *rogi marnewalas* are fast approaching death when they arrive is demonstrated clearly by the short length of time it takes for them to die. Amongst those people who died in the Muktibhavan during the year I was there, the average length of time between arrival at the Muktibhavan and death, was less than five days. (I will elaborate on this in chapter 8).

For the most part, those people coming to die at the Muktibhavan were no longer eating or drinking. As Pandey observed "many old people who are in their last time *refuse* food and water completely." The vast majority of guardians who answered my questionnaire indicated that the dying person they had brought was eating nothing. Those six guardians who reported food was being eaten listed for the most part only milk. Two people were reported to have been eating fruit, one person rice, and one "light food." Often the people I interviewed indicated that the dying person had not been taking food or drink for as long as several weeks or a month.

Virtually all of the dying people are completely dependent on their caregivers. Most often, they are carried to Kashi; they cannot walk or travel by themselves. Generally, they cannot so much as roll over or move by themselves. The majority of them have stopped communicating. Often, they are asleep or unconscious most of the time.

The people dying in the Muktibhavan are also old—according to the records they are extremely old. For reasons that I will fully elaborate in chapter 7, I believe that the reported ages are for the most part estimates, and apart from that are exaggerated as well. However, the average reported age of people dying in the Muktibhavan during the year I was there was 80. All except one person had reported ages of 60 years or higher and almost ten percent of the people were 100 years of age or more. One man was reported to be as old as 118 years.

The *rogi marnewalas* are so far along in the dying process and so totally dependent on their caregivers that they cannot really be thought of outside the context of their families. It is more accurate to say that a family has brought someone to die than to say a dying person has come accompanied by his or her family members. The unit is the family, though the focus of attention is the individual. The people who come are householders *(grihasthas)* and so remain a part of a greater family whole right through the dying process. Nobody ever dies alone at the Muktibhavan.

The number of accompanying family members is quite varied: the records for the year I was there indicate that a minimum of one and a maximum of twelve people stayed with the dying person. However, as can be seen in the chart in figure 4.4, most often between three and six people register with the dying person. The pattern I noticed, and one that is confirmed by medians calculated from the records, is that very often four men and one or two women will accompany the dying person. This is easily understood as it requires *about* four men to move a dying person to Kashi, and *exactly* four men to properly

FIGURE 4.4

Number of family members accompanying a dying person to the Muktibhavan in 1990

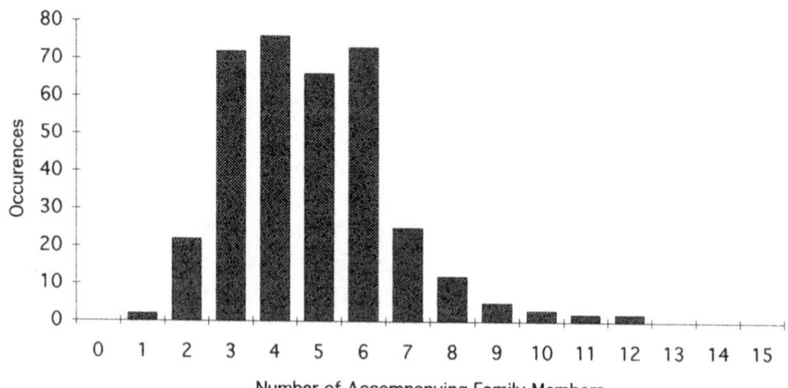

carry a body down to the burning ghat. The one or two women often do the cooking, much of the caring for the dying person, and all the public mourning. Children accompany about one in ten groups and about three percent of families bring along servants of one kind or another.

Although most dying people are in an advanced stage of the dying process, there are a few who are not; not everybody who arrives at the Muktibhavan to die actually dies. However, the "success" rate is impressive. In the year I was there, 365 people registered in the Muktibhavan and of these 305, or roughly 84%, died. Thirty-eight people, or roughly 10%, were recorded as having returned home. The fate of the remaining twenty-two people, or 6%, was unrecorded. There are several explanations for why people return home without dying. Pandey told me that some people are asked to leave because they have stayed more than thirty days. However, according to the Muktibhavan records for the year I was there, this never happened. In fact, as can be seen in figure 4.5, the majority of people who did not die, but "returned home," did so within fifteen days of arrival, and more often within a week. An alternative explanation is that people, themselves, are deciding to leave. Again according to Pandey, those *rogi marnewalas* who are not dying a timely death *(kal mrityu)*, are actually cured by their stay at the Muktibhavan. I suspect, too, that some people who come thinking they are dying, decide to go home when they see how much closer to death all the other people are. But it is also true that some people can simply not afford a long stay. As Pandey said: "A lot of people come thinking that their sick person will die very quickly and only bring a limited amount of money. Sometimes they go home because they have no money on which to live."

Those 84 percent of people who die at the Muktibhavan do so

FIGURE 4.5

Number of days stayed by those people who left the Muktibhavan alive (for one year period between July 1990 and June 1991)

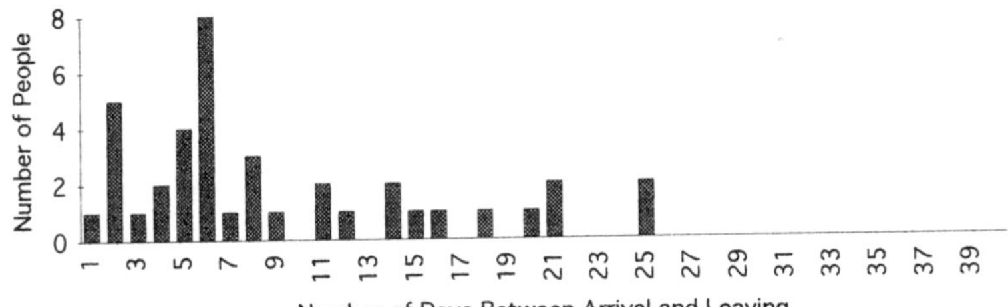

very quickly, the details of which I will discuss in chapter 8. The people who do not die but return home have miscalculated in some way or another, either on the timing of the death or on the *type* of death the dying person is moving toward. However, in a lot of cases, the dying person is unlikely to want to leave, and in the sense of their life goals, perhaps there is no going back. Pandey explained:

> Often when a family brings a dying person and after about ten days the person has not died, the family starts to think that maybe it will take a very long time for him to die and that they should go home. They think "our household affairs and our children's studies have come to a standstill." But generally when they start speaking of going home, the *rogi* refuses to leave. He says "Do not take me. I want to stay here." We [the priest-workers] come to know their wishes and we understand: An old person who has lived in the village and never taken the name of God before now, will not want to return to his house, but will want to stay here taking God's name. When we go to them and read or sing religious songs they want us to stay and read and sing more and more to them.

According to Pandey's understanding, the people who have come to die stop feeling fear once they have reached Kashi. He said; "They are not afraid of death. They take God's name and keep chanting the name of Rama. I think they are not afraid. Rather, they are happy to be dying here." The guardians of the dying people seem to agree; all of them say that the dying person is happy to have reached Kashi and almost all say that the dying person had no fear of dying. They have made the decision to die or at least accepted it and said good-bye to the village and all their worldly possessions. They cannot easily go back. There thus can be some tension between the desires of the dying person and the needs of the family. The family has stopped everything to bring the dying person to Kashi. The dying person has only spiritual goals now, but the family still has concerns in the material world.

There is another manifestation of this tension between material and spiritual needs. At some times of the year it was very busy at the Muktibhavan. During other seasons, such as when it was very hot, fewer people came to die. The pattern seems to be consistent from year to year as the priest-workers knew when it would be crowded and when not. Figure 4.6 graphically shows this seasonality as calculated for all years for which I have records for both bhavans. Though there

FIGURE 4.6

Percentage of total number of people registering at both *bhavans* according to month (calculated on the basis of all available records for all years)

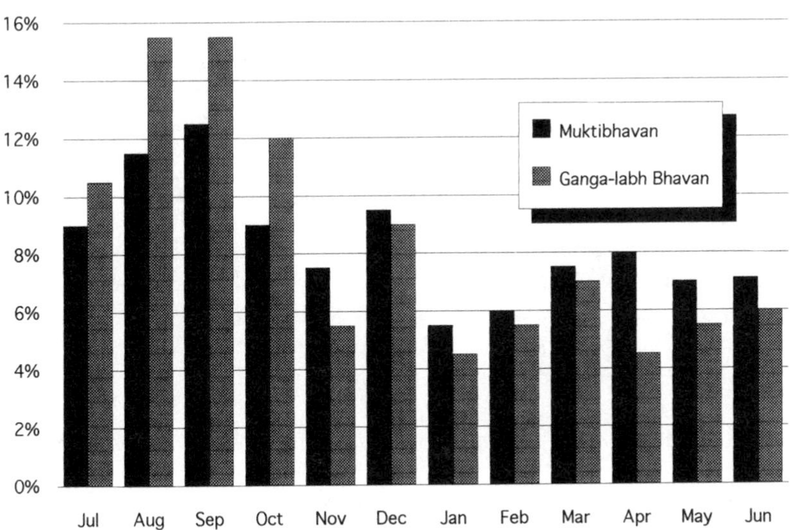

are many possible religious explanations for this phenomenon such as the possibility that people would want to die at particularly auspicious times, as mentioned in many of the texts,[2] I found no evidence for any such reasons. Rather, I believe that Shuklaji is correct that the seasonality is connected to the timing of the planting and the harvest. A family can only be away from its livelihood at certain times of the year. It is a financially difficult chore to bring someone to die in Kashi, and sometimes it is too difficult.

Shuklaji actually laughed when I asked him if people were ever forced by their families to come to Kashi to die. He said:

> No, they come only because of their own desire. When they are still healthy they will say that they want to be in Kashi at the time of death. Or when they are sick they will announce that they want to go to Kashi. [Laughing] Why would people bring someone by pressure when they can save all that money by remaining there in their own house?

This may be the rule but there are some exceptions in which people are forced, in one way or another, to die in Kashi. But often in these cases, too, it is expense that dictates; often people, having brought someone to be treated in Kashi and having found out that there is no hope, decide that it would be too expensive to return to the village, knowing that they will bring the body back to Kashi for cremation.

Although the families stay free at the Muktibhavan, it is quite expensive to come to die in Kashi. Mr. Dalmia, the Muktibhavan's patron, said he is providing charity for the very poor, but what he is really doing is providing it for those who appear poor to him. According to Pandey, himself a man from the villages, it is the rich who come. They are the ones who know about getting *moksha* in Kashi and they are the ones who can afford the time and the travel. Tikka Baba agreed: "For the poor it is an enormous expense, so the poor do not come. Where would they get the money? Only the rich bring people here to die." Tikka Baba estimated that a family must bring a minimum of one thousand rupees (about 30 dollars) to cover the cost of transportation, food, and funerary items, and to pay the Doms at the burning ghat.

The records reveal that slightly more men than women come to die; in the year I was there, 56 percent were men and 44 percent were women. The vast majority of these men and women, like the vast majority of India, are not from cities but are from the small farming villages. The records show that the people who come to Kashi to die and who stay in either the Muktibhavan or the Ganga-labh Bhavan, are from a wide variety of castes (though they are predominately Brahmin and Rajput). Also they are from many of the districts of Bihar and eastern Uttar Pradesh (though predominately from the districts of Rohtas, Bhojpur, and Varanasi), all of which consist of the rich farmlands of the Ganges river basin.

According to the responses to the questionnaire, the great majority of people—almost 90 percent—had been farmers or householders; people with no careers per se. The most significant career type mentioned was "teacher," which was reported by three people. One or two others each reported the careers of business, shopkeeping, pot-making, and laboring. Of the people who reported the education level, two-thirds said that the dying person had no education whatsoever. Of the roughly one-third who did have some education, almost half had finished the equivalent of high school and a third reported having postsecondary education.

Dying in Kashi seems not just a last minute attempt at correcting a life full of sins. Rather, getting *moksha* was a longer-term pursuit of the people who come there to die. The vast majority of people who responded to the questionnaire reported that the dying person had, during the course of their lives, done other things specifically for the purpose of achieving *moksha* (I will discuss the types of things they did in chapter 6).

Most people said that the dying people themselves made the decision to die in Kashi though a significant number said that it had been a family decision. Most said that the whole family agreed that bringing the person to Kashi was the right thing to do, but three people reported some disagreement. One of the people who was reported to *not* want to die had been brought on the basis of a decision by her husband. In one case at the Ganga-labh Bhavan, I actually met a family like this. The husband had brought his wife there to die. She, herself, said she had no interest in dying, didn't believe she was dying, nor would she be interested in dying in Kashi, she said, even if she *were* dying. Her husband knew all this, of course, but thought she was "mistaken." He told me that he thought she was dying and that she should die in Kashi, both for her sake and for the sake of his own reputation. In the end, she did not die, and as far as I know they returned to their village.

My experience is that such occurrences are quite rare. Yet it points to many more subtle difficulties in interpreting the things I was told; the people responding to questions have their reasons for answering as they do, including simply the desire that things should appear to be some ideal way. Interpretation of the questionnaire has the additional complication that the priest-worker who administered it may also have his own reasons for wanting people to answer in the "correct" manner. Some of the information which I have collected is distorted in this way by the guardians and the Muktibhavan staff, each for their own reasons.

My feeling from talking to the priest-workers, from examining the records, and from the questionnaire, is that it is fair to say there is a "type" of person who uses the Muktibhavan, but all these data have essentially been filtered through both the guardians and the priest-workers. The guardians do not necessarily envision a "type" of person who uses the Muktibhavan, but many of them do share ideas of what is a good death and the type of people who die good deaths. The priest-workers definitely do see the people who die there as a 'type,' and as I shall discuss in chapter 7, Muktibhavan policy actively encourages this. I suspect the records and my questionnaire reflect the understandings of the manager and the priest workers, as well as the guardians, in addition to any other underlying reality.

Certainly, part of being the ideal type of dying person at the

Muktibhavan is being brought by your family. In fact, if a man or woman has no family to look after him or her while dying, it is a sign, according to Shuklaji, that he or she is morally corrupt. There were a couple of instances when people came with no family: one time I met an old woman at the Muktibhavan who had been taken there by some relatives and abandoned. Another time a man brought his sister to die at the Muktibhavan. He left saying he was going back to the village to get some things, leaving behind the dying woman and her children. She died leaving no adult members of the family to deal with the situation. Shuklaji and the priest-workers dealt with the cremation and looked after the children until, eventually, a woman came and took the children home. That there is an ideal type of dying person and that they have a family with them is proven by these exceptions; neither of these cases found its way into the record books. Persons with nobody to look after them, those who are abandoned, and those dying at young ages are all people who do not, theoretically, die at the Muktibhavan.

Arrival of the *Rogi Marnewalas*

Dying pilgrims and their families use a variety of forms of transportation to get to Kashi. Some come in hired jeeps, though this is quite expensive. Others come by train and bus, difficult and crowded journeys, and so arrive at stations some distance from their final destination of one or the other of the *bhavans*. From these places, there is not much choice of transportation: either a clanging, bouncy, and noisy auto-rickshaw, or a clanging, bouncy, and crammed journey by cycle rickshaw. So it is that people arrive at the Muktibhavan gates. The priest-workers in the courtyard are alerted to send somebody down with the key to the gate by either the blaring of a little horn, which makes up in startling pitch for what it lacks in power, or the ringing of the elaborate series of well-polished bells attached to every cycle rickshaw.

One time a family pulled in through the gate in an auto-rickshaw so full that two family members were hanging off the sides of the vehicle. The dying *rogi* was lying across three people, themselves squeezed into the back, with her feet sticking out. Another time, I watched an old man arrive by cycle rickshaw. He was too weak to even sit by himself, and was lying curled up on the thin wooden foot support and was being held firmly in place by the legs of his relatives.

It is evident that most of the pilgrims arriving to die have experienced a journey that, in terms of physical hardships, has been extremely arduous. In many cases they are just hours or days away from dying and they have been on a journey that typically might involve a trek in the back of a horse cart to the station, a crowded and hot journey by train, and finally a bumpy and crowded commute from the train station to the Muktibhavan.

People talking in the courtyard seemed to remain unaffected as a rickshaw rolled up the driveway. The conversations carried on but they would watch out of the corners of their eyes what was going on. Usually a family member would approach one of the priest-workers, rather than the other way around, and the approach was often tentative.

The priest-workers are in a very interesting and ambiguous position with reference to the families coming in with a dying person. They are going to enter a relationship, and that tends to mean a hierarchical relationship. The priest-workers have several advantages in terms of gaining the upper hand in the subtle negotiations of relative status, but also several potential difficulties. To the people that come, they are highly paid officials of one of the most fantastic places they have likely seen. Furthermore the priest-workers are wise to the city of Kashi, a place that, while adored, is often also terrifying and completely new to the pilgrims from the villages. The priest-workers have been around death day and night, and to many Hindus this association with death is associated with the gaining of power. On the other hand, the *karmacharya* are from the same villages as the people who come to die. They are mostly from the villages of Bihar and mostly they are from relatively poor farming families. They have not been trained (are not particularly learned in the scriptures) specifically for the jobs they are doing. And they are, to some extent, acting as priests, which by many other Brahmins can be considered a low-status occupation.

It is evident from this early stage that there is an unequal relationship between families and the institution's employees, one which to my mind exists for the reason that the families are inexperienced and do not know what the procedure is, but which is also actively cultivated by some of the priest-workers. Often the family members end up thinking the priest-workers to be very significant "men of God," trust their opinions (of, for instance, how much longer a person will live) and rely on their advice.

I saw nobody turned away, though the manager says that people sometimes are. They may be turned away either because the Muktibhavan is full or because the people are not "acceptable." If the arrivals are to stay, and this seems to be the usual case, one of the priest-workers shows the family to a room which is unoccupied. In the majority of cases, there are enough male family members to carry the dying person up to his or her room, but priest-workers do assist in those cases where the family needs help. The *rogis* are generally moved around by their relatives very roughly. This was also the case at certain other times during their stay, such as when the dying people were rolled over or sat up by their families.

While the family settles in the room, the man who is acting as guardian to the dying person, or the most senior man there, goes through the process of registering. This usually occurs in the front courtyard and often in the midst of a crowd of semi-interested people. This initial check-in is where most of the information for the Muktibhavan records is collected (see figure 4.7). In the cases I witnessed, the form was never given to the guardian to fill out but was filled out by a priest-worker who would read out the questions and write down the answers. Some of the guardians may not, in fact, have been able to do this chore by themselves, but it seemed to me that the priest-workers took the opportunity to publicly demonstrate just how literate they were. In certain cases, the answers were decided upon by a sort of a group consensus, as in the cases when the guardian did not know the exact age of the dying person. In other cases the priest-worker would ignore the response of the dying person's guardian and write down what he thought the answer should be, as when deciding on the sickness of the dying person which invariably was recorded as old age, despite the fact that the dying person's family members often were aware of a more specific sickness.

The Work of the *Kirtan Karmacharya*

> Death is unavoidable; the person who is born is definitely going to die. I see this everyday.
>
> After a sinful life, in order for the soul to be liberated, a person must come to Kashi and take the name of God—Rama's name. Only with this will the person get *moksha*. *Moksha* means reaching the abode of the Gods and receiving the mercy of God. That person will never again have to take birth on this earth again.

These are more of the words of Hridyanand Pandey. As I have described, he has been working at the Muktibhavan for the last twelve years and is the most experienced and gregarious of the priest-workers. His position of assistant to the manger and his many years of interaction with the dying people and their families have made of him a wealth of information and advice.

FIGURE 4.7

Admission form: Translation of the Muktibhavan's admission form showing information required and additional regulations

Shri Hari
Admission Form
(Application form for the family member who brings the patient into the Kashi Labh Muktibhavan

1. *Rogi*'s (sick person) name) ______________
   Rogi's fathers name ______________
   Guardian who will make entry of the *rogi* ______________
   Rogi's age ______________ man or woman
   Explanation of sickness ______________
   Rogi's address ______________
   Number of men and women coming with the *rogi* ______________

Regulations

1. Persons with contagious diseases such as cholera, plague, T.B., etc. cannot be admitted.

2. Even after being admitted, if some contagious sickness is contracted, then they should depart from here on their own accord.

3. The famly of the *rogi,* within three hours of death of the *rogi,* should take the dead body from the Muktibhavan for Antyesthi Kriya (funeral rites).

4. The guardian or the person caring for the *rogi* may stay in the Muktibhavan so long as in food etc. Garlic, onion, meat, and alcohol should never be used. Playing cards, chess, and laughing and joking should also be completely avoided. Spend your own life very purely as possible. Some of your time should be given to the ongoing *kirtan* (devotional song).

I certify to keep attention to the matters given above

Signature of local guardian ______________

Signature of guardian
Date ______________

Pandey's day starts at four in the morning, when he, with all the other *karmacharya,* gets up for *arti* (worship). They assemble in the *puja* room, the central hall of the old mansion; a room that connects rooms and the heart of the Muktibhavan. This is where the gods reside, within their splendid and colorful pictures, framed and behind glass smeared with red powder and white sandalwood paste. Nine gods sit on a table draped with one of the familiar yellow and red cloths that are for sale all over Kashi. Incense is lit and bells begin to ring.

Puja is done twice a day; early in the morning and in the evening. *Puja* is the standard form of Hindu worship, consisting ideally of a long series of offerings and services. It is performed in a huge variety of settings, from home to temple, daily and on festive occasions. In its manifestations, it is variable (Fuller 1992, 66). At the Muktibhavan, amidst chimes and bells and reciting of mantras, a variety of food is offered to the gods and a flame is waved in front of them. The flame is then passed around the room for all to pass their hands over before touching their eyes and hair with their finger tips. On the tray with the flame is a small pot of red powder for application to the forehead. The last stage in this *puja* is the distribution of the fruits and sweets which had been offered to, and are now blessed by, the Gods.

What may be less standard in the many manifestations of *puja*, is what happens next at the Muktibhavan. When the worshippers in the *puja* room are finished, as the food is being divided, the priest-worker who is carrying the tray, and one or two others, leave the *puja* room and enter the inner courtyard toward the rooms of the dying. Walking slowly in single file, they continue reciting mantras and ringing chimes and bells. All is pitch blackness at these times and the priest-workers walk from room to room, lit only by the flickering glow of the camphor flame and its reflections off the brass tray they carry. Into the rooms they go and encircle the dying person. They wave the flame over and around him or her and apply red to his or her forehead. Like this they visit all the rooms where someone is awaiting death.

After morning *arti*, Pandey takes care of his personal needs like brushing his teeth, scraping his tongue, and bathing. Then, as the sun is coming up, he sits down and recites his mantra—the Gayatri mantra. Only after this does he prepare and eat his food (which he does alone). When he has finished eating, his work day begins and he usually starts off by going and sitting outside.

Each person, he said, must work eight hours a day; there is six hours of doing *kirtan* and *bhajan* in three shifts of two hours and approximately two hours for holding religious discourses, reading stories, and distributing *charnamrit*. At other times they are free, but not free to go, as they must be there for unexpected events. In Pandey's case he spends a lot of time registering the new arrivals.

The main function of the *karmacharya*, the duty for which they are primarily there, is the maintenance, twenty-four hours a day, of a continuous musically accompanied chanting of the names of God. At any time there are eight priest-workers at the Muktibhavan and always two are on *kirtan* duty. They work three two-hour shifts a day, so one pair will sing two hours just before noon, two hours in the evening and another two hours in the middle of the night. They never get more than the six hours in between shifts and there are often other things they are expected to do when they are not singing. Consequently the priest-workers are often in need of sleep, and so during any visit to the Muktibhavan one is likely to see several sleeping here or there. The ideal of twenty-four hour continuous *kirtan* is just that: often the

FIGURE 4.8

Priest-workers taking their shift at the ceaseless singing and chanting of the names of god.

beat of the music and the chanting of the names of God will become slower and slower and quieter and quieter as the two on-duty priest-workers drift into a trance-like sleep.

This is not surprising as the music is hypnotically repetitive. Usually there is one man playing a two-ended drum and the other plays a pair of brass chimes. One or both of them will be chanting. Mostly what is chanted is the names of Vishnu (Hari) and two of his most famous incarnations: Rama and Krishna. The usual order of the chant is *"Hari Ram, Hari Ram, Hari Ram Ram Hari Hari, Hari Krishna, Hari Krishna, Krishna Krishna Hari Hari"* but this is chanted in a variety of rhythms and speeds, so that there is seemingly no relation from one time to another. The chimes, very high-pitched, pierce through walls and ears; the drum, very low, rumbles through the building. The voices of the men, untrained but for hour upon hour of singing to their God, are hauntingly beautiful in their roughness and melodiousness.

As Pandey sees it, he is foremost a *kirtan karmacharya;* his prime function is to do this singing. But there are two other hours of the day to be worked, and it is during these hours that the priest-workers perform activities which bring them into personal contact with the dying and their families. Once a day, for instance, one of the priest-workers goes from room to room carrying the huge book which contains the *Ramcharitmanas.* The hearing of religious stories is another way of gaining spiritual benefit. So the priest-worker spends twenty minutes or so in each room reading and didactically explaining passages. The priest-worker often will be sitting cross-legged up on the wooden cot, while the family sit listening on the floor. The readings are done for and are directed toward the dying person but it is usually the family who are the most interested. Often family members will follow the priest-worker, when he has finished reading in their room, into the room of another family. The readings are social events, one of the few times that people from different families spend time with one another.

For the dying person, there are other significant visits by the priest-workers: the morning and late evening *pujas* are not the only time that the shiny brass tray moves from room to room. During the day, every two hours, from eight in the morning until six at night, one of the priests carries the tray from dying person to dying person. On the tray is a small bottle of *charnamrit*—water from the river Ganga which has been used to wash the feet of an image of Vishnu—infused with some dried leaves of the holy *tulsi* plant. In the midst of the family, the priest-worker bends over the dying person and, with a hand full of densely smoking sticks of incense, inscribes the sound "Aum" in the air while reciting a mantra. The function of this is said to be purificatory and is a necessary precursor to what is to follow; the mantra promises purity to anyone in any disease state who merely remembers Vishnu (see figure 4.9). Next, a little *charnamrit* is spooned up by the priest-worker and poured into the mouth of the dying person and a second mantra is recited. Finally, after giving the *charnamrit,* the *rogi* is, ideally, made to utter the name of the god Rama, though often it is not possible for them to do so.

FIGURE 4.9

The mantra for purification and the mantra to ward off untimely death

ॐ

अपवित्रः पवित्रो वा सवविस्थां रातोडपि वा ।
यः स्मरेतू पुण्डरीकाक्षं स बाह्यन्तरः शुचिः ॥

Aum
A person who is impure or pure or who has gone to any condition (disease), who remembers the lotus-eyed one (Vishnu), he becomes pure inside and outside

ॐ

अकालमृत्युहरणं सर्वव्याधिविनाशनम ।
विश्णुपादो पीत्वा पुनर्जन्म न विद्यते ॥

Aum
Having drunk this charnamrit (wash water of the feet of Vishnu), which takes away untimely death (and) which destroys all disease, may there be no rebirth

As Pandey explained, "one spoonful of *charnamrit* and a little *tulsi* leaf, from one to five leaves, will result in everything for the dying person." The second mantra extols and reinforces the power of the *charnamrit* which prevents untimely death *(akal mrityu)* and ensures *moksha* in the case of a timely death *(kal mrityu)*. It has the power not only to distinguish between a good and bad death, but also to completely ward off the bad ones. Thus, the priest-workers attribute both very quick deaths and complete recoveries to the power of the mantra and the *charnamrit* and *tulsi* leaves, though it can also be attributed to the Muktibhavan and to God. As Pandey said, "there is such grace of God here that some people recover when nothing before could help them." Pandey had many stories such as this one which occurred just days before we talked:

> We recently admitted a woman here. She is a very old woman. When her husband died she resolved to let her hair grow long and matted. She came here from the hospital where she was being treated. She could not pass urine and was in terrible pain. She had been given all sorts of medicine at the hospital, but nothing worked. Then she was brought here to die and she was given some *charnamrit* and a mantra was recited. Its result is either that the person will get *moksha* or they will be saved from a premature death. In this case the woman immediately started to pass urine. She was cured, but she was not cured by medicine. So, sometimes people get well here, and even at seventy or eighty, go back to look after their families and houses and to work in their fields.

It is during the many daily visits to perform these rituals that Pandey, or the other priest-workers, talk to and give instructions to the dying person and his family. They do not to talk to dying people about worldly matters: a dying person should not be bothered about such things. Foremost in Pandey's mind is the need to chant Rama's name. Though he says that, in general, the people who come are very religious and chant the name of Rama until their last breath, those who do not are advised to do so. Pandey said:

> We tell the families to make them hear Rama's name to the maximum extent. The family must chant the name to them and so must we. Some (dying) people can chant the name by themselves but others have forgotten his name. So we force them to hear it.

There are many things that they need to instruct the family about. Some people do not look after their sick relatives properly. The priest-workers lecture these people and try to make them understand the need for doing service for the sick person:

> We instruct the guardians. We tell them to bathe the sick person everyday, and to serve him, to make him sit in the sun in the winter, to air their beds. We insist they keep them clean. If not how can we perform our religious ceremonies? How can we read the *Gita* and the *Ramayana* if they do not keep clean?

Though people who behave in *nastik* (irreligious) manner are not admitted, occasionally, some people come who bring country liquor, *ganja*, cigarettes, *bidis* (leaf cigarettes), and go to see films. Then also the priest-workers need to step in;

> When the relatives go to films, or sit around playing chess, and the old, dying person is begging for water, how can we witness such a scene? They should be doing service for their dying relative. We tell them: 'Spend your time singing the praises of God. Make the patient hear these songs and look after him. Only then will your time be spent fruitfully.' " If they do not comply, we are compelled to remove them.

Another thing that the priest-workers are supposed to do is instruct the family on what to do as death approaches. The Muktibhavan, in fact has a small flyer with such instructions (see figure 4.10). The family is told to tell the dying person to keep smiling and laughing for this is a great time of bliss, that they should keep concentrating on God, and that they should say hello to Him for all of us left behind. These flyers are old and are not given out regularly any longer, but they are given out now and then and the priest-workers are well versed in the text of these flyers. Pandey says things like this to a dying person:

> Hey Baba! You have come to Kashi! You should concentrate on God! You should take the name of God! Just chant: "Rama, Rama, Rama, Rama, Rama, Rama." Do not think any more of this world! Now you must go to be with God! So keep taking God's name and concentrating on God!

Or as Tikka Baba said:

> We tell people that when they die they will attain *mukti.* We tell them they will reach the *param gati* [the highest condition] and that they will be born again neither as *manushya* [human] nor *bhut* or *preta* [demon or ghost]. We tell them they will be born in *Deava lok* [the abode of the gods].

Although most of the time the dying person is either all too willing to be compliant or is too far gone to react, sometimes there is some resistance. As Pandey said, it is difficult to tell who has done bad deeds or good deeds in their lives when they first arrive. If they do not want to do as the priest-workers say, then they are compelled to do so. Pandey told me this story of a man who did not like the name of Rama or the religious stories:

> Once I was sitting next to an old man and reciting from the *Ramayana.* I was making him listen to a particular chapter. At first he scolded me and told me to read the *Ramayana* elsewhere. Now this is my work. I said to him "Please listen carefully. I am reading this very important chapter." He had a stick near him and he hit me with that stick while I was reading. Now even though he hit me, I went on reading as it was my duty. A person becomes a little senile when they are old so, even if he does not like it, my job is to forcibly make him listen. It is my job to forcefully give this mantra of the name of Rama.

When I asked Pandey about why he liked his work, he told me that it was because of the spiritual benefits he was accruing from having the opportunity to sing the praises of God. It was only after our conversation about his day-to-day interactions with dying people that he volunteered something else. He thought silently for a time and concluded that it is a great feeling to help somebody behave in a way that will help them obtain *moksha.*

In theory, when somebody eventually dies in the Muktibhavan, it is a source of great joy, for the person has achieved *moksha.* The priest-workers, at least, often recount stories of death as though they were the happiest of endings. Tikka Baba once told me with a proud grin on his face that the day before, six people had come and every single one of them had died. Sometimes, the manager or one of the priest-workers will make a point of talking to the more ambivalent family of the dead person with a big smile and even laughter and,

FIGURE 4.10

Instructions for time of death: Translation of a sheet of instructions which is sometimes given to families to help them deel properly with the time of death

Shri Hari:
Hare Ram Hare Ram Ram Ram Hare Hare
Hare Krishna Hare Krishna Krishna Krishna Hare Hare

When his death is imminent, sit down next to the patient and with a smile tell him:

1. Continue smiling and laughing.
2. Continue to make others smile and laugh. For you this is a great time of bliss. Keep determination—you are reaching the great place of the gods. There too do not feel even a little doubt. For you this is a very great time.
3. God is inviting you for immersion in his undivided bliss. There is no other reason.
4. Here, meeting and separation are the greatest joys.
5. Keep completely full of only the feeling of God.
6. Keep a firm resolution, you are going to that immortal enjoyment that is thousands of times better than here.
7. From your exerience of immortal enjoyment, we will all become very happy.
8. Please definitely give our regards to god.

Shri Gitaji 2:11, 5:29, 12:4, 18:69

subtly scolding them for their attachment, will tell them to rest assured that the dead person is now with God.

Sometimes too they must give advice to the family on the conducting of the last rites and disposal of the body. (Figure 4.11 is a translation of a flyer which they provide for people needing advice on conducting proper funeral rites.) In cases where there are not enough men, one of the priest-workers may help carry the body to the burning ghat. However, soon after a death the connection between the family and the Muktibhavan is severed. In fact one thing which astounded me was the speed with which a body is removed from the Muktibhavan. In many of the cases I observed, within just a couple of hours of death occurring, the body would be washed, wrapped, tied to a bier, carried to the burning ghat, and set ablaze.

FIGURE 4.11

Sheet of instructions given to families for what things must be gathered after a death for the proper celebration of rituals (translation from Hindi)

Shri Hari
Provisions for After Dying

1. Shortly after he or she has died call a barber, a Brahman priest, and the relatives.

2. Gather the following goods—

Two bamboo sticks eight feet in length, six sticks, one *ser* (960 gms) of jute rope, one *tola* (12 gms) cotton thread, one *ser* reed cord, two to four peacock feathers, ten yards cloth for dead body (not from a mill or with blue color), one yellow cloth with *"Rama nam"* printed on it made from cotton or wool (a fancy shawl is not necessary), half *ser* flour of rice or barley, one brass screen filter, one fire pot for fire, ghee according to capacity (at least one *ser*), four or two annas of money, one pot of water, one *ser* flowers, one flower garland, one quarter *ser* of cotton, coconut, or the kernel of coconut having asked the people of the house, wood of *tulsi* plant—at least one quarter *ser*—the more the better, one *tola* of camphor, sandlewood chips—at least one half *ser,* sandalwood (pieces) —at least one half Ser, material for *havan* and powder of camphor having mixed both together—at least one half *ser,* one quarter *ser* "sugandhit" (sweet smelling mixture)—one half *ser.*

For homage, one bundle of green grass and one *chatank* (5 *tolas*) black sesame seeds. The stick for offering the material into the fire for havan.

Do cremation of dead body then do *havan.* For funereal rites and Vedic mantras the instruction text and priest should be taken along.

Eight *man* (320 *ser*) of wood. Banyan, Pipal and Bel—five or ten *ser*— and whatever other wood is available.

Two crowns (Ketiya or Irandi) for the person doing the rituals. One quarter *ser* of cow dung.

Death of a *Rogi Marnewala*

Late in October, I met Mr. Singh at the Muktibhavan. He spoke about as much English as I could speak Hindi at that time, only three months into my fieldwork, but I taped much of what he told me and somehow we understood each other. He said that his mother was in the last stage of life, and that she would die very soon. His mother and he were very close: his father had died when he was four years old and Singh was his mother's only son (though he has brothers from another of his father's marriages). His mother was over eighty years old, he said, and had been in the Muktibhavan for two days. They had come from a village in Varanasi district, not too far off from Kashi. Consequently there were many relatives with them including four women and a man Singh said was his servant.

As I entered their room, all the women squatting on the floor pulled their *saris* over their faces. They were surrounding Singh's mother, who was lying on a blanket on the floor. Only her face was visible and from it, it was evident that she was close to the end. Her face was very thin and contorted. Her mouth was wide open and a rasping sound accompanied the slow upward and downward motion of the blanket over her chest.

Singh told me it was his mother's own desire to be brought to Kashi. She had, one month before, asked the family to bring her there. Two days before, Singh said, she had indicated that it was time to go to Kashi. However, she was "in a coma" when they brought her, and thus I suppose the decision was obvious, though later he said that she knew she was in Kashi and was happy to be there. She had been taking only Ganga water, *tulsi* leaves, and milk, brought from the temple of Vishvanath.

Singh told me his mother was there in order to get *moksha.* This is how Singh explained it:

> This life is full of trouble and sadness. Dying here means never having to be born into this life again. God is everybody, just like the sea. A person is like a little drop of sea water. There is no difference in the sea and a little drop. What matter you will find in ocean, you will also find in a little drop of ocean.

Singh announced that he was going to the Ganges to get a pot of water with which to bathe her after she died. He told me to come with him. We walked through crowded streets down toward the Ganga. It was difficult to keep up with him as he walked quickly, not talking to me but occasionally glancing back to see if I was still there. There was a festival going on in Kashi and the ghat, too, was very crowded. Finding an open spot in the sea of people at the water's edge, he dipped his *lothi* into the river and then headed back to the Muktibhavan at the same furious pace. He knew there was reason to hurry.

We arrived back at around five in the afternoon and he went

upstairs to his mother. Within ten minutes, the wailing of the women signaled that his mother had died. I met him coming out of the room. Without a trace of expression on his face he said, "She is gone, expired." He told several other male relatives (who seemed to have shown up from somewhere) in the same unemotional manner. They in turn betrayed no emotion on hearing the news.

Despite his unaffected countenance, Singh was discernibly shaken. For a while he walked around aimlessly, a bit confused. The women covered up Singh's mother's face and stayed in the chamber with her, weeping loudly. The men all left the chamber and were downstairs arranging the necessary materials for disposal of the body. Shuklaji had written out a death certificate and gave it to Singh. Shuklaji, when speaking to him, was all smiles and cheer, and even laughed about something. The mood of the men was serious but they seemed to feel obliged to return his grins.

The body was brought down and placed outside on the ground, undressed but shrouded from view. Singh washed her body with the water we had collected from the Ganga. A large piece of white cloth was folded about her and a couple of the men carefully tied it to conform to the contours of the body. She was then tied on to the bamboo bier and covered with a large piece of gold cloth over which were draped flower garlands.

The bier was picked up by four of the men and the whole party, nine or ten in total, chanting *"Rama nam, satya hai"* began the kilometer or two walk through the narrow lanes down toward Manikarnika ghat. The women stayed behind.

At the burning ghat, the body was taken to the edge of the Ganga and was splashed with water. It was then leaned on the steps while arrangements were made. Singh stripped down to his underwear and found somebody to shave his head. Then he dressed in a fresh white *dhoti* and wrapped a white piece of cloth around his neck which draped down over his back. While he walked up to the office where deaths are officially registered, wood was arranged in a large pyre on the edge of the river near the smoldering remains of some earlier cremations. The body was carried over and placed on the top.

Singh went to collect the flame. Carefully guarded and sold for a high price, this special fire is said to have been burning continuously since time began. Singh came back with a burning ember smoldering away in a bundle of grass. Under the instructions of a funeral priest, he passed it in several circles over his dead mother's head, the motion of which ignited the grass. Then he shoved the burning bundle into the pile of wood.

He stepped back and watched. Others attended to the kindling

FIGURE 4.12

A body being dressed and prepared to be carried to the burning ghat

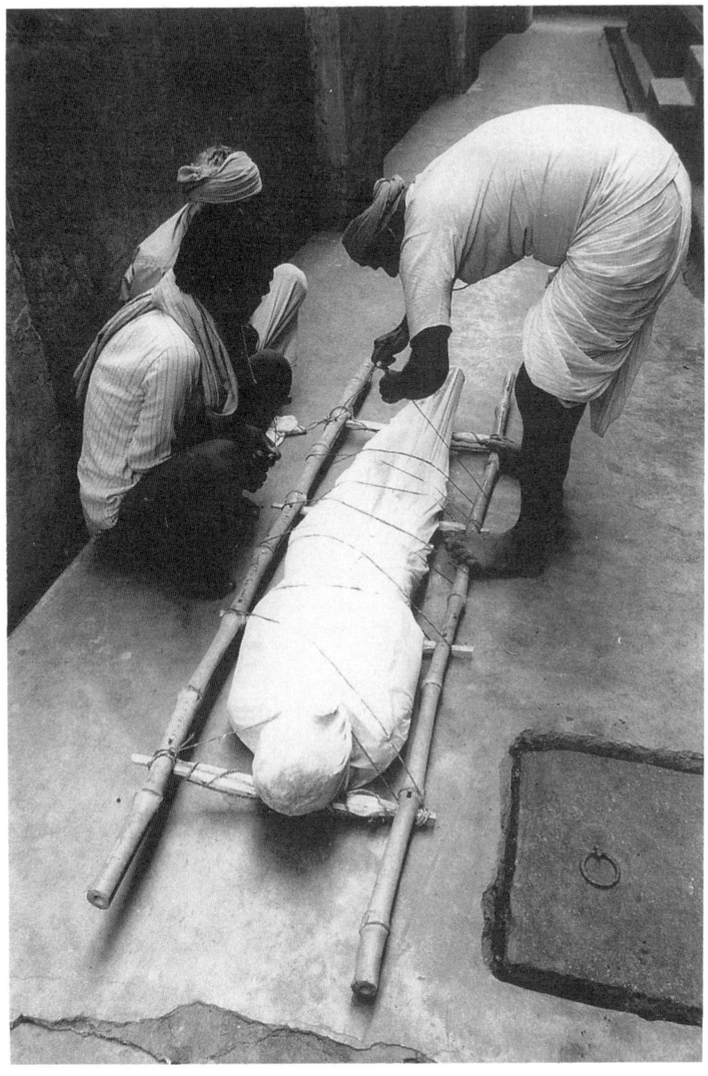

of the fire and threw in a powder which perfumes the air and enhances the flames. I stayed and watched his mother burn with him and still I saw no emotional reaction or expression, though once or twice he stared forlornly into the fire. He said to me at one point "Do you know what the body is worth after death? It is worth nothing." When the end of his mother's leg fell out of the fire sizzling and crackling, he watched it being picked up with a stick and thrown back on the fire without so much as a break in what he was saying to me. He was saying this:

> The body is made from five matters. One fire, second air, third water, fourth soil and fifth sky. Under burning you will find . . . that the five elements . . . separately they are going away. . . . The spirit is already gone . . . the spirit is immersed in Shiva. . . . Vishvanath Baba, Shiva! Her spirit merged in Shiva. This is the opinion . . . that if you die in Kashi the spirit of your dead body is merged in Shiva.

5

Dying as Tradition

In Chapter 3, I described the death of an old man who was brought to die at the small room on the bank of the Ganga at Tulsi ghat by his son, a surgeon at Banaras Hindu University hospital. I characterized this mode of dying in Kashi as being part of an old tradition, as opposed to the newer tradition of dying in the large institutions set up for that purpose. In this chapter I will examine the act of coming to die in Kashi as tradition. I will start by recounting the surgeon's own characterization of the "tradition," the word he used again and again, of bringing people to Kashi to die.

The surgeon said his family had a tradition of coming to Kashi to die on the bank of the Ganga. The surgeon's grandfather, years before, at the age of 82, had been brought to die in Kashi. He believed, too, that his great-grandfather died there before that. More recently, his uncle died suddenly in the village but they brought his body to Kashi and cremated it at Harischandra ghat. Then his "cousin-grandfather" was brought and he died on the bank of the Ganga. The most recent was the surgeon's father who was brought only when it looked like death might be imminent. He was taken first to the hospital and only when there was no chance to save him was he brought in to Kashi.

The surgeon maintained that everybody from the village would like to come to die in Kashi. "It is not just my family," he said, "it is a tradition." However, very few people actually come from his village; only the well-off people can manage it. He maintained, too, that it is not just his village but that all the people in the surrounding villages have the same desire to come to Kashi to die: "It is the culture of eastern U.P. and Bihar," he said. The people of this region "try to bring everybody." At least this was so in the past—these days, he said, people are becoming less interested.

The surgeon's story is the only one that I have from somebody whose family tradition still is to die on the bank of the Ganga. Now, the people who come to Kashi to die stay in one of the two large institutions and not on the river bank. For many of the people staying in these institutions, as for the surgeon's family, coming to die in Kashi is often a family or village tradition.

When I asked Shuklaji where all the dying people came from he told me that the pattern for both the Kashi Labh Muktibhavan and the Ganga-labh Bhavan was the same. He knows this because it had been investigated; the story goes that somebody made allegations that there was some kind of bribery occurring at the Muktibhavan and that was the reason so many people were coming from Rohtas district. The representative of the Charitable Trust that owns the Muktibhavan investigated by checking out the records of the Ganga-labh Bhavan. Finding that the same proportion of people going to that *bhavan* were from also Rohtas, the matter was dropped. Shuklaji said that 75 percent come from Rohtas district, 5 percent from Bhojpur district and 20 percent from all over India. Shuklaji's explanation for the similar distribution of dying people from particular districts is that the Ganga-labh Bhavan is merely taking the overflow of the Muktibhavan.

My analysis of the records of both *bhavans* confirms that Shuklaji is correct about the distribution, though his idea of "all over India" really means all over eastern Uttar Pradesh and Bihar. However, the records do not confirm his contention that the Muktibhavan's overflow is spilling over to the Ganga-labh Bhavan. Rather, as I argued at the end of chapter 3, it appears that people who might once have gone to the Ganga-labh Bhavan, are now going to the Muktibhavan.

In 1990, the people coming to Kashi for *Kashi-labh* came from thirty-four different districts in three states (see Figures 5.1 and 5.2). About 80 percent of all people came from the state of Bihar. Most of the remaining 20 percent came from Uttar Pradesh, though approximately 1 percent come from the state of Madhya Pradesh. Though both *bhavan* managers told me that occasionally people come from "all over India," in 1990 nobody came from outside of these three states.

Though people come from many of the districts within these states, almost three quarters of all the people who came to die in one of Kashi's two *bhavans* came from one of only three districts: Rohtas, Bhojpur (both in Bihar) and Varanasi (in Uttar Pradesh). Rohtas district is by far the most important. Although it is in a different state than Kashi (which is in Varanasi district, Uttar Pradesh), Rohtas is very close to Kashi. Roughly 60 percent, or 281 out of the 458 people who registered in one of the two *bhavans* in 1990, came from Rohtas. About 6 percent came from Bhojpur and 7 percent from Varanasi.

When I compared the figures for 1980 to those of 1990, I saw that the decrease in people coming to Kashi over the last fifteen years is

FIGURE 5.1

Map of North India showing districts and proportion of total number of people coming from each. Based on Muktibhavan and Ganga-labh Bhavan data for 1990

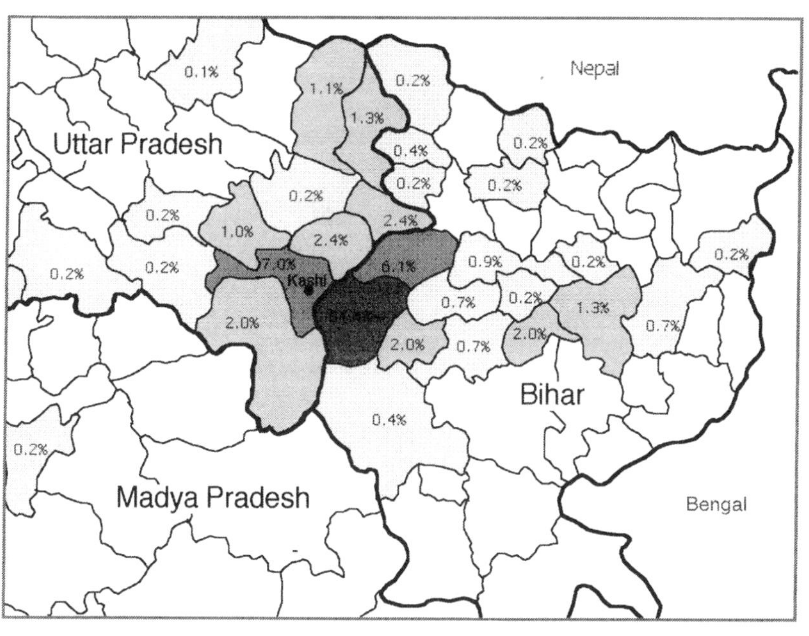

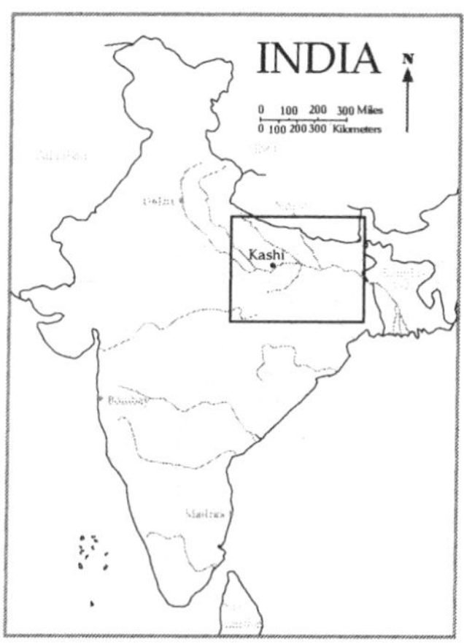

FIGURE 5.2

District: Pie diagram illustrating the proportions of all people going either to Muktibhavan or Ganga-labh Bhavan in 1990 by district of origin

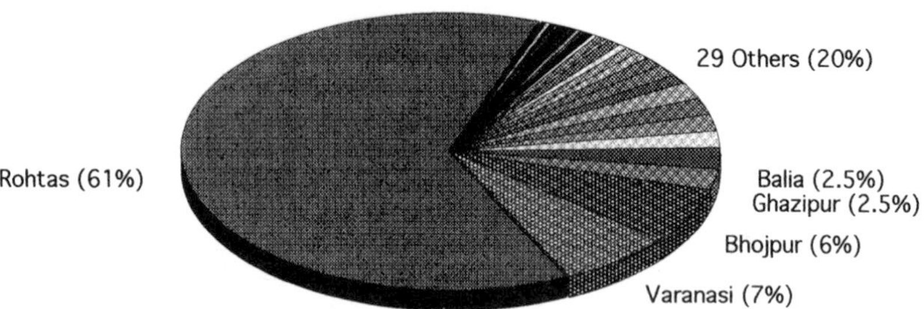

mainly accounted for by fewer people coming from the "big three"—Rohtas, Bhojpur, and Varanasi. However, decreases from these districts are not of the same relative proportion, and are not evenly distributed, between the *bhavans.* The number of people coming from Bhojpur district to Kashi, for instance, has decreased by 50 percent since 1980. This decrease is due entirely to a decrease in people from Bhojpur going to the Ganga-labh Bhavan. The trend from Varanasi district, on the other hand, is just the opposite of Bhojpur; fewer people are going to the Muktibhavan than before, and the number has not changed at the Ganga-labh Bhavan. From Rohtas, there has been a huge decrease (of 61 percent) in people going to Ganga-labh Bhavan, but at the Muktibhavan the number of people from Rohtas increased. Of the many other districts, from which just a few people come every year, there was no real change in numbers coming to Kashi between 1980 and 1990. However, there was a significant shift amongst these people from the Ganga-labh Bhavan to the Muktibhavan.

The trends by which people of particular castes are using the two *bhavans* show the same general pattern. In 1990 people from 42 different castes[1] came to one of the two *bhavans* (see Figure 5.3). The picture is not straightforward, however, as some people tend to identify themselves with their *jati* (caste), whereas others tend to identify themselves with their *varna* (grouping of castes, or class). Brahmins, for instance, are always identified as "Brahmin" and not as whatever subdivision of Brahmin they belong to. According to the records, people calling themselves Brahmins accounted for just under 50 percent, while people calling themselves Rajputs made up almost 25 percent. About 20 percent of all people were from the fairly low castes such as Kurmi and Yadav—castes which Omji identified as "touchable Shudras." In

FIGURE 5.3

Caste: Pie diagram illustrating the proportions of all people going either to Muktibhavan or Ganga-labh Bhavan in 1990 by reported caste

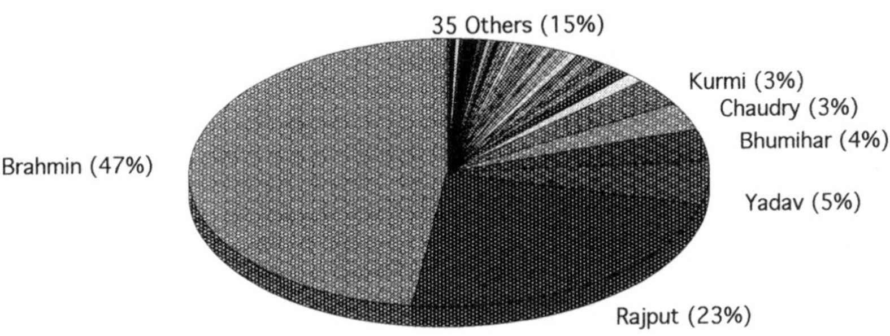

1990 seven people belonging to one of four "Untouchable" castes came for *Kashi-labh,* all of whom were registered at Ganga-labh Bhavan. Only four had come in 1980.

Despite the overall decrease (of over 15 percent) in the number of people coming to Kashi for *Kashi-labh* over the last decade, the number of Brahmins registered in 1990 is exactly the same as for 1980. The decrease is accounted for by all the other castes, most significantly by Bhumihars and Rajputs. However it would be incorrect to conclude that there is less diversity in castes now. In 1990 the same number of castes (though not all the same ones) showed up in the records as in 1980.

Though the number of Brahmins coming to Kashi remains the same, they are not evenly distributed between the two *bhavans.* Brahmins, now, overwhelmingly end up at the Muktibhavan. In 1990, 52 fewer Brahmins went to the Ganga-labh Bhavan than in 1980, and 51 more went to the Muktibhavan. In 1990, 185 Brahmins went to the Muktibhavan while only 29 went to the Ganga-labh Bhavan. In general, the shifts in who is using which *bhavan* over the last decade has resulted in the Muktibhavan having a "higher average" caste, and the Ganga-labh Bhavan, a "lower average" caste.

From the above figures, one trend is quite clear. The Ganga-labh Bhavan is losing its "support" from the biggest categories of users, namely, Brahmins and Rajputs and those from Rohtas and the rest of the state of Bihar. The number of people coming to Kashi Labh Muktibhavan from these castes and from Rohtas district, on the other hand, is either unchanged over the last decade or is increasing. In order to move toward an explanation for this trend, in the following section I present an account of a Brahmin man who brought his dying mother to Kashi from their village in Rohtas. They came knowing about the Ganga-labh Bhavan, but through a series of circumstances ended up at the Kashi Labh Muktibhavan.

Mr. H. H. Dubey and His Mother

In late July 1991, just days before I left Kashi, I met Mr. H. H. Dubey at the Muktibhavan. He had heard from one of the priest-workers that I had been taking people's photographs and sending them back to the village at no cost, and so he asked me to take his dying mother's picture. After doing so and letting him write his mailing address into my notebook, I asked him if I could come back and interview him. "Of course," he said, "why not?" But when Omji and I arrived on schedule he was not to be found. Again I arranged a time and again he disappeared. Finally we showed up without notice and, having no time to hide, Dubey invited us into his room. He turned out to be quite a talker and he recounted things in incredible detail; when I asked how big his village was, for instance, he described each and every *jati,* their jobs, and other characteristics, how many houses they had in the village and roughly where they were situated.

Dubey described his mother as "an ideal woman." She was the type, he said, who would tolerate people saying rude things. Her behavior with the family was always excellent; she had constantly done service *(seva)* for them and looked after them. She lived a simple life and ate simple food and had done many pilgrimages to places like Brindhavan, Ganga Sagar, Jagarnathpuri, and Gaya. Dubey's father had not been very rich. They kept both buffaloes and cows and used the milk as food in their house. They also made ghee which they sold to pay the school fees for the children. Dubey said that milk was very important to his mother; she relied on milk and she said it would cure anything. On the other hand, she did not trust medicine; she never took any medicine or had any injection into her body. And, Dubey said, she never became sick.

That is, until two months before. At that time she was eating rice and drinking milk normally. Then one day, she told her son that she had decided that she wanted to do the donation of a cow *(gau dan).* Now Dubey had just done the wedding of his daughter and incurred a lot of expenses so he thought that it was better to wait for a while. He said to his mother that during the coming *navaratra* (nine nights of the Goddess), which was a couple of months away, they would do the donation of a cow. Also, at that time, they would feed the neighborhood people and the Brahmins. But within a couple of days of this conversation, Dubey's mother became "slightly paralyzed on one side." Also at this time she started to eat less and less rice and stopped being able to speak very well, though she could still listen. So Dubey bought a cow (for Rs. 350) and a new *sari* for his mother to wear. He sent for a barber and "some *guruji*"—a learned person of some kind—and, when all was set, they performed the cow donation. Then, after that, they did a grain donation *(ann dan)*, giving ten kilos of unhusked rice, eight kilos of threshed rice, and some black beans. Many of the village people came and helped out by giving his mother things for her to give away.

These donations are done in anticipation of death; it had become clear that Dubey's mother was dying. Dubey said that she quickly "became very old" and started to experience "pain and weakness." They went to a doctor in the village. The doctor said that he could "give her some injection," but it would save her for only twenty-four hours or so. The doctor said to Dubey, "It is better if you take her right away to a hospital in Kashi." The doctor also told Dubey that he should not take her to the Banaras Hindu University hospital because it is outside of Kashi and if she dies there she will not get *mukti*. He said it would be better if he admitted her in a hospital that is inside of Kashi and he told him how to get to such a hospital.

On their way to Kashi, Dubey thought to himself that it would be no use to "give an injection" to his mother. She could not eat properly or swallow water very well. If tablets are given to her, he thought, that would be painful for her. He decided not to go to the hospital. At the same time, he said, she also was saying to him "I want to see the Ganga. Take me to the Ganga." Dubey thought to himself "it will be better if I take her down to the river side."

Dubey had actually been to Kashi with dying people on several earlier occasions. He had, in fact, brought his own father to die in Kashi. Later he had brought his father's brother's wife and, at least one other time, had accompanied a neighbor or friend who was bringing somebody to die. During those times, he stayed at the Ganga-labh Bhavan at Manikarnika ghat. This time, however, he decided against going back to the Ganga-labh Bhavan because, he said, his mother could not really move and Manikarnika ghat was difficult to get to. Also he was interested in finding a "better place," and one where his mother could see the Ganga. Dubey knew that one of his friends from the village was working in a temple near to Dasashwameda ghat. So he went there with his mother, hoping to be able to arrange a place to stay.

They slept the first night outside on the steps near Dasashwameda ghat. At that time his mother was still in her senses, he said, and that is what she wanted. The next day, "by the grace of Rama and Sita and Hanuman," the temple provided a little room up some stairs where they could stay. But this turned out to be no good because it was very difficult to move her up and down the steps and because, inside, the water which was poured over the temple's image, constantly dripped on them during the night.

The third day, after Dubey again took his mother down to see the Ganga, she became totally uncommunicative. He had heard from someone that there was another *muktibhavan* somewhere nearby. So he left his mother and walked up the street to Gowdolia. There he went to a *dharmsala* and explained to them that he had brought his mother to get *mukti.* They said that they do not take such cases but they told him how to get to the Kashi Labh Muktibhavan. He went to the Muktibhavan and talked to one of the priest-workers, who told him that if he came quickly he could have a very nice room with electricity. Dubey brought his mother to the Muktibhavan that evening.

They had been there for two days when I met Dubey. Since admitting her, he told me, he had watched all her power "slowly, slowly go." She had not eaten for some time and just the day before our conversation it became impossible for her even to drink water. Dubey did not know how long she would last. He said, "until her time is up and she has permission from God, she will not die." I was leaving Kashi at that time and I never found out what happened with Dubey and his mother, though it is probably safe to assume that she did not last long. I sent Dubey the photographs of his mother after I arrived back in Canada, but have never heard back from him.

Though Dubey said that he set out from the village, having spoken to a doctor, with the aim of finding a cure for his mother, there is some indication that this was not his only expectation. At least on the part of his mother, who had done the cow donation and stopped eating, there was probably an understanding that the trip to Kashi would not involve a return leg. The doctor had advised that they go to a hospital inside of Kashi (that is within the zone of liberation), in case she died, and Dubey himself had come to Kashi with dying people on several previous occasions.

In my sample of the *bhavan*'s records, there are three other records of people coming from Dubey's village of Ghelari. Two of these were Brahmins and one a Harijan. Dubey told me that ninety percent of the Brahmins in his village bring either the very old people to die in Kashi, or their bodies for burning. About half come alive, half dead, he estimated. The journey is arduous with a live person. Most people have to carry the dying on their shoulders for many kilometers to the railway station. Then, too, the train is very crowded. The very rich people, on the other hand, bring the dying by jeep or by car. By Dubey's estimation, it is about twice as expensive to bring a dead body to Kashi than it is to bring a dying person; the price of transportation is very high where a corpse is concerned. There is, therefore, some economic incentive, if one is going to bring a body to Kashi to burn, to bring it before its resident has abandoned it.

General and Specific Knowledge of Dying in Kashi

According to Shuklaji, there are two reasons why so many of the dying come from Rohtas district. The first reason is custom; the people from Rohtas, he says, have always brought bodies to burn in Kashi, or have come to die in Kashi. He says this is because the Ganga does not flow through Rohtas so people have to go out of the district anyway. The second reason so many people come from Rohtas, according to Shuklaji, is that the first manager was from Rohtas. During the early days he formed a lot of contacts in Rohtas: a lot of people there came to know about the facility through him.

These are examples of two different types of knowledge about dying in Kashi on the part of the people coming to Kashi to die, which can be thought of as general and specific knowledge. General knowledge refers to the broad cultural understanding that it is spiritually beneficial to die in Kashi. This results in a general desire among some, though not all, to die in Kashi. Specific knowledge, on the other hand, is the understanding from either past experience or the accounts of others, that dying in Kashi is do-able.

The districts from which people come have several things in common. Certainly, they are close to Kashi by all-India standards: the people who come the farthest, from districts such as Katihar and Bhagilpur, travel four hundred kilometers, but the majority live within one hundred kilometers of Kashi.[2] Linguistically, roughly 85 percent of all people coming to Kashi to die are from the predominantly Bhojpuri-speaking districts, which span the border between Uttar Pradesh and Bihar, and roughly 10 percent come from the Magadhi-speaking districts of central and southwest Bihar.[3] Essentially all the districts from which people come are within the rich and fertile flood plains of the Gangetic basin. The people from these districts are thus from a similar economic culture of agriculture and thus are probably part of a large cultural area which shares, among other things, understandings about the importance of dying in Kashi. I will leave a discussion of these shared cultural understandings until chapter 6.

FIGURE 5.4

Rogi marnewala and his family at Kashi Labh Muktibhavan

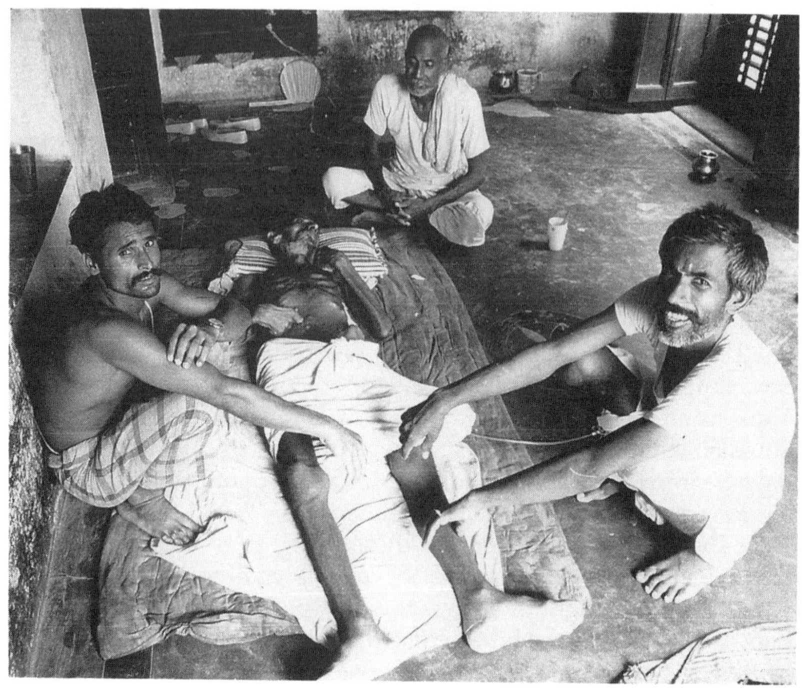

From my encounters with families at the Muktibhavan, I got the impression that many of the people who come to Kashi to die have, in addition to a broadly similar understanding of the importance of dying in Kashi, specific knowledge of just where in Kashi they will find a place to stay. Many of the people with whom I talked had, at least, heard about the Muktibhavan before coming. Mishra (whom I discussed in chapter 4) had planned to die at home but, at the last moment, decided to go to Kashi. They found out about the Muktibhavan back in the village. Kapil Deo Singh, whom I will talk about in chapter 6, said that they were going to take their mother down to the Ganga near their village, but also decided at the last moment to come to Kashi. They knew about the Muktibhavan because their father's sister's husband had gone there once before with somebody and had told them about it. Another family told me that, though they have a family tradition of bringing people to Kashi to die—they had brought their grandmother after she died and their father had died *en route*—they had never been at the Muktibhavan before, but had learned of it before coming this time from some other people in their village.

From the accounts of these people, it seems as if families come to Kashi to die as part of larger village units. At least there seems to be an increased likelihood of a person coming to die from a particular village if somebody else from that village has come before. There are two other types of data which support this notion: the questionnaire responses and the registration records of the two *bhavans*. In the questionnaire, 82 percent of the guardians said that they knew about the Muktibhavan before coming to Kashi while 56 percent said that they actually knew one of the Muktibhavan workers before coming. This means that only a minority of families arriving at the Muktibhavan have come to Kashi with no ultimate destination in mind. Most know exactly where they are going: the Kashi Labh Muktibhavan.

In fact, when asked in the survey questionnaire, almost 50 percent of the guardians said they themselves had been to the Muktibhavan at least once before with some other dying person. Out of these, several people said they had been there three or four times before and one person reported coming eight times previously. However, I am inclined to not fully trust these particular responses. The person who said he had been there eight times before is from a district that shows up so very rarely in the Muktibhavan records that I do not think it is possible that he brought so many people. I suspect that, in some cases, this question may have been interpreted by the respondents as meaning how many other times had they been *to Kashi* as opposed to its intended meaning of how many times *to the Muktibhavan with a dying person*.

A high rate of return visits would say something significant about the tradition of coming to die in Kashi. To see if there is clustering by place of origin, I sorted my samples of the records (over 1,600 of them) by district and village so that all entries of people from a particular village were grouped together. Figure 5.5 shows the number of times villages are represented in the records. It seems the majority of people are from villages from where no other people have come though as I only have roughly 10 percent of all records, it is possible that many of these single occurrences do in fact have hidden doubles. Looked at from the opposite perspective, the records show that at the very least 35 percent of dying people come from villages from where others have come previously or subsequently.

Another point of interest is the presence of obvious "outliers" at the center and on the right-hand side of the graph. People from these

FIGURE 5.5

Repeat visits by village: Graph showing the number of records (people) for villages represented in the records once, twice, three times, etc. Calculated for all available records from both Muktibhavan and Ganga-labh Bhavan.

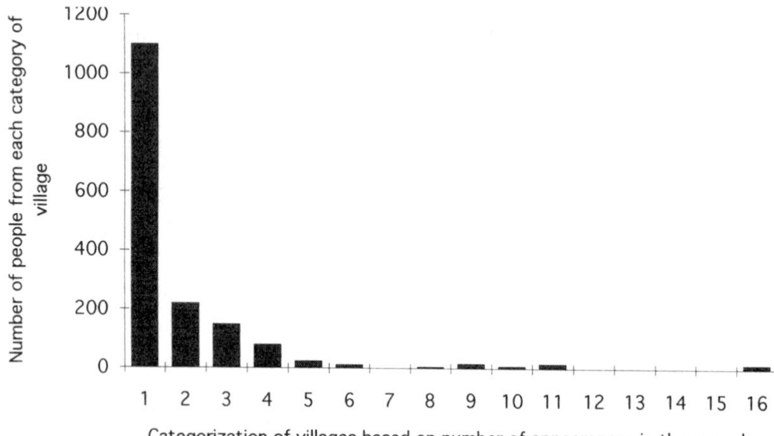

villages regularly come to Kashi to die. There are seven villages clustered at the center, from which between 8 and 11 records were captured in my sample. The village represented on the far right is Ghodra, on the main railline into Kashi from Rohtas, from where the records of sixteen people found their way into my sample. Their distribution over time[4] suggests that every year several people from Ghodra come to Kashi to die, and that this has been going on for some time.

There are some patterns *within* these village clusters from the center of the graph which further suggest a general pattern of people coming by village. For instance, in the one year 1990–91, five people came to the Muktibhavan from a village called Aghalchar, which is in Balia district, Uttar Pradesh. I have no records in my sample of anybody from that village before. The five were all women and they all arrived at different times, separated by between one and three months. They were Rajputs and Brahmins and their ages ranged from seventy to ninety-six. Intriguingly, all five of them died on the very day they arrived at the Muktibhavan; in fact, they all died within eight hours of their arrival. All five of them had come with four male and two female family members. The similarities amongst these people and what is known from the records about their coming to Kashi and their deaths, suggest that the people in this particular village, anyway, share in the *manner* by which they go to Kashi to die.

I know a little about one of these women whose guardian filled out the questionnaire. This woman was reported to have been a 96-year-old Brahmin who had postsecondary education and had been a teacher. The person who brought her had come before, though he did not say how often. The dying woman was not taking medicine, nor was she eating or drinking anything but water from the Ganga. She arrived at eight o'clock in the morning and died about two that afternoon. Admittedly, with only circumstantial evidence, I envision this sort of scenario: One woman in Aghalchar, perhaps a very respected or pious woman, went to Kashi to die. The relatives told others in the village of the place that was available, about what a good death the woman had had and the spiritual benefit of that death. As a result, other old women of the village also wanted to come to Kashi to die. Perhaps somebody in the village has a jeep and so transportation has become easy. The fact that all five of them died so quickly after arriving suggests that they were able to wait until the last possible moment before setting off.

Another thing that became evident from sorting the records by village is that there is different patterns of clustering between the two *muktibhavans*. This appears to be so for all sets of comparable data, including the 5 percent sample of all records and the complete years of 1980 and 1990. However the absolute numbers of records are only comparable for the 1980 year in which 243 people went to the Ganga-labh Bhavan and 288 people went to the Muktibhavan. The records for this year are compared in Figure 5.6. At the Muktibhavan in 1980, 25 percent of all people were from villages from where *at least* one other person had also come *in that same year*. The comparable figure for the Ganga-labh Bhavan is only 7 percent. One explanation for this is that the Muktibhavan is getting better reviews from the family members returning home after a death and thus more people are deciding to go there on this basis.

The village is one of the units of communication of information about such things as the Muktibhavan and how good a place it is for dying. From looking at clusters of records from single villages, the pattern is for several castes to come from a particular village. This indicates, among other things, that the people coming from a particular village are not relatives, and may not even be acquainted. Of the 16 records from Kudra, for example, 6 were Brahmins, 3 Kurmis, 2 Rajputs, 2 Gareris, and 1 Kahar. This again suggests that the village, as opposed to intervillage caste connections, is a unit of information dissemination.

To reiterate, there seem to be two kinds of understandings about going to die in Kashi. On the basis of general knowledge, people come

FIGURE 5.6

Repeat visits by village: Graph showing proportions of people (records) from villages from which no one else came, one other person came, two other people came, etc. For one year (1980) comparing Muktibhavan and Ganga-labh Bhavan.

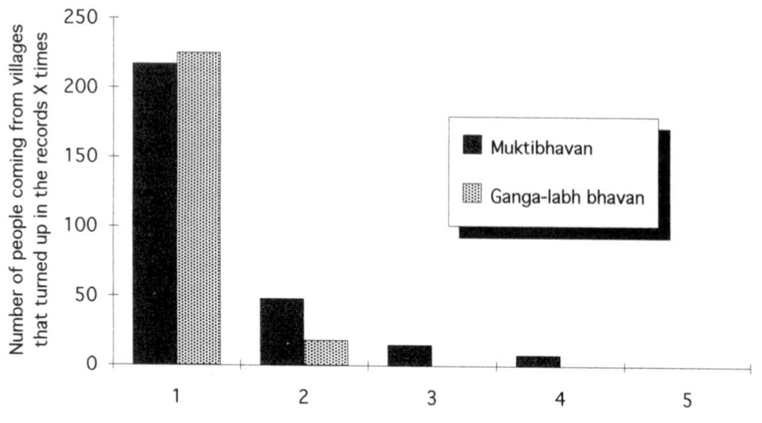

to Kashi to die on an almost random basis in the sense that they do not know people who have done this before and do not know specifically about the institutions in Kashi until they arrive. This is reflected in the large number of villages that are represented in the records only once. These people coming to die primarily on the basis of general knowledge might go to one or the other of the institutions, but make up the bulk of the people in the Ganga-labh Bhavan's records. The overall decrease in the numbers of people coming to die in Kashi and especially at the Ganga-labh Bhavan, is due to a decrease in the number of people coming primarily on the basis of general knowledge. This decrease is occurring simply because it is getting more complicated to make the trip to Kashi. As the manager of the Ganga-labh Bhavan himself said, there are increased costs and the city is getting more difficult for outsiders.

Those people who come to Kashi to die with specific knowledge of a place to stay that is free, spiritually conducive to dying a good death, and pleasant in other ways, may actually be increasing in number. For these people, being from the cultural area might be considered a necessary but not sufficient condition for (considering and acting on the possibility of) going to Kashi to die. The "sufficient" condition, in addition to having the time and finances, is having the specific knowledge that there is a place in Kashi where they can stay and that that place is not going to be difficult or unpleasant. These people account for the steady increase in numbers of people dying at the Muktibhavan over time despite the overall decrease in numbers coming to Kashi.

The End of a Tradition?

At the end of chapter 3, I noted that the overall trend for both institutions is a steady decrease in the numbers of people coming for *Kashi-labh.* About thirteen fewer people, according to the figures represented in Figure 3.6, have been arriving in Kashi to die each year. Here, in the light of the above analysis, I examine the possibility that this general trend, when extended forward in time, suggests that the phenomenon of coming to Kashi for *Kashi-labh* may be coming to an end.

If the people going to Kashi for *Kashi-labh* are acting on what I have called general knowledge and are going primarily to Kashi, as opposed to going because one or the other *bhavans* is there, then the cause of this decrease would likely be located in larger societal forces. In this case, the decrease in numbers coming to Kashi will likely continue unabated. The general decrease in overall numbers coming would have to be seen as coincidental to the "switching of allegiance" going on from the Ganga-labh Bhavan to the Muktibhavan.

On the other hand, if the people coming to Kashi are coming with what I have called specific knowledge of one or the other *bhavan,* the situation is quite different. If people set off for one or the other *bhavan,* then the *bhavans* may increase or decrease in "popularity" independently of one another. In this case, the overall decrease in numbers of people coming to Kashi for *Kashi-labh* might be expected to end when the decrease in numbers going to the Ganga-labh Bhavan ends. The increasing numbers of people going to the Muktibhavan every year, will continue to increase, and so too will the overall number of people going to Kashi for *Kashi-labh.*

According to this analysis, everybody comes with general knowledge, but a proportion have specific knowledge also. I have shown that there is a difference between the two *bhavans* in terms of numbers of repeat visits by village, which I take to be proportionally representative of the degree of specific knowledge. The implication is that people at the Muktibhavan are those who know the ropes. I suggest that this difference between the two user populations is correlated to the decreasing numbers of people going to the Ganga-labh Bhavan and the increasing numbers of people going to the Muktibhavan.

Why the decrease at the Ganga-labh Bhavan while the increase at the Muktibhavan? There are several possible explanations. Dubey, who had a family tradition of going to Ganga-labh Bhavan, had sought out a new place. His explanation was that it was difficult to get his mother to the Ganga-labh Bhavan. Getting to Manikarnika ghat—a difficult task for the young and healthy—requires a walk of perhaps a kilometer through steep and slippery, maze-like alleys which are so thin that a dying person would have to be carried in on someone's back or brought around by boat. The Ganga-labh Bhavan is located at Manikarnika ghat which, while being more awesome in a spiritual sense, is also more awesome in the sense of being sensually overpowering. It is crowded with all manner of people and filled with the smoke of burning bodies. The people coming for *Kashi-labh* and the family who has brought them, are village householders many of whom have likely never spent much time outside of their villages. The Ganga-labh Bhavan is also in a state of relative disrepair and very little money is available to the manager. Dubey, and probably others, simply want someplace "better."

The Muktibhavan is a relative paradise. It is in a less crowded area of the city with relatively easy access from the main road to the railway station. It is a beautiful mansion with a spiritual atmosphere and priest-workers who sing the name of God and read religious songs to the dying people. The lesser spiritual location is certainly made up for by the spiritual activities. In fact, some people who were staying there with a dying person appeared to be having such a (religiously) good time—singing to God and visiting temples—that they might have been on a holiday of sorts. There is no doubt that those who have stayed there tell stories of a wonderful experience as well as a successful bid for *Kashi-labh* when they return to their villages.

This process is, in fact, just as Shuklaji sees it. He believes that the steady increase at the Muktibhavan is due to people returning to their villages and telling others about what a good facility was available. In Shuklaji's words:

> When a family has been here with a dying relative, afterwards they tell everybody about their experiences. They will tell all the other village people, and word will spread in this way. They tell them what the place is like and that everything is available. They tell them about the *karmacharyas* being good and the ongoing *kirtan* and *bhajan*. So more and more people want to come. Some people also come from Banaras Hindu University hospital and from the Marvari hospital and the Ramakrishna Mission hospital. In these places the doctor tells people that there is this place they can go for dying. And these people too, having learned about it, start to send one another.

It is possible, too, that the priest-workers are responsible for a growing number of people knowing about the Muktibhavan. People from the priest-workers own villages come there occasionally, and sometimes too their relatives come to die in the Muktibhavan. In the questionnaire, over 50 percent of people said they knew one of the priest-workers before coming, though it is not clear whether this was from village ties or previous visits, as all but one person who reported knowing one of the workers also reported having come before.

It may be that the days of people who wander into Kashi with a dying relative with no idea where they will find shelter, are coming to an end. But if this is so, there is a corresponding increase in those coming to die in Kashi because they know there is an available institution which meets and far exceeds their minimum standards. Shuklaji feels that if there were no restrictions on who could come to the Muktibhavan and the amount of space they allowed people to stay in, one would see many more people dying there. He said, "If we allowed people to stay on the verandahs or in the courtyard or near the gate, people would come and start dying there also. A hundred people a day would come." Though I think this is an exaggeration, I think too that the evidence suggests that, at least at the Muktibhavan, the phenomenon of coming to die in Kashi is in no immediate danger of disappearing, despite the overall numerical trend.

Up to this point, I have been generalizing from individual cases and arguing that there are general patterns of coming to Kashi to die that can be called tradition. But to generalize is to miss individual variation. In the section that follows, I want to return to the detail of the individual. As Shuklaji pointed out in the quotation above, there are also people who are directed to the Muktibhavan by hospitals. The case of Masterji and his mother illustrate how, within the tradition of coming to Kashi to die, individuals act within economic constraints, problems of transportation and with desires, not for death, but for cure.

Masterji and His Mother

He is called Masterji because he tutors the neighborhood children in the early morning before going off to work as a construction supervisor which he does from nine in the morning till nine at night. He speaks English and has an M. A. in Hindi. Masterji is from Rudravar village in Bihar, which is one of the seven "outlier" villages on the graph in Figure 5.5 from which people regularly come to die in Kashi. Now Masterji lives in Kashi, just a short walk from the Muktibhavan. He lives in a part of a large, old house in one of the small winding alleys. There are about twelve rooms around a central courtyard in this house, and in each room lives a separate family. Masterji, his wife, and their two young children live in a room which measures about nine by nine feet. I met him at the Muktibhavan, where he sometimes visits and participates in the *kirtan* singing. This time, however, he was there because his mother had come to die.

Masterji took me by the hand and lead me into his mother's room. From the door, he pointed to two women squatting on the floor and told me that one was his mother's sister and the other one her brother's wife. Both women pulled their *sari* trains over their heads as we walked in. He took me over to the wooden bed on which his mother was lying curled into foetal position, her back to the room, covered head to toe with an old blanket. "This is my mother," he said as he pulled back the blanket to reveal only the back of her head; a head which was covered in black hair, not the usual grey. "She is only 57 years old," he said.

Vimla Devi lived in Rudravar village, in the district of Rohtas, Bihar. She was a Brahmin. Her husband, Shiv Murat Pandey, had died in 1986. Two of Vimla Devi's living sons were in Kashi then; another had died of meningitis in 1988. She had several daughters also. "There were I think eight issues, eight or nine issues. But only five lived. One was married this year," Masterji said. He told me that his mother had had no education and could neither read nor write.

Masterji had gone to his village for a visit and found his mother complaining of "pain in her bones." He asked his brother who lived in Rudravar to bring their mother to Kashi and he did so, spending 370 rupees on a rented jeep. Masterji took her to a "bone specialist" who gave her some treatment and she seemed to improve. After four days, however, she started deteriorating. She told Masterji that she was feeling a burning pain in her stomach. After three more days, she started feeling that her stomach was filling up with something. Masterji gave her some medicine:

> I gave her two tablets and motions, loose motions started. After five days the motions were coming very quickly. They would not stop. Then I consulted a doctor at this Ramakrishna Mission Hospital. He told me to admit her in his private clinic or in the hospital. I took her to the Ramakrishna Mission. There the medical treatment went on. One bottle of glucose and one bottle of blood. The doctor said that her heart and stomach are quickly ceasing to work. Her lungs were filled with water. The doctor took out one or two bottles from her lungs, and he told me that

> "if you want your mother to live longer, just use the treatment I suggest." But I don't have enough money to pay for this medical treatment. So I told him: "I can't keep her at the hospital." I brought her to the Muktibhavan because the doctor said that she would not live much longer

He had been at the hospital for seven days. It costs fifteen rupees per day to stay at the hospital and the medical treatment came to about 2,500 rupees. This would be several months pay to Masterji and he simply could not afford the cure. So he took her to Kashi Labh Muktibhavan. "In our religious faith, if anyone dies in this area of the Kashi, they will go to the heaven." He said, "For this reason my mother wants to [stay here and] die in Kashi." However, though ultimately Vimla Devi may have wanted to die in Kashi, it is not quite so simple. She was not ready to die. The reasons she was at the Muktibhavan and in Kashi, in a more proximal sense, were based in economics in turn tied

FIGURE 5.7

Rogi marnewala and her family at Kashi Labh Muktibhavan

into a village and family tradition. The following is from a conversation I had with Masterji just three days before his mother's death.

Masterji said that his mother did not desire anything anymore. He was always asking her "What is your wish?," but she would not reply. She was conscious, he said, and he talked to her everyday. She wanted to go home:

> Sometimes she worries. She wants to go to the village . . . she wants to go to the village. But I think that if we go to the village, then later when she dies I will bring her back to Kashi for burning. So it will be expensive. If I spend the money to bring her home again, I will waste our money. So I don't want to take her back to the village.

Vimla Devi was not resolved to dying. Masterji said that though she knew that her body was not strong, she wanted very much to get better. "She has will power to live, but her body does not. There is no blood, the lungs are not working, the intestines are damaged. How can she live?," Masterji asked. She was very sad and complained of the pain caused by the weight of her body lying on the bed. She did not like to be lying there in that bed. She was not afraid, he said, though he seemed to change his mind as he explained to me:

> Only some people are afraid, those people who caused some trouble in their lives, like "I want to marry his son, daughter, etc." These type of people want to live and they are afraid. But not everyone. Some people say that "I am suffering from many types of pain and so I want to die." But everyone is afraid of the . . . "death" is a very fearful word. So everyone is afraid. But she [mother] cannot bear the pain of the body, so she is sad.

When I asked how long he thought she would live, he said he thought another one or two months. She was taking some food and so, according to Masterji, she would not die quickly. Though Vimla Devi was not ready to die, she was interested in attaining *moksha.* Masterji said that she has done many things in her life which people do in order to attain *moksha.* She has worshipped God, and sometimes she kept fasts and propitiated minor deities. And before coming to Kashi, she did several *dans* (gifts):

> She has the faith that when a man goes to heaven . . . there is a river, in our *atma* (spirit), in heaven and hell, there is a river. The name of that river is Vaitarni. So before dying, we give a cow to a Brahmin. The cow will help to cross the river.

Just as had Dubey's mother, Vimla Devi had given a cow to their priest *(purohit)* before coming to Kashi. She had also given some other types of gifts—rice, flour, and lentils—to some Brahmins. The fact that she had done these things suggests that she knew or suspected that she might not be returning from Kashi, though Masterji said, as had Dubey, that they had come to Kashi to find a cure.

Vimla Devi died on the eve of the Holi celebration, a time when it was very difficult to move about in the city. I did not see Masterji until he had returned from the village a couple of weeks after his mother's death. I went to his house to see if he had returned. There I found him alone and asleep in his little room. He looked thinner than before and a little worn. His head had been shaved and the hair had grown back about an eighth of an inch. With tears in his eyes, he greeted me saying that he felt very sad, and that nobody could fill the gap left by his mother.

He was with his mother when she died. He had asked her what she wanted just before she died. She had said that she wanted nothing. He asked again and again, he said. She was speaking but said she had no needs. "She knew she was going to die and she was very sad. She was suffering from pain but she was not afraid." He had woken up at about 3:40 or 4:40 in the morning and heard the *bhajan* and *kirtan* going on. His *bhua* (maternal aunt) was also there, sitting. He gave a spoonful of water to his mother and asked what she wanted. She said that she wanted nothing. "*Hare Rama Hare Krishna* was going on," he emphasized. "*Bhua* is very deaf, so she was just sitting there." He lay down. After half an hour he awoke with the feeling that something had happened. He looked at his mother's face; there was no movement. He moved her face; there was no response. He talked to her; and there was still no response. He told *Bhua* and she told him to align the body with north and south.

Was it a good death? "Everyone in the Hindu faith," he answered, "believes that *moksha* will come from dying in Kashi. Our family dies in Kashi. My father died in the village suddenly of a heart attack, so we brought his dead body to Kashi and burned it at the Manikarnika burning ghat." His mother, he said, had also wanted to die in Kashi. But for his mother, it had not been easy to do so. His mother had felt very lonely. She had wanted to return to the village one more time but there was the problem of money. In Kashi there had been nobody, only him. (*Bhua* was also there but does not seem to count.) "If she had been at the village, everybody would have been there," he said. "But at five in the morning, when she died, she would have been alone anyway." Though the words were not spoken, it was not a good death.

He left for the village immediately after she died to get his younger brother. Masterji was a middle son and only the youngest or eldest can give the fire to the body. His younger brother had gone to the village just five or six hours before to celebrate the Holi festival. Masterji encountered many troubles because it was Holi and there had been a train accident and he couldn't get a bus. So he had to go in a truck. He came back with everybody in a jeep. The body had stayed at the Muktibhavan with Masterji's wife and *bhua*. They came and wrapped the body in cloth and strapped her on to the bamboo ladder and the men carried her down to Manikarnika. His younger brother had his hair shaved off and then approached the Doms for the fire. They set her ablaze at about 5:00 in the afternoon, twelve hours after her death. By 7:30 the body was completely burned, he said. Then they moved to Dasashwameda ghat where they bathed and went to a sweet shop to break their fast. Finally, everyone left for the village where the *shraddha* would be celebrated.

Here is Masterji's account of what happened in the village:

> There is a pipal tree and a clay pot was hung on that tree by a string. People went to the river and bathed and then brought water in a pot. After coming back from the river, the cooking started. The ladies also bathed but did not go to the pipal tree. They made special food that day; rice and *kesari* without certain spices. For ten days—no soap, no oil, no washing clothes, or cutting nails. Everyday we went to the river and put *kusha* grass on the riverside and poured water onto it. In ten days, my younger brother ate only once—it is like doing *tapas* [ascetic practice]—he slept on a wooden cot, and he cannot touch the other family members, as he is pure.
>
> On the tenth day, we made sixteen altars *(vedis)* and an extra one for *Yamaraj* (God of death). Each *vedi* was worshipped and given a name. That day too *Mahapatras*, another caste, came to take the gifts; money, wheat, rice, cloth, bed, sheet, blanket and everything that my mother wore. The *Mahapatras* are unholy priests who take such gifts. Thirteen were invited and came. They take the things and go, nobody wants to see their faces in the morning as they are very low.
>
> On the twelfth day we put out 360 clay pots for the soul to drink everyday on its way to heaven. They were put out by the river, filled with water, and then left there. The thirteenth day, there was also a *dan* at my house. Our *purohit* (priest) took the gifts. It is holy. There was also *dan* for the people who had come to read *Garuda Purana*. And also that day we invited the Brah-

mins and gave a feast, a bit of money and some other little things. That was the end. All things were done according to the instructions of the *assarj*. His instructions come from *Garuda Purana* and some other books.

Masterji was very disturbed by the money he had had to spend. He mentioned the cost of the jeep (Rs. 400) and the fire and wood (Rs. 455) and shook his head commenting how expensive the *shraddha* had been. This type of money is a real problem for Masterji—it is not because he felt little for his mother. He had wept at her loss and even now felt the lack of his mother: "There is only one person who cares about her son, that is mother. Even today, I think and tears come to my eyes. The love of mother is very important."

Masterji understood coming to Kashi to die as a type of tradition. It is, at one level, a family tradition. His grandfather had died in Kashi thirty-four years before. He came from the village and lived in Kashi for two months at the Muktibhavan. His grandmother also died at the Muktibhavan in 1974. His father had not, because he died suddenly in the village. But one of his father's brothers died in Kashi as did one of his father's brother's wives.

On a second level, the family tradition is part of a village tradition. Masterji's village, Rudravar, is one of the few villages from which people very regularly seem to come. Masterji estimates that two to three people per year come from Rudravar to die in Kashi. This is fairly impressive for a village of approximately one hundred houses and about two thousand people. In fact, while Masterji's own mother lay dying in the Muktibhavan, another woman from his village came to die there. She died the morning after she arrived. Masterji's explanation for the high numbers of people from Rudravar coming to Kashi to die is that Mr. Chaubey, the first manager of the Muktibhavan, lived in a village near Rudravar.

Masterji clearly has a sense of the place of tradition and culture in determining what people believe. Masterji thinks about it. He knows why he believes what he does, though he is less clear on why he does not believe other things. I heard this same thing from several other people outside of the context of the Muktibhavan; the reflection by young people that while they do not fully believe certain things when they are young, that they probably will believe later on. Day by day, according to Masterji, his ability to believe what the traditions and culture tell him are increasing. I will continue to draw on Masterji's insights in the next chapter, where I discuss these beliefs.

6

Dying in a Spiritual System

> The marvels of nature have no end. The earth itself is round, and so it rotates. Time is also circular, so what can you say of the universe?
>
> —Shuklaji

The Americans had just begun bombing Bhagdad; the Gulf War was officially on and the alarming news—what little was available in Kashi —was that both sides were suffering casualties and that it looked like the beginning of a long and bloody fight. I arrived at the Muktibhavan with this on my mind and met Pandey and Shuklaji sitting in the shade by the well. I said to them that it looked really bad over there in Iraq. "Why?" Shuklaji asked, "what is so bad?" "Well . . . many people will die," I responded. Pandey looked at Shuklaji and grinned. Shuklaji looked at me as if I were a child. He made a "tschh" noise which I translated as "Haven't you been paying attention to anything I have been teaching you?" Then, smiling he said, "The *atman* can not be killed. It is merely bodies that die. The *atman* will again take birth."

At a literal level the *Bhagavadgita,* perhaps the closest thing to being *the* Hindu holy book, is an incitement to war. In it, Krishna explains to the faltering Arjuna why he must fight. His reasoning is, in part, that death is not the end of life but merely of the body. To Shuklaji, as to many others this is not *only* lore. Similarly, the families who come to Kashi bringing somebody to die do not *just* recount the lore of their culture, though they often can do so quite skillfully. People also tell of how the world seems to them, a world on the basis of which they act. In the case of bringing somebody to die in Kashi, it is in a profound manner that they act: for the dying person leaves the comfort of kith and kin, of home and of village, and travels on his or her deathbed to an unfamiliar and far away place to die.

Texts and Life

As I discussed earlier, there is a complicated relationship between lived reality in India and the long textual tradition of Hinduism. This complexity presents a methodological problem to scholars of Hinduism which, I argued, has generally been adequately dealt with neither by people studying "on the ground" Hinduism, nor by some textual scholars who write as if their subject is lived Hinduism. I will discuss one more example of the latter, by way of briefly introducing "traditional" Hindu eschatology.

Generally, there are three periods of thinking, three historical periods in the development of Hinduism: the Vedic, Upanishadic, and Puranic. The three famous paths *(margs)* of Hinduism correspond to the three periods of thinking. The *karma marg,* the path of ritual action was developed and practiced in the Vedic period. The *jnana marg,* the path of knowledge, in Upanishadic times. And since the beginning of the Puranic times, Hindus have had the opportunity to follow a devotional path, the *bhakti marg.*

According to Hopkins' writing on death and afterlife in Hinduism (1992), the Vedic conception of afterlife focused on the "World of the Fathers" (or realm of the ancestors). This was something which was attained not as a gift from the gods, but as a result of proper ritual action, both by the deceased before death and by his descendants after death (148). These ritual actions included cremation *(antyesthi kriya)* and post-cremation actions *(sapindikarana)* which would establish and maintain the deceased in the realm of the ancestors. Later, the Upanishads created a new metaphysical system which challenged the permanence of the "World of the Fathers" and proposed a new conception of afterlife (149). *Samsara,* the ceaseless cycle of birth, death, and rebirth, lead to the conception that residence in the realm of the ancestors would not be permanent, but would be followed by rebirth. The goal of the Upanishadic path of knowledge *(jnana marg)* was to escape the ceaseless cycle through the realization of the nature of self and the universe. Later, during the period when the Puranas were being written, release from rebirth became possible not just from knowledge alone, but also as a "divine gift to faithful devotees" (152). Afterlife for people on the *bhakti marg* became a life of devotion to God in heaven *(svarg),* as compared to the Upanishadic view of merging with the infinite, or the Vedic view of residence with the ancestors.

This schema is helpful as a means of organizing ideas and texts. It is, however, misleading when applied to *people* in India. Hopkins recognized that all three paths exist concurrently, but it is stated as an afterthought and, for him, it meant the Hindu can *choose* the path. "The question of personal choice," he said, "is perhaps the most basic feature of the Hindu view of salvation and afterlife" (154). But it makes little sense to ask what path of Hinduism the people coming to the Muktibhavan are on. As I shall show, their actions with regard to death can be fitted into all three of these paths. They are largely devotees of Rama, and yet the type of release that they seek is sometimes Upanishadic in its conception of an unmanifest afterlife. Furthermore, having secured *moksha* by dying in Kashi, the family goes on to do all the ritual action which supposedly establishes and maintains the soul in the "World of the Fathers."

The complexity on the ground in India is a result of the availability of many ideas from different periods of time. As Klostermaier (1989, 162) stated: "Hindu practice and belief does not simply follow from an extension of one basic idea but of a plurality of basic notions from which, quite logically but not always in mutually compatible fashion, specific beliefs and practices flow."

As I argued in chapter 2, the number of available ideas, and the manner in which they are "selected" and combined, makes necessary a different approach to lived Hinduism than simply borrowing textual classifications. In this chapter, I will look first at the specific beliefs and understandings held by the people who come to Kashi to die. After presenting a picture of the relevance of Kashi from their perspective, I will try to relate these world views to the specific texts which the people read, hear and see performed.

Spiritual Understanding and Beliefs

When I talked to members of a family who had brought somebody to die, I asked them about the dying person's beliefs. There is a number of philosophical and methodological difficulties in such an endeavor. Is the concept of belief translatable? Is it reasonable to accept a son's statement of what his mother believes? And what kind of range of commitment to an idea can be meant by belief?

Byron Good (1994) has warned us that belief as an analytical category, especially in anthropology, often has the effect of calling into question the validity of that to which it refers. Beliefs of others may seem reasonable though quite mistaken (18). We do not often refer to what we ourselves take for granted about the world as belief, though we do so for others. Also the concepts of others which we translate as belief may refer more to unquestioned or unquestionable understandings of how the world is. Having said that, the people I met at the

Muktibhavan regularly used the Hindi word *vishvas* to describe such things as their opinions of what happens after death and those who spoke English used belief as translation for *vishvas.*

When I asked whether they knew what their father or mother believed, the answer was, generally, "of course." As this is something I cannot honestly say myself, I have had to wonder about the validity of accepting these "proxy" statements of worldview. Masterji explained to me how he could speak for his mother in this way. He said he talked many times with his mother about belief. Though he did not believe in a lot of it himself, he felt he knew what the people of his village believed because they basically all shared the same understandings. His feeling was that, for the most part, these beliefs and understandings are village level phenomena; variation in belief is more a matter of degree than of difference.

Perhaps the most significant issue with belief is that of level of commitment. For instance though many people may believe enough to say that dying in Kashi results in *moksha,* fewer believe it enough to act on it. People can "believe" things in a lot of different ways and it can be difficult to determine what a person means when they use the term. What I heard from some could be Hinduism as they think it should ideally be, what they think the scriptural texts say, or what they want an outsider to know. It could be their conception of what "the common man" believes or it could be a personally held deep-seated understanding. In my interviews, I made a habit of asking whether or not what the person was saying was their own, personal belief. Sometimes the answer was yes. Other times the answer would be something like "Oh, you want to know what *I* think. *I* do not think that. . . . What I am telling you is what most (other) people think."

Many of the people I met were reflexive about their beliefs and had obviously thought about the process of believing in addition to the substance and complexity of Hindu beliefs. Masterji described his beliefs in this way:

> It is our tradition, our religion and our culture. So I also must believe in this way. It is an effect of education. If a man changes day by day and his faith in our gods grows like that, then he will also have faith in the reward of Kashi. But I, myself, do not have faith in these particular conditions. Just like you believe in Christ we believe in our gods, like Rama and Krishna. I believe, my son believes, his son will also believe. But at the present time, I can't *really* believe. However, as time passes, and according to the surroundings and traditions, day by day my faith in the Hindu

> religion, culture, and other mysteries grows. Sometimes I think to myself "Is it right? . . . Is it really?" But still these things—what men do and its results *(karma)* and what he will find after death —I can't believe. I believe only in the gods' power and might.

Masterji knows the tradition and the culture but is only somewhat immersed in it. He only sort of believes it and he believes selectively, in certain aspects of it. He knows he has no choice because he was brought up in it. It is a matter of education, as he said. He also expects that as he gets older he will start believing more fully. He has seen this happen to others and noticed that older people are more pious than young people.

Although some people come to die in Kashi, to varying degrees, because it is a tradition to do so, they also hold beliefs and understandings which allow the tradition to exist. People do come to Kashi in order to die there and they say, in explanation of the act—more often it is said for them—that the reason that they came was to obtain *moksha.* Though to a certain degree level of belief can be checked against such action, ultimately what people say they believe has generally to be taken at face value.

Kapil Deo Singh

Kapil Deo Singh was a squat man with slicked-back hair and a beautifully groomed, oiled, and curled mustache. He intercepted me one day as I was leaving another room and invited me into his. He was there with seven or eight family members; they had brought his mother to die at the Muktibhavan.

Singh's mother looked very old. She was lying on a wooden bunk, curled up in the foetal position. Her eyes were open and moved about the room. The skin on her face looked as if it were struggling against her strong and distinctive bone structure; losing the battle to wrinkle by being stretched taut. She had lost all her upper teeth on the left side and all her lower teeth on the right; those that remained stuck out of her mouth at all angles and fit with one another like an old puzzle. One of her arms was wrapped thickly in clean white bandages. Singh told me she could still speak, but that she wasn't really aware of what was being said to her.

Singh described his family using the English term "middle class." Most people, however, would probably think of them as rich, as they own sixty acres of land. Singh is one of four brothers who live together as part of a joint family. There are thirty-five of them living in a single house. The two older brothers work the land; the two younger work "outside." Singh is one of the younger brothers and in his work as a contractor builds bridges and dams.

The second time I visited Singh, the family were doing a *dan* ceremony in their room. Two of the priest workers were standing over the old lady chanting. A couple of the women were propping her up into sitting position. Singh was holding his mother's hand out and in her hand was placed some money, flowers, and a few drops of water. Eventually this money was given to one of the priest workers who shook off the wet flower petals and slipped it into his *dhoti.* Singh told me later that this had been a special *banarsi gau dan,* with money substituting for the cow; a ritual he had heard you should do when you bring someone to die in Kashi.

The formal interview Omji and I held with Singh was quite public as the racket from a generator next-door, ubiquitous during the many power failures of the hot season, forced us to talk in a back room where many other people had gathered. When I asked Singh where he learned the rule about conducting the *banarsi gau dan,* the first I had seen or heard, there was laughter from the others who were listening. Singh did not say where they learned of the ritual: "It is something that helps to get *moksha,"* he said. "We gave the *cost* of a cow." Fifty-one rupees.

They had also done a *gau dan* with a real cow before coming to Kashi. They had also done readings from the *Bhagavadgita* and *Ramayana.* After his mother's death, he said, they would give a donation of some land. He would not say how much land or to whom. Singh said they would do the cremation ritual *(antyesthi sanskar)* in Kashi at Manikarnika ghat, but they would return to the village to conduct the eleven days of post-death rituals *(shraddha).*

His mother, he said, was 105 years old. But her eldest offspring was 72, her youngest 52, so I judge that she was probably closer to 90. Singh said he didn't know too much about his mother's life. He knew that with her husband she had done many pilgrimages, such as to Haridwar and Vrindhavan. Her husband, Singh's father, had died in 1966.

The family had recognized that she was dying when she stopped eating: "In old age when the senses stop working there is no use to eat. So she has decided like that." They had also talked to a doctor who had said that medicine would no longer help her. When they decided to go to Kashi, the village people all came and touched his mother's feet. They all gave her a spoonful of Ganga water. She said nothing at that time as her speaking power was gone; she was not really aware of what was going on. Now at the Muktibhavan, she asked for individuals once in a while. If they were there, they went to her but, otherwise the family would tell her that the person was coming soon. At the Muktibhavan she was taking no food and no medicine, though she was drinking water with some vitamins. She had not eaten for fourteen days before arriving. Singh thought her to be in a "very peaceful condition" though he also thought she was anxious to "leave her body." She sometimes would say, "Lord, give me *moksha,* Lord give me *moksha (Bhagavan, moksha dijie).*"

Singh said that it was not really his mother's desire to die in Kashi: it was the desire of her sons. They wanted their mother to die in Kashi, Singh said, "because Kashi is a religious place *(dharmik sthan).* It is the city of Shiva. The advantage of dying in a *dharmik* place is that you will get *mukti.*[1] Especially Kashi is accepted for this and it is because it is the city of Shiva." He said they would stay for as long as it takes. They would not go home until she died.

There is some family precedence for at least trying to die in Kashi. Their father had wanted to die in Kashi and they tried to bring him, but he had died on the way. Their grandmother had been brought to Kashi after she died. Before this, Singh could not remember though he thought there were others. Singh thought that almost everybody would like to come to Kashi to die but that the cost is prohibitive. The Singhs came in their own vehicle; the expense was not a lot for them. People from the village who had come previously had told them about the Muktibhavan and Singh was pleased with the place. He described his time there as peaceful; "no trouble at all." He regularly sat with the priest-workers and participated in the singing of the *bhajan* and *kirtan.* "Where else would you get such a place to stay where always there is *Hari Ram Hari Ram* going on?" he asked, "This helps for *moksha.*"

Singh understood *moksha* in this way: "When a person becomes free of death and birth. There is no birth again. Forever." His mother desired *moksha,* he said, but for him and his brothers there was an added dimension. "It is every child's wish to give *moksha* to their parents," he said, "because there is so much pain during the time of death and birth." He did not know whether or not his mother would get *moksha* if she died outside of Kashi. "Everybody tries to do religious work in their lives like donation and pilgrimage *(dan aur yatra)* with the hope of getting *moksha.* But dying in Kashi is a sure way to get it." For Singh and his family, it was simply not worth taking the chance. For in their understanding, if you do not get *moksha* this time, it may be a very long time before there is another opportunity. This is because:

> The next birth will not be that of a human being. This comes after many lives. In our culture we believe there are 8,400,000 different lives *(charasi lakh yonis)* into which you will take birth first. Nobody knows where your next birth will take you.

When I asked Singh where he had learned about *moksha,* he answered that he had read both the *Gita* and *Ramayana.* But also, he said, "from very early on, the old people always tell you that you should do such and such a thing in order to get *moksha.*" He has heard the *Garuda Purana* being read many times, whenever there is a death. He listened to the whole thing after the deaths of his grandfather and his father.

Moksha

As I discussed in chapter 2, within textual Hinduism there are different understandings of the nature of *moksha.* At the Muktibhavan, while everyone says that *moksha* is the aim of dying in Kashi, what they say they understand about *moksha* is varied.

Mishra's (chapter 4) *moksha,* according to his family, was not escape from the eternal cycle of birth, death, and rebirth. What he wanted was a *decent* next birth. He would be a Brahmin, perhaps a saint. And he would be avoiding the common fate of taking rebirth in the form of an animal, ghost, or devil.

Singh (chapter 4) had a different conception of *moksha.* "This life," he explained, "is full of trouble and sadness. Dying here means never having to be born into this life again. God is everybody, just like the sea. A person is like a little drop of sea water. There is no difference in the sea and a little drop. What matter you will find in ocean, you will also find in a little drop of ocean. . . . This is the opinion . . . that, if you die in Kashi, the spirit of the dead body is merged in Shiva."

Masterji (chapter 5) explained *moksha* differently again. The meaning of *moksha,* according to his mother's belief, is the bringing to an end the cycle of rebirth. "To come on to the earth, to die and to again take birth. Again and again. This is a result of man's work—his *karma.* The Hindus want to become free of taking birth and dying again and again. This is called *moksha.* In our holy book, the *Gita,* Krishna explains about this matter. If a man takes *moksha* he will not be born again. That is the meaning of *moksha.*" But also, "In our religious faith, if anyone dies in this area of the Kashi, they will go to heaven *(svarg),*" he said. "For this reason my mother wants to [stay here and] die in Kashi."

Amongst the people coming to the Muktibhavan to die, *moksha* is variously understood to be rebirth into a good life, merging with the infinite (unmanifest God) and residence in heaven alongside a manifest God.

The Pursuit of *Moksha* While Living

Ideal Hinduism, textual Hinduism, prescribes four aims of life *(purusharthas)*. They are the following of moral law, the achievement of material wealth and family, enjoyment of life and, eventually, liberation *(dharma, artha, kama,* and *moksha)*. These goals are correlated with the ideal life stages such that, as a student, one should study and practice moral law and, as a householder, one should acquire wealth and enjoy oneself while raising a family. The last two stages of life, ideally, should be focused on the final, and most spiritual of goals, *moksha*.

The people who come to the Muktibhavan to die are coming in pursuit of *moksha*. However, as I have suggested, they are not people who conform to the ideal system in any strict sense. These people are, throughout their lives, householders. Their pursuit of *moksha*, though probably something that gains precedence with age, seems to be a life long, but by no means full-time, religious endeavor. I asked people in the survey what things the dying person had done toward obtaining *moksha* throughout his or her lifetime. According to the responses, everybody except one person had done other things toward getting *moksha*, (see figure 6.1). About half of the respondents reported the general answer, "righteous deeds and giving gifts" *(dan punya)*.[1] Forty people reportedly had "done pilgrimage" and several others were reported to have had done specific pilgrimages. Sixteen people reportedly had undergone fasts, five people had built temples, and two people had constructed schools.

It should be noted that these specific acts are a part of "everyday Hinduism" and are done by people for many religious reasons. As Klostermaier says, "The inextricable conjunction of the rather impersonal Vedic and the highly personal Puranic traditions make it impossible to clearly differentiate in the activities of traditional Hindus among acts done to obtain ritual purity, to gain merit, or to win the grace of God, which, in a certain sense, obviates everything else" (1989, 163). Achieving *moksha*, can be added to this list. It is quite possible that many of the acts said to have been done for *moksha* were done for other religious reasons and only as death approaches were being reinterpreted.

FIGURE 6.1

Compilation of responses to the survey question: "Which other things has the dying person done in life to obtain *moksha?*"

Righteous deeds and gifts *(dan punya)*	42
Pilgrimage, unspecified *(tirtha yatra)*	4
Pilgrimage to specified destination	
Gangasagar	3
Badrinath	1
Haridwar	1
Mathura	2
Brindavan	1
Avadh	1
Rameshwar	1
Four Hindu pilgrmage centers *(char dham)*	2
Fasting *(vrat)*	17
Religious gifts, unspecified *(dan)*	5
Religious gifts of specified item	
of cloth *(vastra dan)*	1
of grain *anna dan)*	4
of calf *(gav dan)*	2
of a bed *(seji dan)*	2
Was a freedom fighter *svatantrata senani*	1
Constructed a . . .	
temple	5
school	2
well	1
Held good views *(acche vichar)*	1
Spoke the truth *(satynisht)*	4
Sang devotional songs *(bhakti bhajan)*	2
Did religious work *(dharmik kam)*	1
Read *Ramcharitmanas*	1
Associated with good people *(satsang)*	1
Listened to *Bhagavadgita (githa path)*	2
Did worship and sacred reading *(puja path)*	4

From my interviews, it seems that the gifting of a cow *(gau dan)* as an activity done for getting *moksha,* was much more widespread than the questionnaire indicates. This is an activity which is performed, in addition to other times, specifically as death approaches.

Kapil Deo Singh's family gave a cow while still in the village, and (symbolically) another while at the Muktibhavan, saying it would help their mother achieve *moksha.* Several other people were more specific and said that the gifting of the cow helps the soul on its post-death journey to the realm of Yama (the god of death) at the time when the soul has to cross the terrible Vaitarni River. Often, amongst the people dying at the Muktibhavan, as I will show, the gifting of a cow marks the self-recognition of the beginning of the dying process.

The active pursuit of *moksha* is a prescribed goal of ideal, textual Hinduism. People learn from early childhood that they should be striving for *moksha* though most probably have only a vague ideas of what it is, and why they should want it. From several family members I got a standard answer to the question of why the dying person desires *moksha.* The answer is that life is a miserable affair full of sadness and pain. The unending cycle of one life after another is a perpetual, unending misery. And the only way out of the unhappiness is *moksha,* However, it is not very likely that the people dying at the Muktibhavan actively pursue *moksha* because their lives have been miserable or that human life generally is miserable. I learned this by telling people that I could think of nothing better than to get another birth. That, I was told, was because I assumed I would be born a human being again. This would not be the case.

For many, another human birth will not come until after eight million four hundred thousand nonhuman births *(charasi lakh yoni).* As Dubey (chapter 5) explained, according to what good and bad things a person has done during his or her life, that thing will the person bear —pain or happiness—at the time of death. After death, those people who have done nothing but good work will get *moksha.* But "those people who have done the bad deeds, they have to be born again. They come back into the 8,400,000 life forms, and are born according to their *karma.*" Life in human form is a very rare event. It is also the one opportunity to end the cycle. Even if human life was good and rich, the driving force for achieving *moksha* is that if you don't get *moksha* this time, it may be a very long time before there is another opportunity.

Clearly, for many it is not what *moksha* is in specific detail which is important. *Moksha* is not a sought-after goal for its own merits, nor an escape from human misery. It is an escape from the alternative fate of living and dying a virtual eternity of miserable nonhuman lives from which there is no chance of escape. This life is the one opportunity and it better not be wasted.

The Pursuit of *Moksha* While Dying

At the time of death, there is a sure way of attaining *moksha.* As Masterji expressed it:

> In the middle of this city there are three areas: Vishvanath, Kedar, and another. . . . I don't know. Those who died in these areas are very lucky. In our faith, those who die in Kashi go to heaven, but for those who die outside there is no *mukti.* So people feel that if they die in Kashi there will be no rebirth. So they want to die in Kashi.

Or as another man said:

> It is our belief. It is the opinion of the people, mine and all people's, that in such places as this, one can get *moksha.* Especially in Kashi. But the Banaras Hindu University hospital is outside of the boundaries of Kashi. *Moksha* is not available there.

Kashi and its *moksha*-giving properties are mentioned in many scriptures. Many of the things that these texts say about Kashi have been collected by various people, translated from Sanskrit into Hindi, interpreted and presented in the form of small booklets. One example is *Kashi Moksha Nirnaya* by Swami Shivanand Saraswati, which is widely available at the small shops that cater to pilgrims in Kashi. The textual tradition of Kashi's *moksha*-giving properties—statements of the special properties of Kashi and arguments as to how this can be meshed with the more general principles of Hinduism such as *karma* —is thus available to all. For instance:

> Where else does a creature obtain liberation as he does here, simply by giving up the body, with very little effort at all!
>
> Not by austerities, not by donations, not by lavish sacrifices can liberation be obtained elsewhere as it can be obtained in Kashi simply by giving up the body!
>
> Even the yogis practicing yoga with minds controlled are not liberated in one lifetime, but they are liberated in Kashi simply by dying. Kashi Khanda 60.55, 57, 58, cited in Eck 1982, 331

Here I rely on Eck (1982, 324–44) for a summary of the textual tradition regarding the attainment of *moksha* by dying in Kashi. All creatures, it is written, including insects and germs, become liberated by dying in Kashi. In all other places death is under the terrifying jurisdiction of Yama, the god of death. But Yama is banned from Kashi by Shiva. When one dies in Kashi, Shiva whispers the *tarak mantra* in his or her ear; the hearing of this mantra at the time of death is the mechanism by which *moksha* is granted. There is a difference of opinion about what Shiva whispers; it is either "Brahman is *Aum*" or "Rama, Rama" depending on the subtradition. It is not the mantra itself that grants *moksha,* but the flood of knowledge that results from hearing it. The texts have had to grapple with the problem of how justice is given out and how *karma* can prevail when everybody including the worst of sinners get *moksha* by dying in Kashi. Some say that such people will simply not get the opportunity to die in Kashi. Others describe a torture dished out by Kashi's gatekeeper, Lord Bhairava *(bhairava yatna)* at the moment of death.

The textual tradition, as summarized above, has concordances with the views of the people coming to the Muktibhavan to die but it is by no means an adequate description. For some, Kashi simply gives *moksha;* there is no reason. For others it is because it is the city of Shiva, and that is enough. For some people, Kashi is just one place where *moksha* can be obtained. As Singh said above, it is "because Kashi is a religious place *(dharmik sthan)."* Dying in any *dharmik* place results in *mukti,* in his view. Generally, people say that if they do not achieve *moksha* while in human form, they have missed their opportunity, implying that, unlike the traditional idea, only humans can get *moksha* from dying in Kashi. Nobody I talked to expected that any punishment would be forthcoming. Finally, as I shall show, it is not the flood of *knowledge* resulting from a mantra, but the power of the *name* of Rama, which is the mechanism of the granting of *moksha* for the people dying at the Muktibhavan.

The Importance of the Muktibhavan

The Muktibhavan is considered to be a good place to die primarily because it is located in Kashi. But, for most people, the Muktibhavan itself has some features which help in the obtaining of *moksha.*

Singh, who brought his mother to die (chapter 8) said of the Muktibhavan that, "all the facilities are guaranteed and if people will die here their future is guaranteed." This, he said, is because in the Muktibhavan, there is twenty four hours a day chanting of the name of God. Masterji said the Muktibhavan is a good place to die, "because it is neat and clean, the management is very peaceful, and there is always *hari kirtan, bhajan,* and the name of god Rama."

Masterji compared the Muktibhavan to the Ganga-labh Bhavan saying that there, there is not the same type of good atmosphere and the name of God is not heard. In his view, the atmosphere is important and the *kirtan* and *bhajan* helped his mother to get *moksha.* "She heard Rama's name and other religious songs and chanting," he said. "In our faith, if the dying people hear the name of god—Narayan, Hari, or Rama—the god helps those people. I will tell you a story about this":

> There was a man who was a butcher. His son's name was Narayan. This butcher never chanted God's name and never worshipped God. But when he was dying, he called his son, "O Narayan." Now Narayan happens to be another name for the god Vishnu. So Narayan appeared in front of the dying butcher and said "What?" (As a result of calling the name) the butcher went to heaven to be with god. For this reason we give our children names like bhagavan's names—Krishna, Rama, Vishnu, Maheshvara, Shiva. You find amongst Indians these types of names. These are the names of God. For this reason too *kirtan* and *bhajan* is done (at the Muktibhavan). The names of gods are sung, and in the morning and the evening, the *Ramcharitmanas* is read.

Another thing that the priest-workers at the Muktibhavan do is readings from the *Ramcharitmanas* and *Gita.* Masterji said of this that "the reading of these Hindu holy books, the books that the Hindus have faith in, hearing these verses *(shlokas* and *chaupais),* we find courage and peace in our heart and minds. If there is any kind of *maya* (delusion), we become free from hearing these verses."

The importance of the twenty-four hour singing and the stress on the name of god, situate the *institution* in the devotional movement of Hinduism. Klostermaier (1990, 223–24) noted that this type of singing is an aspect of "taking the name," one of the essential steps of becoming a *bhakta,* a follower of the devotional movement *(bhakti marg)* of Hinduism, reflecting the majority of Hindus. At *bhakti* religious centers it is quite common to have people, often paid, chant the name(s) day and night. The importance of "the name" suggests a parallel to the importance of the universal sound: "As creation owes its origin to the 'word' *(Aum),* so the sacred names of Rama, Krishna and Hari are the vehicle that bring the individual back to him" (Swami Rama Tirtha, cited in Klostermaier 1990, 223). Many of the people staying at the Muktibhavan said that hearing the name helped in the

FIGURE 6.2

Priest-worker reading religious stories over loudspeaker system at *Kashi Labh Muktibhavan*

dying person's pursuit of *moksha.* Several of the priest-workers at the Muktibhavan say that they themselves receive spiritual benefit from doing the *kirtan* and *bhajan* singing.

Another way in which the Muktibhavan assists people to obtain *moksha* is by administering water from the Ganga and the leaves of the holy *tulsi* plant regularly to the people who are dying there. Both these substances are widely thought to be conducive to obtaining *moksha.* Masterji told me this well-known story, one which I heard several times, as an explanation of why *ganga jal* is given to a dying person:

There was a king whose name was Sagar. Sagar had sixty thousand sons. He had done the *ashvameda yajna* (a special horse sacrifice) ninety-nine times. Now if anybody completes the *ashvameda yajna* one hundred times he will become like Indra, the king of gods. So Indra played a trick with Sagar. Indra thought that if anybody completed the *ashvameda yajna* 100 times, he would take his place, so he played a trick.

Now Sagar's horse was wandering very far. (If anybody takes the horse then he must fight with the king. If the horse becomes free, the victory of that king is supposed.) Indra put Sagar's horse under the earth at an ascetic's ashram. The name of this ascetic was Kapil Muni. Kapil Muni was meditating on God.

The sixty thousand sons of Sagar searched for the horse all over the world. They could not find the horse. So they began to dig through the earth. When they reached Kapil Muni's ashram, they found that the horse was there. They became very angry. They said "You have seen us and you have gone into this position (and are pretending to be meditating)." The ascetic became angry and cursed them all to die. Soon all of the sixty thousand sons lay dead.

King Sagar was upset. All his son's were lying in hell *[Nark]*. He had to figure a way of obtaining *mukti* for them. Now there is only one way: if Ganga will come from heaven and if Ganga's water will fall on them, then they will become *mukt* [liberated].

So the descendants of Sagar tried to bring the Ganga from heaven. But no one succeeded. At last Bhagiratha tried. He worshipped very hard, he did ascetic endeavors *(tapasyas)* day and night. Brahma became pleased. He said "I will send Ganga, but if Ganga comes straight from heaven, if she goes straight on to the earth, she will go right into the earth. So who will hold up the Ganga, and save the earth?' " So he suggested that he go and worship the god Shiva, who will bear the load of Ganga. Bhagiratha prayed to the god Shiva. Shiva became happy and pleased with Bhagiratha, and told him "Tell Brahma to send Ganga. I am ready." He parted his hair and stood on his *trisula* and waited for Ganga.

Her sound was roaring coming from heaven but Shiva was silent. The water of the Ganga came and missed Shankar (Shiva). She moved round and round, she was very proud, but she missed Shiva's head. After that Bhagiratha said "I have prayed for years and years and now Ganga is missing Shiva's head. What was the

> purpose of the bringing of Ganga?" So he again prayed to Shiva so that Ganga would flow to his ancestors. So Ganga flowed off Shiva's head and followed Bhagiratha from the Himilayas, through Rishikesh, through Gangotri and finally on to Ganga Sagar where Kapil's ashram was. Every year on the fourteenth of January the Hindu's go there, bathe there, and see Kapil Muni. Sagar's sixty thousand sons became free with the Ganga's water. So we say that the Ganga's water gives *mukti* from the hells. So this is why the people take the Ganga *jal*.

Masterji's story is a version of the most well-known and oldest of a series of myths recounting the origins of the Ganga which, according to Kinsley (1986, 189), all tend to stress the river's heavenly origins and connection to the great male deities, Brahma, Vishnu, and Shiva. Water, in general in India, is known for its great purifying powers, and the great rivers, especially, are revered for this quality. As Masterji's story makes clear, the river Ganga is a conduit from heaven and is of sufficient purificatory power that contact with it guarantees *moksha* for the dead. Another story I heard several times from people at the Muktibhavan concerned the death of some corrupt and evil man who was certainly bound for the worst of fates. His body was torn up and consumed by vultures. One vulture, flying over the Ganga, accidentally dropped a small fragment of bone from its talons. The moment the bone hit the waters of the Ganga the evil man, who was enduring torture in hell, found himself transferred to heaven.

There is also a story which explains the use of *tulsi* leaves for the dying at the Muktibhavan, as told by Masterji:

> Tulsi! What is the story about Tulsi? I will tell you about the story of Tulsi!
>
> There was a kind of giant we call *rakshasa,* you know? His wife was Brinda, Brinda was a very holy lady *(sati).* So her husband could never be killed, not by any god. No god could kill him because of the power of that *sati,* Brinda. He did many bad things and the gods became fearful of his actions. They prayed to Vishnu, "Please save us from that *rakshasa.*" Vishnu said that he would do something.
>
> Vishnu made his own face look just like that *rakshasa* and went and slept with his wife, Brinda. Her *sati* power was finished and so Brinda's husband was killed by Shiva. Brinda heard the news. "How could my husband be dead? It means something is wrong with me." So she cursed the god Vishnu. "You cheated me

so I am giving you the punishment that you will become a stone." Now we pray to the *saligram,* that black type of stone we call *saligram.*

But god Vishnu also gave a punishment "You will be worshipped by the people. Because I slept with you, you have become my wife. So you will become on the earth a *tulsi* plant." And so Brinda became a *tulsi* plant. "And those that take your leaves in their mouths, because you are so holy—like the worship of Lord Vishnu—those who keep the *tulsi* leaves in their mouth or use the leaves, will also be holy." That is the reason to use the *tulsi* leaves.

Anandi's Dadi

Anandi Prasad had come with his two uncles and one cousin to bring his *dadi* (paternal grandmother) to die in Kashi. They stayed on at the Muktibhavan after her death to do the *shraddha* rituals. They had discussed it with a pilgrimage priest *(panda)* who had advised them that it was best to celebrate the *shraddha* in Kashi. He had told them that a particular text recommends that all the ritual work should be done in Kashi; since their grandmother had died in Kashi, they should do her rituals in Kashi. Anandi and the others also thought that if they went back and celebrated the *shraddha* at their village they would have been inviting her soul back to there too. They said it was better if her soul remained in Kashi. They were, however, planning to go to Gaya to do *pinda dan.* Gaya is the best place to do *pinda dan,* Anandi Prasad said, because it is where Lord Rama came and offered the rice balls for his father Dasharath.

Dadi, their grandmother, had been 105 years old. Anandi Prasad said that she had produced over 100 descendants. She herself had had five sons and five daughters. Her husband died in 1967 at 80 or 85 years of age. *Dadi* had had no education. She had done a lot of religious work during her life: she kept a fast on the eleventh of every month and celebrated all the festivals. She had done "all the important pilgrimages."

Toward the end, she was undergoing some medical treatment which lasted for about six months. She gave up taking her medicine about twenty days before she died. At first they had tried to make her take it, but she would spit it out. She gifted a cow *(gau dan)* ten days before they left for Kashi. The family knew it was her last time *(antim samay)* because she stopped eating and was taking only juice. She had abandoned food the day before she did the *gau dan.* Her body had become weaker and weaker, Anandi Prasad said. She did not eat anything until the day before her death. But the day she died she had asked for some *kicheri* and had managed to eat it with her own hands.

At first, the family had planned to take her to die near the Ganga somewhere closer to their district of Nevada. Only at the last moment had they decided to come to Kashi. They knew to go to the Muktibhavan as their father's sister's husband had been at the Muktibhavan once before and had told them all about it. Many people came to see *dadi* in the house before the family set off for Kashi. They all touched her feet, and everybody was in tears because she was well liked in the village and had done many things for people. Everyone wanted her blessing that they could live as long as had she. But she was not able to respond to them. She had been only barely conscious. However, once they reached the Muktibhavan she became more lucid and was able to sit up and talk to them through signals.

The death had been very good, in Anandi Prasad's view. He said she was happy until the end. At the point of death they were asking her if she wanted a bath with Ganga water and she said yes. They asked her if she wanted to return to the village. She did not want to return to the village.

They had brought their grandmother to Kashi in order that she secure *moksha.* The person who gets *moksha,* in their view, will become free from death and birth, Anandi Prasad told me. "He will not come again on this earth. There is no other birth afterwards. And if the person does not take birth then how will he die?" The person who gets *moksha* "goes to a place called *svarg-lok* [heaven]. There, there is no pain or difficulties, only happiness." On the other hand, in their view, if you don't get *moksha* then you will have to live through the 8,400,000 *(yonis)* before you will have another chance at getting a (pure) human body.

> He will be born in one *yoni* and then die, then be born in another and then die. He will cycle through all 84 *lakh* life forms. When somebody dies, they change bodies, immediately. It is just like changing clothes. This is what Krishna said in the *Mahabharata,* in the *Gita.*

The person who gets *moksha* will not come into this cycle of life forms and will have no more experience of pain. Anandi Prasad understands that Kashi immediately grants *moksha* to those who die there. There are eight places that do so, he says, but Kashi is the best place. There are two reasons for this. First, Kashi is standing on the trident of Shiva and so is a special place. Second, King Harischandra did duty at Harischandra burning ghat, so people are interested in being cremated there. (He is referring here to a story of king Harischandra who had to give up everything and take a job as a burning ghat attendant. He is respected for doing this.) In the village they had heard these stories. When their grandmother died, they took her to Harischandra ghat and cremated her—not in the new electric crematorium, he emphasized—but with wood.

Both Anandi Prasad and his cousin felt that they know more about *moksha* than most people. Their parents were always teaching them about it when they were young and later in school they were taught about *moksha.* Now they are in university and taking philosophy and so know much about it. They have, for instance, studied the *Ramayana* and the *Gita.* As part of their *shraddha,* one of the priest-workers at the Muktibhavan was reading them the *Garuda Purana.* They read all sixteen chapters within three days. "Reading the *Garuda Purana* gives satisfaction to the soul," Anandi Prasad explained. Neither of them have themselves read the *Garuda Purana* but they were familiar with it because they have heard it many times. When anybody dies in the village *Garuda Purana* is read.

Relationship of Beliefs to the Textual Tradition

Masterji thought that mostly the knowledge about dying in Kashi and achieving *moksha* is passed down from generation to generation. He heard about Kashi and *moksha* when he was young, not from lessons, but just from overhearing conversations that were going on. Also, he said, the village people "go here and there." He, for instance, lives in Kashi and regularly visits the special places. When he goes back to the village, he tells the others about these places. Sometimes, too, "learned people" go to the villages and they explain the history and culture to the villagers. Also, learned people come occasionally from places like Kashi and Prayag and describe these holy cities. Finally, there seems to be three important books to the culture of his village which teach about death and dying, *moksha,* and getting it in Kashi.

The following is a transcription of part of a conversation I had with Masterji in which we were discussing how people come to know about *moksha* and dying in Kashi:

CJ: Where did your mother take her knowledge about *moksha?*

Masterji: She heard the story from the priest of our village. After death there is a funeral system in our village, or in Hinduism. After death a person's son—his or her eldest or youngest—gives fire to his mother or father. For ten days that son sleeps on the ground or on a wooden bed and hears a story that is called *Garuda Purana.* In *Garuda Purana* there are stories about what will happen after death and how to live; how to do these types of things. A priest comes to the village and reads this story at the house when a person has died. The priest brings the book and reads the story and the people sit around and listen.

CJ: So most people will have heard the *Garuda Purana* many times?

Masterji: Yes, because many people die and so they hear it often.

CJ: And in *Garuda Purana* it tells about Kashi?

Masterji: Yes, and also in some parts of other holy books like *Gita,* and *Ramayana* or *Ramcharitmanas.* There is also *yagya* (sacrifice). At this time the priest tells the stories during *havan* (fire sacrifice). *Ghee* and other holy things like sandalwood and camphor are mixed and put in the fire. On these occasions the priest speaks about the stories. They do the *yagya, havan* and *puja* in the evenings . . . mornings sometimes . . . and they explain about the holy deeds of the saints and the holy books.

What people know about is a matter of culture and is passed down verbally, through face to face interaction, from generation to generation. And yet in Indian society there has long been another source of knowledge. There is the body of scriptural texts which complicates the knowledge flow in profound ways. In India, people are exposed to particular texts throughout their lives either first hand—by reading and hearing the texts, and by seeing them performed—or second or third hand, through lessons and conversations with people who know the texts.

At some point the substance of the texts must become indistinguishable from other aspects of cultural knowledge, having no known connection to a text. In this manner, I envision particular texts percolating into various levels of cultural understanding. The flow is not only one way; historically the texts are products of society though there were likely wide gulfs between the composers of the texts and the people they have "trickled" down to.

The process by which scriptural texts become cultural knowledge is not the same as Shrinivas's idea of Sanskritization by which the lower castes are thought to acquire textually based ideas and behaviours by aspiring to those of Brahmins. From a more distant perspective, the texts are a media form which affect all castes, allowing social interactions to transcend time and space and adding simultaneously variability and conservatism in thought. Sanskritization is a unifying process, one in which castes supposedly become more similar by virtue of their connections to the texts. However, there are so many textual traditions that, through a historical process of picking and choosing, they can actually be responsible for cultural differences at regional or caste levels.

Masterji's village is representative of other villages in the region, in terms of the particular texts to which they have direct and important connections. Amongst the people coming to die at the Muktibhavan there are consistently three texts which are well-known, all of which contain information relevant to coming to Kashi to die and getting *moksha*; the *Ramcharitmanas*, the *Garuda Purana*, and to a somewhat lesser extent, the *Bhagavadgita*.

The *Bhagavadgita*

Many people said that they listened to readings from the *Bhagavadgita*, often referred to as simply *Gita*. Masterji said that he thinks people generally are familiar with the *Gita*, as it is a part of the famous epic *Mahabharata*. Sometimes people arrive in the region of his village and perform the *Krishna Lila*, a play based on the *Mahabharata*. Also in the primary school books there are many stories of the *Mahabharata* and so people who learn to read even a little get to know these stories. Sometimes, *pandits* come and tell the stories of the *Mahabharata*. At the Muktibhavan, the priest-workers regularly read the *Gita* to the dying people, especially the eighth chapter which deals with achieving *moksha*.

The *Bhagavadgita*, according to Klostermaier (1989, 94) is "unrivaled" in popularity and authority in the history of Hinduism. However, it is not an easy scripture. From an analytical standpoint, looking at the *Gita* as a philosophical treatise, it seems to be a synthesis of a number of different traditions. Masterji also said the *Gita* was a difficult text and, though most village people know some of the words of the *Gita*, he thinks many do not understand the meaning. "They just believe that the *Gita* is the holy book. They don't read it because it is very difficult," he said. "They know the basic story only, particularly the story of Krishna and Arjuna on the battlefield. In each of the chapters there is a lot of detail. They only know that to hear the *Gita* is enough for *moksha*."

From the people I talked to at the Muktibhavan, I heard things which are almost direct quotes from the *Gita*. One of the messages of the *Gita* which I heard several times is the understanding that the self is immortal and moves from body to body. Often this was expressed using a variant of the following metaphor:

> Just as a person casts off worn-out garments and puts on others that are new, even so does the embodied soul cast off worn-out bodies and take on others that are new. (2:22; Radhakrishnan 1982, 108)

The goal of life, according to the *Gita,* is perfection, the realization of the nature of self. It is this realization which results in the liberation of the soul. However, movement along the path to perfect understanding and behaviour is slow and one must pass through a long series of lives before reaching the end. The efforts made in one life are carried over into the next life and, step by step, progress is made:

> There he regains the (mental) impressions (of union with the Divine) which he had developed in his previous life and with this as the starting point, he strives again for perfection. (6:43; Radhakrishnan 1982, 209)

The soul, according to the *Gita,* goes to that which is thought about at the last moment of life (Radhakrishnan 1982, 229). By this mechanism, the previous life influences the next. However, the *Gita* also implies that simply thinking of God at the time of death can achieve the goal of liberating the soul:

> Those who know Me as the One that governs the material and the divine aspects, and all the sacrifices, they, with their minds harmonized, have knowledge of Me even at their time of departure (from here). (7:30; Radhakrishnan 1982, 225)

> And whoever, at the time of death gives up his body and departs, thinking of me alone, he comes to My status (of being); of that there is no doubt. (8:5; Radhakrishnan 1982, 228)

The *Bhagavadgita* also prescribes certain times to die. During half of each day, half of each month and half of each year, liberation is not possible no matter what realization the dying person has had or what his or her final thoughts.[3]

> Fire, light, day, the bright (half of the month), the six months of the northern path (of the sun), then going forth the men who know the Absolute go to the Absolute. (8:24; Radhakrishnan 1982, 235)

> Smoke, night, so also the dark half (of the month), the six months of the southern path (of the sun), then going forth the yogi obtains the lunar light and returns. (8:25; Radhakrishnan 1982, 235)

The *Gita,* a text which advocates the path of devotion over the other methods of realization of God, tends to view *mukti* as *equivalence* with God as opposed to *identity* with God. The soul *(atman)* does not merge with the infinite *(Brahman)* but rather adopts the "mode of being" of God, in which "the freed soul is inspired by Divine knowledge and moved by Divine will" (Radhakrishnan 1982, 76). This resonates fairly well with the thoughts on the nature of *moksha* of many of the families who have brought someone to die at the Muktibhavan.

The *Ramcharitmanas*

According to Masterji, everybody in his village knows the *Ramcharitmanas,* even the illiterate people. They know the story and they know some of the verses *(dohas)* by heart. Sometimes people sit around at night and somebody who can read reads out the *Ramcharitmanas* and the others listen. Also there are *Ram Lilas* (plays enacting the events of the story) performed by people who go from village to village. Occasionally people will collect money and then perform a *Ramcharitmanas navapath,* a *puja,* and lesson on the *Ramcharitmanas* which lasts for nine days. The *Ramcharitmanas* is thus well known and is an important text. This seems to be the general case for the entire region from which people come to the Muktibhavan for dying.

The *Ramcharitmanas* contains many references to getting *moksha* by dying in Kashi as well as to the relationship of Shiva and Rama and to the importance of Rama's name in achieving *moksha.* Toward the end of the book, Rama himself addresses the citizens of his city in the following manner:

> Give ear to my words, all you people of the city. . . . Listen to me and act as may seem good to you. . . . It is great good fortune that you have secured a human body, which—as all the scriptures declare—is difficult even for the gods to attain. . . . [H]e who receives it and still wins not heaven, reaps torment in the next world and beats his head in vain remorse. . . .

> Sensuous enjoyment, brothers, is not the object of the human body; why even heavenly enjoyment is short-lived and ends in sorrow. Those born as men who give themselves up to sensual delights are fools who would choose poison in exchange for nectar. No one will ever speak well of him who picks up a peppercorn and throws away the philosopher's stone. His immortal soul wanders endlessly through eighty-four lakhs (8,400,000) of living species by the four modes of birth. . . .
>
> Sometimes God of his mercy, and without any reason for the affection, bestows on him a human body, a raft to carry him across the ocean of mundane existence, with my grace for a favourable wind. . . . [T]he man who, though equipped with such means as these, fails to cross the ocean of birth and death, is an ungrateful, dull-witted wretch, bent on his own destruction. (Tulsidas 1990, 601)

FIGURE 6.3

Private reading of *Ramcharitmanas* in the room of a *rogi marnewala* at Kashi Labh Muktibhavan

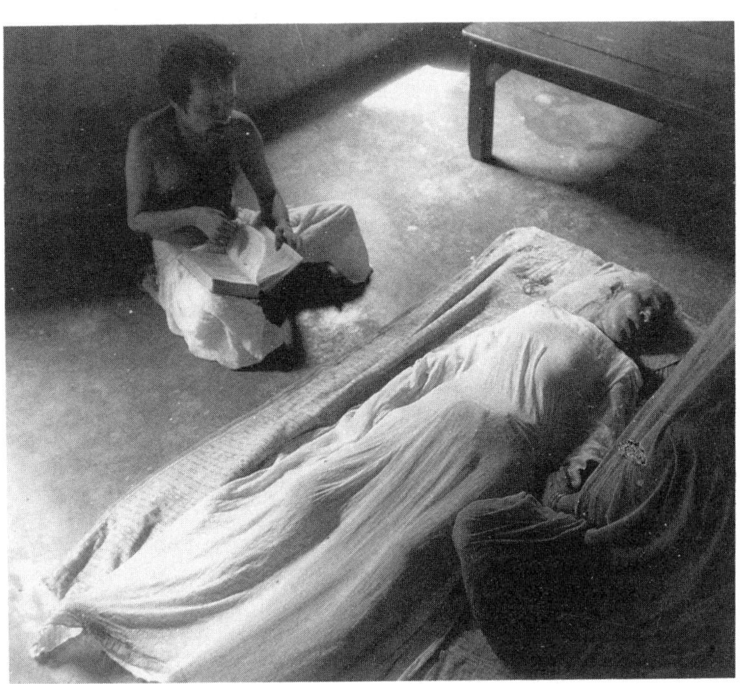

The *Ramcharitmanas* thus prescribes the pursuit of *moksha* with some urgency. It must be accomplished in this very lifetime. If not, a great opportunity, life in a human body which has come about through the grace of God, has been missed. It may be as many as 8,400,000 more miserable, nonhuman, lives before another such opportunity is available.

There are several other principles outlined in the *Ramcharitmanas* which seem to relate directly to the people dying at the Muktibhavan. Several of the relevant citations from the text are listed in Figure 6.4. The *Ramcharitmanas* states that *moksha* is available by dying in Kashi. This is so, it says, because Shiva mutters the Great Spell in the ears of a dying person there. The spell is the name of Rama and the power of this name is such that even demons in battle with Rama, and screaming at each other to kill Rama, attain *moksha* merely by this mention of his name. The *Ramcharitmanas* also describes the death of Dasharath, who, thinking of Rama as his life faded away, died a "glorious death."

"It is absolutely certain that even those people who have done bad deeds all their lives will get *moksha*," according to the priest-worker Pandey. He believes this, he said, because Tulsidas wrote in the *Ramcharitmanas* that one may be a great sinner, but if, in the last stages, one says "Rama, Rama" or even just in the last breath, then the person will get *moksha*. But, Pandey said, the name must be said properly:

> There is the story of Valmiki [the composer of the original version, the *Ramayana*]. Early in his life he was a big *dacoit* [outlaw]. To make up for his sins he was told to chant *"Rama, Rama, Rama, Rama, Rama."* But he didn't do it properly and went around chanting *"Mara, Mara, Mara, Mara, Mara"* (which happens to mean "Die, die, die"). So he was born again.

FIGURE 6.4

Selected citations from the *Ramcharitmanas* (Tulsidas 1990)

"[T]he Great Spell muttered by Siva, who enjoins it as effecting salvation at Kashi." (15)

"Why not dwell at Kashi, the abode of Shambu and Bhavani, knowing it to be the birthplace of salvation, the mine of spiritual wisdom and abolisher of sin?" (425)

"When I (Siva) see any creature dying in Kashi, it is by the might of his (Rama's) name that I rid it of all sorrow (liberate it)." (72)

"[T]he potency of the name 'Rama' is measureless. The immortal Shankara (Siva), who is a fountain of joy and a storehouse of all wisdom and perfection, continually repeats it. There are four kinds of living beings in the world; such of them who die in the holy city of Kashi (Banaras) attain to the highest realm. This too marks the glory of Rama's Name, for it is this very Name that Siva in his compassion imparts to the dying soul in Kashi." (33)

"Crying 'Rama, Rama!' and again 'Rama!' and yet again 'Rama, Rama!' and 'Rama!', the king cast off his body in his agony of separation from Raghubara and ascended to the abode of the gods. . . . Living, he gazed on Rama's face, fair as the moon, and dying for his loss, had a glorious death." (289)

"(The demons bid defiance to one another, shouting 'Kill him! He is Rama!') Thus crying 'Rama! Rama!', they left their bodies and attained beatitude *(kaivalya-moksha* or final emancipation). By this means the compassionate Lord slew the enemy in an instant." (403)

The death of Jatayu the vulture. "Said Rama, 'No friend, you must not die.' But he answered with a smile, 'He by the mention of whose name at the hour of death the vilest sinner wins salvation, so declare the Vedas, is present now in bodily form before my eyes. What purpose, Lord, will my body serve when there is nothing left to desire? With his eyes full of tears Raghunatha replied, 'It is your own meritorious deeds, friend, that have brought you salvation. There is nothing in the world beyond the reach of those who have others' interests at heart. Casting off your body, friend, ascend now to my realm. What more shall I give you, when you have all you desire? But on reaching there, friend, say nothing to my father of Sita's abduction." (412)

"Listen, O enemy of serpents, the Kaliyuga is a storehouse of pollution and vice. Escape from the cycle of birth and death is easy (in this age). . . . [T]he goal which in the first three ages is reached by solemn worship, sacrifice, and austerity men are able to attain in the Kaliyuga only by Hari's name. In the Satyayuga everyone is possessed of mystic powers and wisdom too; in that age men crossed the ocean of birth and death by meditating on God. In the Tretayuga men perform sacrifices of various kinds and escape rebirth by dedicating their actions to the Lord. In the Dvaparayuga men have no other expedient than the ritual worship of Raghunatha's feet. But in the Kaliyuga men sound the depths of the ocean of mortality by merely chanting the story of Hari's perfections. In the Kaliyuga austerity, sacrifice or spiritual wisdom are of no avail; one's only hope lies in hymning Rama's praises. The power of the Name is manifest in the Kaliyuga." (637)

"In the Kaliyuga no action *(karma)* avails nor devotion *(bhakti)* nor knowledge *(gyana)*; the name of Rama is the only resort." (20)

> "In this terrible age the Name is the wish-yielding tree, and when one thinks on it, it puts an end to all the illusions of the world. It is the name of Rama that grant's ones desired object in the Kaliyuga." (20)

The *Ramcharitmanas* is the colloquial version of Valmiki's *Ramayana,* which is popular in various versions throughout India. The *Ramcharitmanas* is the Hindi (Avadi) version composed by Tulsidas in Kashi itself. According to Eck (1982, 87), it was, at first, attacked by the orthodox *pandits,* but was loved by the general populace, and remains today the "Bible of the Hindi-speaking people." Especially in the villages in the regions around Kashi it is popular. Masterji explained it in this way:

> There are two *sampradayas:* devotion to Rama and devotion to Krishna. Both are *avatars* [incarnations] of Vishnu. Before they were separated. The people of the area around Krishna's birthplace kept faith in Krishna, and the people around Kashi and Ayodhya kept faith in Rama. Now they are merged and so people now say *'Hari Rama Hari Krishna.'*

But they are not totally merged. As Saraswati said, each region has its own favorite god. From central Uttar Pradesh to Bihar, roughly the area from which people come to the Muktibhavan to die, it is Rama who is "the idol of the people" (1983, 35).

As early as AD 200–400 the idea that Rama was an *avatar* of the god Vishnu who had descended to the earth in human form to slay the demon Ravana in combat had been developed (Bakker 1986, 61). The text *Agastyasamhita* (c. AD 1200) discusses the *moksha*-granting properties of Kashi and takes the position that Shiva performs worship and propitiates Rama by the repetition *(japa)* of his mantra, and that it is, ultimately, Rama that empowers Shiva with the ability to bestow *moksha* on those who come to die in Kashi (Bakker 1986, 69). The thirteenth to the sixteenth centuries witnessed a spread in devotion to Rama, concurrent with a growth of emotional devotionalism *(bhakti)* all over North India. During this period the "cult of the name" developed in which the repetition of the name Rama, among others, became accepted as a means *(sadhana)* to gain liberation (75).

Eck (1991, 65) called Shaivism the "ancient layer" beneath medieval and modern Hinduism. The Vaishnava *bhakti* movements, such as that of Rama, are superimposed upon a predominantly Shaiva milieu in village India (65). Tulsidas, who wrote *Ramcharitmanas,* was clearly a devotee of both gods and integrated praises of Shiva into the text of the *Ramcharitmanas*. The relation between Rama and Shiva is articulated in a popular saying which is attributed to Tulsidas: Shiva's best *bhakta* is Rama, and Rama's best *bhakta* is Shiva. This literature, according to Eck, has become an architecture of pilgrimage to the extent that the two types of worship are intertwined in much of North Indian pilgrimage. The *Ramcharitmanas*, as the most well-known texts in the region around Kashi, is very much an architecture of the pilgrimage to die in Kashi.

The *Garuda Purana*

The *Garuda Purana* was read during the *shraddha* ceremonies after Masterji's mother's death. People from other houses came to hear it read in its entirety. It was read for about two hours per day, at various times, according to the wishes of the priest, for about ten days. This seems to be generally the case with the people coming to the Muktibhavan. Singh, described above, for instance, has heard the *Garuda Purana* being read many times, whenever there was a death. He has listened to the whole thing carefully on two occasions on the deaths of his grandfather and his father. In the reading of the *Garuda Purana* that I witnessed, done as part of the *shraddha* for Anandi Prasad's grandmother, all sixteen chapters were read within three days. Anandi also had said that he was familiar with the *Garuda Purana* having heard it many times in the village.

What I am referring to here as the *Garuda Purana*, and what is taken in the villages to be the *Garuda Purana* is, in fact, a small portion of the *Garuda Purana* proper which is known as the *"Uttarakhanda"* or *"Pretakalpa"* (the period of nonliving). This section has been shown to be a later addition to the *Garuda Purana* proper, and probably was a separate work in itself (Gangadharan 1972, 122). The *"Uttarakhanda"* is a highly variable section and the differences in the editions are many (1972, 111). The version I have cited here is the one that was read at the Muktibhavan and which, as far as I know, is generally used in the villages surrounding Kashi. It is published by a small press in Kashi with the name *Garuda Purana* and contains no information as to version or its relationship to the *Purana* proper.

The *Garuda Purana* is essentially a conversation between the bird Garuda and the god Vishnu. Garuda asks many questions relating to death and Vishnu reveals to him, in some gruesome detail, all that happens, from the time when death approaches, to life in the womb as rebirth is imminent. It begins like this, with a description of what it is like to die:

> While dying, the person's eyesight will become like a god's. He can see the messengers of Yama (the god of death) in the realm of death *(Yama lok)* as well as in this realm. Having seen this he will become very anxious. His senses become muddled, his knowledge destroyed.
>
> The soul, on seeing the messengers of Yama, will become afraid and want to run away. When the five different types of winds *(pran, ushan, udan, vyan* and *saman)* start to leave their places, for the sinner this one second will last for one epoch *(yuga)*. Like a hundred scorpions the messengers will fall on him.
>
> From the fear of the messengers, the dying person's mouth will start to exude spittle. The soul will leave the sinner people from the lower regions. Those virtuous people, their souls will be released from somewhere in their heads, like their eyes. At that time the sinner will see the messengers of Yama standing there with red eyes and in an angry mood, with fearful faces and holding iron clubs. They are naked and they are gnashing their teeth. The hair of their head is like that of the arm, they are black like crows, their faces are twisted, and their fingernails are like swords.
>
> In fear he will become totally incontinent. And crying in this condition, and getting the result of his previous deeds, the soul will leave the body and acquire a new body the size of a thumb called *"angusta."* Seeing his family and friends, he will be dragged off tied to a rope to the realm of the dead *(Yama lok)*. (*Garuda Purana* 1:26–32)

Having adopted an ethereal thumb-sized body, one can next expect to be tortured. The text goes on to describe the long journey to the realm of death, the many punishments dished out along the way, and the many types of "hells" along the route. It describes the sins during life that land you in a particular hell, especially the awful Vaitarni River which runs with blood, pus, and urine and contains gnashing serpents and fish with sharp needle-like snouts. The text tells of why you might become a ghost, and it tells about standing before Yama, the God of death, waiting to be judged as his bookkeeper Chitragupta weighs out your good and bad deeds. It tells of the importance of all the rituals and donations and the things which are important for avoiding repeating the hellish journey through death, or at least making the next trip the last. The *Garuda Purana* (GP) is a work on morality but, also it is a teaching in how to get *moksha* which it portrays as permanent residence in the realm of Vishnu or Brahma, or in some other heaven.

> With great holy work, the soul will take birth as a human being, the person who will follow the order of religion in the body of a human being, he will get *moksha.* Not knowing the religion, the human being comes and goes in this sorrowful world. If you want to make success out of this human being life, then you have to collect religious merits. (GP 8:95–96)

Your relatives and all your wealth will stay behind when you die. The only things that will accompany you are your religious (good and bad) deeds. For this reason, the *Garuda Purana* recommends that wealth be donated during life to accumulate religious merit.

> When he is going to the other worlds, for expenditure along the route, that is the donations, having done so he goes with great happiness along the route. Without these donations that creature will have many problems on the route. (GP 8:93)

Specifically, there are several donations that should be done right before death, called *atur dan* of which there are several types (sesame seed, iron, gold, jute, salt, seven grains, land, and cow). There are five types of cow donation, according to *Garuda Purana:* three are supposed to be done for dying: one at the time of death *(antdenu),* another for achieving *moksha (mokshadenu),* and one for crossing the Vaitarni River *(vaitarnidenu).*

> O Garuda, having given the *gau dan,* the great river (Vaitarni) never comes in the middle of this great route, therefore it is better to give the donation in good time. (GP 8:86)

The Vaitarni is, at one level, a metaphor for the body. Falling into the Vaitarni River is falling into the womb and taking rebirth; successfully crossing the Vaitarni is achieving *moksha.*

> Meat, bones, blood; the Vaitarni River is like the body, because the Vaitarni River is also full of meat and blood. Those who give a cow to a Brahmin, they never fall into the Vaitarni River. And those people who are chanting the name of God never fall into the Vaitarni in the form of a body, meaning that they get *mukti.* (GP 8:24)

Several people I talked to thought in these metaphorical terms. People regularly used the term *nark* (hell) in the sense of a possible destination after death, but when asked to explain *nark,* they would say that it is here on earth; as the body is the Vaitarni, life is hell. Most everybody at the Muktibhavan agreed that giving a cow before death helped the soul to cross the Vaitarni river, which by extension of the metaphor, means avoiding rebirth.

In order that this be the last life, many things must be done. It is thus important to prepare for death and the *Garuda Purana* lists several signs by which people should recognize that their death is approaching:

> Having seen his body grow old and become sick, seeing that the stars and planets are against him, and becoming weak in the senses, the wise person will know his time of death is coming and without fear or hesitation should do work to pardon his sins. (GP 9:3)

There are several things which are mentioned throughout the *Garuda Purana* which can be done toward achieving *mukti*. The method which is most stressed is hearing and saying the name of Vishnu:

> The person who chants the name of Vishnu, the destroyer of sins, or chanting of the *Gita*, or chanting the 1,000 names of Vishnu or hearing it from others, or fasting on the eleventh day, *Gita path, Ganga jal, tulsi* leaves, water from the feet of Vishnu *(Vishnu ka charnamrit)* and the name of Vishnu; these things give *mukti* at the time of death. (GP 8:25–26)
>
> Hearing the name of Vishnu in one's ear destroys many sins. (GP 9:8)
>
> The person who will say my name (Vishnu) at the time of death, their millions of great sins will be burned to ashes. (GP 9:12)
>
> The relatives must say the ten names of Vishnu to the dying person. (GP 9:11)
>
> If the son forces the dying person *(marnewale manusha)* to say the name of Vishnu, he will get *mukti.* (GP 9:13)
>
> O Garuda, the power of the name of Vishnu to destroy sins, human beings cannot otherwise realize this power. (GP 9:15)

The *Garuda Purana* contains several teachings which are of direct relevance to the pilgrimage to Kashi to die and to the ritual and other behaviour surrounding the dying process at the Muktibhavan. For instance, Kashi is promoted as a place (though not the only place) in which dying results in the attainment of *moksha:*

> At the time of old age, he who becomes detached and leaving all feelings and he who remembers me, that happy soul will definitely get *mukti.* Those persons who, wanting to die, leave their homes to live *(vasa)* in Prayag or some other *tirtha,* or to die in Kashi, etc. he will definitely get *moksha.* (1) Ayodhya, (2) Mathura, (3) Maya (Haridwar), (4) Kashi, (5) Kanchi, (6) Avantika (Ujaina), (7) Dvarka: these are seven *moksha-* giving *puris.* (16:112–14)

The *Garuda Purana* teaches the proper methods of leaving the body that results in a good situation *(sadgati).* Dying on a platform on which sesame seeds and *kusha* grass have been spread, dying near to an image of Vishnu, dying in the shade of a *tulsi* plant or holding *tulsi* leaves, all result in the attainment of *moksha.* Of specific relevance to dying at the Muktibhavan are the following passages:

> The person who is going to die should be made to sleep on a pure place and jewels should be put in his mouth along with water from the feet of God *(Vishnu Bhagavan ka charnamrit).* If one drop of this water will go inside the mouth of the person he will become free from all sins and achieve liberation. (GP 9:20–21)
>
> The *Ganga jal* [Ganges water] that destroys all sins gives the same benefit as religious work done in the holy *tirthas.* (GP 9:23)
>
> The person who listens to one *shloka* about God, he will never come back from the realm of Brahma *(Brahma lok).* (GP 9:32)
>
> Chanting the Vedas and Upanishads or the prayers of Shiva or Vishnu, for Brahmin, Kshatriya or Vaishya, gives liberation. (GP 9:33)

The purificatory rituals, the giving of *charnamrit* and *Ganga jal* with *tulsi* leaves, and the recitation of verses from the holy books are all activities which occur at the Muktibhavan and are done in the time immediately preceding death or at death. According to the *Garuda Purana,* if they are done, the dying person will certainly get *moksha.* This will be evidenced, as several people at the Muktibhavan mentioned, by the life's breath and where it proceeds from the body

> The person who at the last time does these activities, the soul of these religious persons comes out through a hole in the top of the face. The mouth, nose, eyes and ears: the life's breath *(pran bayu)* of religious people comes out through these seven doors. (GP 9:36–37)

Several people told me that a lack of air coming from the lower regions at the time of death may be taken as a good sign. Conversely, a bad fate is evidenced by the voiding of the bladder or bowels at the time of death. Incontinence, at the time of dying, according to the first passage I cited from *Garuda Purana,* is from the fear that a sinner feels of seeing the frightful messengers of death approaching.

Conclusions

The people who come to Kashi and the Muktibhavan to die are participants in many levels and layers of culture. They come, ultimately, because of their understandings and beliefs about dying. These beliefs and understandings are a part of larger realms of religious or spiritual beliefs. The people who come to die at the Muktibhavan are Hindus who share a rich textual tradition with other Hindus. But these people are also members of a more regional culture which has chosen (in the historic sense) to favour particular aspects of the larger Hindu (textual) tradition, ideas from which move from the texts into the culture of "face to face interaction" in a complicated manner. People are also both members of castes and residents of villages that have particular beliefs and understandings not shared by outsiders. And, finally, people are individuals and have, to varying extents, selectively taken and analyzed aspects of the Hindu, regional, caste and village traditions available to them.

My analysis was driven by my sense of wonder at the degree to which people's explanations regarding coming to Kashi to die can be found in the very texts they say they know and how these explanations differ from textbook Hinduism. My analysis of the Muktibhavan records shows that the people come only from districts in Bihar and western Uttar Pradesh, an area roughly concordant with that area in which Saraswati (1983, 35) said Rama is "the idol of the people." The analysis has thus been an attempt to get at an aspect of culture at a regional level. It is not a full explanation of why people come to Kashi to die and cannot explain why only a small number of people in the region come.

The people who come to the Muktibhavan to die, as is probably the case with people all over India, know some things from the *Bhagavadgita.* After most deaths, the *Garuda Purana* is read and thus people hear again and again about the horrors of the hells and of rebirths, and how to avoid them. Most importantly, the people coming to the Muktibhavan to die are devotees of Rama and are greatly influenced by the *Ramcharitmanas* which they read, are taught, and regularly see performed.

7

Dying and Morality

The *Garuda Purana* clearly embodies a system of morality. It is a long description of punishments for the people who sin *(pap)* and rewards for the people who do good work *(punya):* after dying and journeying to the realm of the dead, and standing in front of Chitragupta, the bookkeeper of Yamaraj, one's accumulated good and bad deeds are tallied up and the appropriate reward is decided upon. Two chapters of the *Garuda Purana* are essentially lists of particular sins and the punishments they entail. For instance:

> Those people who criticize the Vedas, Puranas, Mimamsa . . . those people who become happy at other people's misery . . . those people, crying day and night, going to *Yama lok* will receive punishment from the messengers of Yama and will be thrown into the Vaitarni River. . . . Or people who insult their mother, father, or respected people, they will have to live in the Vaitarni River. (c4: 9–11)

For the people coming to die at the Muktibhavan, death is entwined in a system of morality not simply because the punishments for bad behaviour are received after death. A death in the village involves a reading of the *Garuda Purana.* People are thus reminded, at the time of death, of the proper ways to live and of the sins that will land them in a terrible afterlife.

This chapter explores the themes of morality and death, especially in terms of the system of morality built into the rules and operational structure of the Muktibhavan. The people coming to the Muktibhavan to die are, in a sense, opting out of the moral system by receiving the reward of *moksha* regardless of how they might have behaved in their lives. They are managing to avoid the "immutable" rules of karmic retribution. The owner who wrote the Muktibhavan rules, and the manager who runs the Muktibhavan, see things differently. From their perspectives, and for separate reasons, *karma,*[1] which is inseparable from the Hindu moral code *(dharma),* operates in Kashi as everywhere else. Dying at the Muktibhavan, from their perspective, is therefore an exercise in morality. The rules and day to day operation of the Muktibhavan form the structure and environment in which the pilgrims who come to the Muktibhavan to die spend their last days.

Heaven and the Muktibhavan Rules

Jaydal Dalmia, the man who started the Muktibhavan, said that he had wanted to give the dying a place to stay in Kashi but even more to give them a religious atmosphere in which to die. This meant that in addition to providing a place where relatives can stay and cook their food, as is similarly provided at the Ganga-labh Bhavan, he provided *kirtan karmacharya* (priest-workers) who are responsible for a number of things, the most important of which is the chanting of the name of God twenty-four hours a day. The reasons for Dalmia's wanting to provide these particular services fit well with his understanding of death and *mukti;* an understanding which both overlaps with and is different from the understandings of the priest-workers and the pilgrims who die in the Muktibhavan.

For Dalmia, it is important to die in Kashi because this act results in *mukti,* an "exemption" from the cycle of birth death and rebirth. This is desirable because life for most (meaning the poor[2]) is miserable and there are much better places to be than this world. Dalmia's *mukti,* then, has two dimensions. It is escape from this world and it is entry into another world. These two aspects of *mukti* are influenced by different aspects of the way in which one dies.

Dying in Kashi is enough to guarantee *mukti,* to guarantee that the cycle of rebirth will come to an end—eventually. *Mukti* can be either immediate *(sadya mukti)* or delayed. It is possible to die in Kashi and get a delayed *mukti,* meaning that you will have to be born again a specified number of times, "perhaps seven or three" before the process is permanently ended. In this manner, according to Dalmia, dying in the other six *puris* of India also results in *mukti* by providing that one's next birth is in Kashi, and by guaranteeing that one will, next time, die in Kashi. Whereas it is the physical act of being in Kashi that results in the guarantee that rebirth will come to an end, it is one's mental condition at the moment of death which determines whether *mukti* is immediate or delayed.

Dalmia also said that one's dying thoughts determine which of four *types* of *mukti* one will get. The type of *mukti* refers to the state in which one will exist for all eternity, and while all four are considered to be blissful, there is definitely an order of good to better to best. The four types of *mukti* are: *salokya* in which you reside in the same world as god, *samipya* in which you remain near to god, *sarupya* in which you take the same form as god, and *sayuja* where you actually become merged with god.

There is one other element which is determined by the moment of death: the punishment that one will receive after death. The punishment may be simply delayed rather than immediate *mukti,* but it also can be something which happens to you in between death and heaven *(svarg).* A murderer, for example, who dies in Kashi, and who at the moment of death is repentant, who hears the name of god and is concentrating on him, will certainly get *mukti.* The *mukti* may even be immediate and high level, depending on his mental state at the moment of death, but the murderer will certainly have to undergo punishment on his way to heaven.

"Heaven" was one of a few English words that Dalmia used every once in a while to make sure I was understanding. For Dalmia, *mukti* meant going to heaven and heaven, like Hindu society, is hierarchically divided into four levels. Attaining liberation from the cycle of death and rebirth is one step in reaching heaven and though it is an important step, it is as important to minimize the punishment after death and to maximize one's level in heaven.

The Kashi Labh Muktibhavan has been set up in order to facilitate those aspects of dying which Dalmia understands to yield the maximum spiritual benefit. Being in Kashi is not the all important condition: it is necessary but not sufficient for full spiritual benefit. The amenities provided by the Muktibhavan which help maximize spiritual reward include the specific rituals and a host of rules and performances designed to create a religious atmosphere *(dharmik vatavaran).*

Jaydal Dalmia, then an old man, did not remember who wrote the rules of the Muktibhavan. But his entourage, the many men who sat with us through our interview, all agreed that he himself probably wrote them as he was "famous for his strict rules and regulations" within his corporate structure. Shuklaji also said that Dalmia was responsible for the rules. The rules of the Muktibhavan are shown in Figure 7.1.

Among the rules are several restrictions on the behavior of people staying at the Muktibhavan. The families coming with the dying are restricted to eating vegetarian foods without onions and garlic. Playing games, such as cards and chess, is not allowed, and laughing and joking are discouraged. The families must be courteous to others staying in the *bhavan* and thus should not fill the place up with smoke from their charcoal stoves, write on the walls, or spit on the floors.

FIGURE 7.1

The Muktibhavan rules: Translation of the rules printed on a large signboard at the main entrance of Kashi Labh Muktibhavan

Shiva's Name is Aum

Entering regulations for those staying at Dalmiya Kashi—Muktibhavan

1. In this Kashi-Labh Muktibhavan only those faithful believers and sick people on the brink of death will be able to stay; only the ones who have come for the benefit of Kashi. Sick people desiring to be cured with the use of medicine should stay in a hospital or someplace else.

2. In here only those good people of Hindu *varnashrama* will be able to stay.

3. In here a place to stay will be available for fifteen days. Also after this, if there is special need and only with the permission of the manager, then one will be able to stay.

4. The work of making food must be done on a closed stove using charcoal. There shouldn't be any type of smoke in the rooms or verandas.

5. Sick people afflicted with tuberculosis, cholera, plague, and also with any other infectious diseases will never be able to stay. If such a disease is contracted when staying here, then the manager will not give permission to remain.

6. From the people staying here, if some contemptable or indecent or even reprehensible behavior will be done, then the manager has the authority to make them immediately depart.

7. People staying here must give the matter special attention that what they do is not in any way disturbing or inconveniencing to other people.

8. In the "Muktibhavan's" stairs, walls, courtyards, and verandahs, to spit or also to write something is completely prohibited.

9. People accompanying the *rogi* should take great care with their things. If any article becomes lost or stolen, then for this the "Muktibhavan" is not responsible.

10. People staying here should not give rewards to the Muktibhavan employees.

11. If from the staff of this place there is observed some impolite or improper behavior, then one should stop in the Muktibhavan's manager's office and write in the complaint book.

Dalmia saw all these behavioural restrictions as necessary for the creation of a religious atmosphere in which the dying can, undisturbed, "remember God, hear his name and concentrate on him at their dying moment." Playing chess and other games takes the mind off God. The smell of food must not permeate the building and remind people that they have not eaten. Part of having the right mind-set for maximum spiritual reward, in Dalmia's view, is by *withdrawing* from the material world: the smell of food pervading the Muktibhavan would definitely not be conducive to such withdrawal.

For Dalmia, a good death is defined in both moral and spiritual terms: a good death is one which results in the maximum spiritual reward after death and the least punishment. Though it is the fact that the Muktibhavan is in Kashi that guarantees *moksha,* Dalmia said it is dying in a religious atmosphere, dying hearing the name of God, dying focused on good thoughts, which yield an immediate *mukti,* a high level of *mukti,* and a short period of punishment before reaching heaven. These are the elements of a good death.

The Muktibhavan manager, Shuklaji, has a different understanding of how the spiritual benefit is won. For him, it is not only important that the families do not disturb the dying person but they must also *participate* in the creation of the right atmosphere and mind-set for a good death to occur. Thus, family members are encouraged to participate in the ongoing *kirtan* or devotional song and themselves repeat the name of God to the dying person. As I shall show, Shuklaji's understanding leads to a more moral interpretation of what is a good death, and the exclusion of certain classes of people who are not dying such a death.

The Thoughts of Shuklaji

> Everybody cannot get *moksha;* if they did, the game *(lila)* of God would be over.
>
> —Shuklaji

As I said earlier, the Muktibhavan manager, Shuklaji, helped me with this research and became a good friend. He took it upon himself to teach me many things. Yet he was, in fact, much more concerned that I learn how to behave in the proper manner than learn how the Muktibhavan was run. Part of the reason he was interested in talking to me was that he felt that I would spread his teaching. Part of the reason I am interested in talking about him is to honour this desire. However, his thoughts, though uniquely his own, represent the *context* in which the people coming to the Muktibhavan die and explain several features of Muktibhavan operation and policy. I am thus using his teachings slightly differently than he might have imagined I would, though I believe I am not misrepresenting them.

Shuklaji seems to understand religious belief at several levels. He said he believes himself, but he also thinks that it is imperative that other people believe for the general good of society. This is illustrated by the following conversation between Omji and Shuklaji, captured on a tape before the resumption of our more formal conversation:

Omji: What happens is connected with previous births. This is believed by the deities also. . . .

Shuklaji: . . . [A]ctually rebirth is definite. But when an ancestor passes away a death anniversary rite is done in Gaya. And after that they become gods [*devata*].

Omji: Yes, they become gods. . . .

Shuklaji: But till the time they become gods, we do not believe they are reborn. We consider them to be ancestors. But we do not know how long they remain ancestors and what they do.

Omji: No, they can not be seen. . . .

Shuklaji: It is a matter of tradition.

Omji: Yes.

Shuklaji: But this *is* certain. With good deeds [*karma*] and good destiny [*sanskar*], good thoughts [*vichar*] come. And this can be felt. If everybody understood this [the matter being discussed], then people would stop doing good deeds altogether. There would be a loss of piety [*punya*].

From Shuklaji's perspective, the details of what happens after death are not known absolutely. For the vast majority, it is a matter of faith and a matter of tradition. What is sure, for him, are the social functions of what individuals believe. After-death beliefs, as he said, lead to good deeds and piety.

On the other hand, Shuklaji, himself, *does* have a strong set of beliefs which are based on his own contemplation of what some of the great seers of history have written. For instance, he believes there is a reward for dying in Kashi. According to Shuklaji, "in Kashi the results are surely positive every time." He has to believe this, he said, because he has studied the works of the saints, *mahatmas*, *rishis* and *maharishis* who have written down their experiences. They have said that Kashi has special properties, that Kashi is different from all other places: "A person who dies in Kashi, he is neither on this earth or in the sky nor in the nether-world *(patan).*" But while a special reward accrues to all who die in Kashi, according to Shuklaji, it is within the rules of *karma.* "Even in Kashi people always get the results of their actions. Good deeds *(accha karma)* may either result in *moksha* or have a good influence on subsequent births. Sins *(pap)* will have the opposite effect": in Shuklaji's understanding, *karma* is always played out. He said:

> You have a very nice shirt. If I force you to give me your shirt, will I get the pleasure of your shirt while you feel the loss? No, because the amount of pain you are getting and the amount of pleasure I am getting are being entered into the record book of the eternal Brahman, and we will both get an answer.

At one level, Shuklaji does not believe that dying in Kashi results in *moksha* at all. Though he often *says* that dying in Kashi results in *moksha,* when he explained the process, he said that, really, what one gets for dying in Kashi is a spiritual lesson which is helpful in the pursuit of *moksha.* The lesson will lead to new knowledge and the desire to do more good deeds, which in some unspecified time will end rebirth. He said:

> Both the repenter and the sinner must face those who protect this city. The chief sentinel of Lord Shiva is Kal Bhairav and there are also some other demi-gods [*yakshas*] and creatures like snakes and scorpions, who all give punishment. And after the punishment the soul takes birth again. After the punishment, he will slowly gain some knowledge and the understanding that he should do some good deeds. He will come to see that, just as a businessman gets rich, those who do good deeds get happiness and peace. So too the person who chants God's name is immersed in God and so too the student who studies becomes knowledgeable and slowly merges with God. In this way it is certain that the person who lives in Kashi obtains the results of his good and bad deeds in Kashi itself. This is what is meant by getting *moksha* in Kashi. The evidence of this is in the writings of the saints which are as true as God himself.

Just as dying in Kashi does not necessarily secure *moksha,* in Shuklaji's view, the person who dies after doing good work will get *moksha* whether or not he is in Kashi. Here is Shuklaji's story of Kabir:

What is *moksha?* Just like me, Kabir Das had not seen it himself but believed that if one dies in Kashi then one will obtain *moksha.* So he cut off his hands and his legs thinking that if he had no legs he would not be able to leave Kashi, and that if he had no hands then he would not be able to commit any bad deeds.

[Shuklaji interrupted the story, as he often did, to explain to me: "But there is often hindrances even to such great determinism."]

The divine soul said, "It is true that if one dies in Kashi, one gets *moksha.* But I am God [*ishvar*], the divine soul [*paramatman*], the leader of all [*sab ka nayak*], and the protector [*raksha karnewala*]. So I should demonstrate that the importance of Kashi is everywhere, that every place is Mathura, that every place is a pilgrimage center [*tirtha stan*], that I am everywhere."

So, taking a particular form, the form of a horse, he came.

["The divine soul is happy to undergo many trials to protect man."]

He said to Kabir Das, "Please sit on me and I will show you Kashi. Your hands and feet are gone so you have not seen Kashi yet. How will you get *moksha* if you have not seen Kashi?"

["The merciful divine soul sometimes tells lies for the sake of protecting man," Shuklaji explained to me.]

The divine soul, the formless Brahman, took the form of this particular animal, and in this way took Kabir Das onto his back. Having shown him Kashi, however, he took him [outside of Kashi] to Gorakhpur.

Kabir Das [understanding what was happening] said "*Moksha* is certain for those who see God and those who contemplate on God. If everyone came to Kashi then the rest of God's game [*lila*] would be useless. Good deeds are good everywhere and, if one's thoughts are good, one is sure to get *moksha.*"

Kabir started doing worship there. He had the opinion that people from all religions had the same God, and that if there is good, that is God, and if there is bad, that is God. Orthodox religion [*sanatan dharma*] is God, your religion is God, Buddhism is God. He never cried when he was sad or laughed when he was happy; he was always in one state of mind. He was fully immersed in God.

But that was him, now what about us? . . . Kabir Das was not attached to any particular religion. He was like God. When he achieved *moksha* he converted his body into the form of a flower for the benefit of others to know. And both Hindus and

> Muslims divided that flower. In this way he showed that Kashi was everywhere.
>
> ["What our thoughts are like and what our destiny is like, *these* will determine our future wherever we are."]

The greatness of Kashi, like other pilgrimage centers, in Shuklaji's opinion, is that people can go there, live and learn there, and come to know its greatness. The benefit of Kashi is that you can accumulate *knowledge* and *good deeds* from spreading the knowledge to others. In this way, Kashi can contribute toward obtaining *moksha* but, in the end, "if there are good deeds there will be *moksha* and if there are bad deeds there will be pain."

So Shuklaji does not believe in getting *moksha* by dying in Kashi in the *immediate* cause-effect sense of either Dalmia or the people who come from the villages to die at the Muktibhavan. He, instead, sees it metaphorically, and understands the good coming of the trip to Kashi to die as leading to *moksha* through the improvement of one's *karma.* Ultimately, Shuklaji's understanding is very important in terms of how the Muktibhavan is run. His understanding that you can never really escape *karma,* even by dying in Kashi, makes him concerned with behavior and morality and who is or is not dying a good or bad death.

Thoughts on Life and Death

Shuklaji does not believe that the rituals done after death have any effect on the soul. "People," he said, "because they cannot *see* whether or not their relative has attained *moksha* or has been reborn, do everything according to the religious scriptures [*shastra*]." Even still Shuklaji, himself, is doing all the *karma* for his father and other immediate ancestors. It is a matter of acting correctly, not of what is believed to be true: he said, "All these last rites we do are nothing. . . . [W]e perform the last rites because, until such a time, we remain indebted. People will say 'his Grandfather expired but last rites were not performed. We should not even drink water in their home. We should not touch them.' "

What Shuklaji says he believes is that generally the soul *(atman)*[3] takes rebirth after death of the body. The *atman* has progressed through 8,400,000 births in various life-forms *(charasi lakh yoni),* and either through good deeds or by the grace of God, human form has been attained. If the *atman* "gets into a good family, lives in a good environment, and gets a good healthy body," then it will rise higher, both throughout life and from one human life to the next. If it misuses the opportunity, then it will "fall down" and have to again suffer through the cycle of nonhuman births. This is a small but significant variant of the belief of many people who come to the Muktibhavan to die: that there is only *one* chance as a human. Whereas they feel there is only the one opportunity to achieve *moksha,* Shuklaji believes that you keep getting chances at being a human and thus gradually improve toward *moksha,* depending on how your lives are lived.

Human and non-human rebirths are not the only possibilities, according to Shuklaji's understanding. Figure 7.2 shows my conception of a spectrum of after death fates as Shuklaji sees it. On the good and bad ends of the spectrum are *moksha* and ghosthood respectively. Whereas bad behavior results in a nonhuman rebirth, becoming a ghost is a result of *very* bad behavior which results in a bad death. According to Shuklaji, "If a person dies in an accident, or gets burnt, or dies in some other bad manner, then the *pitr* (ancestor) becomes a *preta* (ghost) and must undergo diverse torture for perhaps a thousand years." Shuklaji told me the story of Gokarna which illustrates how bad work can end up in ghosthood, but also how the good work of others can rescue them.

> Gokarna used to drink, eat meat, and go to prostitutes. His brother was an ascetic, was unmarried, and was always immersed in prayer. Because of his brother's good destiny, he went to *Badrik Ashrama.* When the ascetic returned he found that Gokarna was not there but that many prostitutes were living in their house. The prostitutes told him that Gokarna had died a long time back.
>
> Now he knew Gokarna had done a lot of bad things [*galat karma*] and so was concerned over what had happened to him.
>
> [Shuklaji took time to explain to me "His attachment to Gokarna was not selfish but reflected his brother's debt *(rin),* just as you are my friend and I have a friend's debt to you."]
>
> So he decided to give Gokarna his good deeds and to nullify the evil effects of his brother's crimes.
>
> [Again breaking from the story, "In the same way one can give a poor person money that has been acquired by fair means and eliminate his suffering."]
>
> The ascetic meditated and came to know that Gokarna had become a ghost and was living in a bamboo thicket near the house. The ghost was greatly afflicted; day and night he would dream about prostitutes and meat and eggs.
>
> Now the *Bhagavata Mahapurana* is a scripture which helps to attain salvation by nullifying sins very quickly. The brother

FIGURE 7.2

The spectrum of cause and effect in Shuklaji's understanding of dying and what follows.

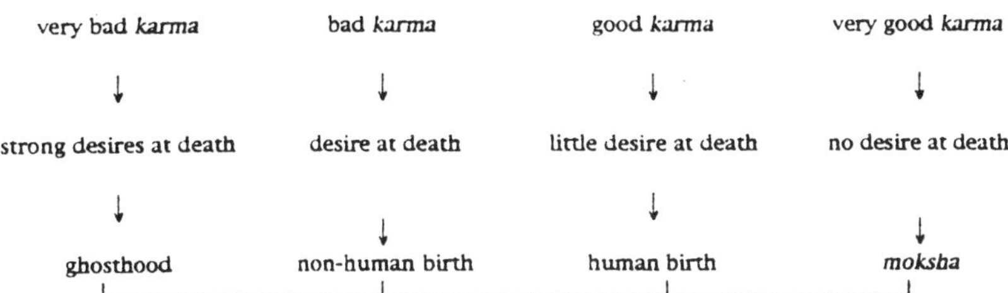

acted quickly so Gokarna would all the sooner attain *moksha.* Many people have attained *moksha* in this way. There was no need for a pandit and he himself, having sat down, started reciting from the book. In the mornings discourses were held. Gokarna, even though he was a ghost and should have run away, listened because of the effects of his brother's good deeds.

The effects of years of bad deeds became nullified with each passing day. When seven days had passed—on the seventh day of the *Bhagavata Purana*—the bamboo thicket burst open and a splendid light came out. This is known as *moksha.*

Thousands of people had come to listen to his brother's discourses. Gokarna, though he had committed many sins, had also listened and contemplated upon them.

[Here Shuklaji paused and said to me "In this same way when you hear something, you write it down then translate it and contemplate upon it. Afterwards you will tell others what I have told you and you will have elaborated on it. I have also elaborated on it slightly. And so it slowly progresses."][4]

Realizing that Gokarna had achieved *moksha* he continued his discourse for seven more days. In that week, about one hundred people achieved *moksha.* In the same way, when the current flows many thousands of bulbs light up. So this is an example of how a brother clears his brother's debt and how, with good deeds and good destiny, *moksha* is easily attained. The important things are good deeds, good destiny, good thoughts and good form.

The good rescuing the bad seems almost a parable for what happens at the Muktibhavan in Shuklaji's view. In some ways, the story he told is about himself as Gokarna's brother. Shuklaji gives afternoon

FIGURE 7.3

Broadcasting lessons from the *Bhagavata Mahapurana* throughout the Kashi Labh Muktibhavan

sermons from the *Bhagavata Mahapurana.* The object of the sermons, like many of the things done at the Muktibhavan, is to help people toward *moksha,* by transferring to them the results of good work.

Moksha is at the other end of the spectrum of fates after death. According to Shuklaji, *moksha* is "going to be with God." God, in Shuklaji's view, among other things, is a device for focusing attention on a reality that is beyond comprehension. It is a human creation of form which stands for the formless. "God too has worldly forms,"

Shuklaji said, "like Krishna, Rama, and Durga, who people *believe* in, but He is also unknown, and without form, which people must *meditate* on." Ultimately, said Shuklaji, it is the formless *Brahman* into which people will merge; *Moksha* ultimately means dissolution of the life force *(atman)* into the infinite *(paramatman),* just as a cup of water becomes part of the sea. "Residence with God" is a way of understanding something that cannot be understood. Meditating on God can help in getting *moksha* but, ultimately, in Shuklaji's view, people *must* understand the formless to attain *moksha.* He said:

> So we force the *rogis* [dying people] to understand that they must meditate on the formless God; that there are no houses or buildings, no material life, no family; that he came to the world alone and that he will leave alone; that he came out from the *Brahman* and that he will also merge there.

Freedom from Desire and the Last Thought

According to Shuklaji, freedom from desire *(iccha)* is the key to getting *moksha.* He told me the following story to illustrate how it is that one should become free of desire, even of one's close family.

> In the *Bhagavadgita,* the story is told of how Abhimanyu was killed in the absence of Arjuna (his father). Arjuna was very grieved and desired to be reunited with his son. The lord Krishna tried to console him in many ways. Finally he said "OK, I will allow you to meet with Abhimanyu again." So they went to heaven and when they arrived Krishna pointed to the moon and said "See, recognize him. It is Abhimanyu, he is immersed in the moon." Arjuna tried to take him in his arms and said, "Oh, son!" Abhimanyu replied, "Many *krores* (tens of millions) of times you have also been my son, but I have not followed you and greeted you like this."

Shuklaji explained that Abhimanyu had come to the world with a duty and having performed it had gone back without any attachment. Krishna took Arjuna to see Abhimanyu to show him that nobody has any relationships, that it is all illusion. A son is just another soul who arrives with a duty to perform. He has been on the earth many times before. Like everyone he must perform his duty and try to obtain *moksha.* To achieve *moksha,* he must be completely detached, even from his own son. Of course this theory of family is difficult to practice, as attachments are great. As Shuklaji said of his own endeavors, "On the one hand, I say to God everyday that everything is him, that nothing matters. But there is the other side of me which, when my son is sick, is searching for a cure."

Desire affects the future by influencing one's thoughts at the moment of death. "If one is thinking about God at the time of death, then one will go to be with God." But, if a person is thinking about a son or some other desire at that very moment, then he or she will take on another form. The trouble is that it is not at all easy to think of God at the moment of death. Thinking of God at the moment of death can only come about by eliminating all other potentially interfering thoughts. This in turn can only be achieved by eliminating all desires for worldly pleasures. And this is why one must first come to the realization that, "one has no friends, no enemies, no family—that everything belongs to God."

Here is a story that Shuklaji told me to illustrate how the final desire and thought can affect the next life:

> There is a good example of how rebirth takes place and how destiny [*sanskar*] is made. There was a great saint. His five disciples knew that he was in contact with the divine soul [*paramatman*] and was thus certain of obtaining *moksha.* They asked him how they would know that he got *moksha* when he left them. He said he would tell them about this when the time came.
>
> Many days later, the time came. They were in front of a plum tree on which there were many plums.
>
> He said to his disciples, "Now I am going to leave my body."
>
> The disciples said, "Guruji, now you are going to merge with God."
>
> "It is certain," was the reply of the saint.
>
> "If we ever get to stay in heaven," they asked, "how will we know that we could meet you there? [that you will be there?]"
>
> The saint then said, "If I obtain *moksha* you will know in this way: A brilliant light, like the sun or the moon, will be emitted from my body. You will be able to see this with your own eyes. If I don't get *moksha* and end up getting rebirth then the brilliant light will not come."
>
> ["But *karma* is so strange," Shuklaji said turning away from the story to explain things to me. "How do you get the fruit of your actions? No one really knows what is good and what is bad, when the time comes. We think we have friends and we think we have enemies. But in the end, we reap what we have sown. Now see what happens."]

When the saint gave up his body, when the soul was leaving his body, it was about to go to Brahman. But at that very last moment his eyes fell upon the plum tree. The plums were absolutely ripe, yellow, and very tempting. His mouth started to water and he became greedy and thought, "If I get that plum, it will be very tasty!" Now if he had got that plum his desire would have been fulfilled. But because the plum tree was very far off and because the saint's body was immobile, his desire was unfulfilled. When the soul left the body there was no brilliant light.

The disciples were confused as they knew that their master had performed sacrifices, contemplated on God and served other people and yet there was no brilliant light. After the last rites, the eldest disciple, through Yogic powers, attempted to learn the exact state of affairs of what birth their master had taken.

[Shuklaji said to me, "It is important for lesser ones to closely pay attention to great men and their journeys through life."]

They desired, too, to fulfill their master's wishes and to liberate his soul. So through divine knowledge they came to know that, "Oh! Our master has become an insect!" And where was that insect? Inside that very plum! Because it was the master's wish to have that fruit he was reborn as an insect inside the plum. The eldest disciple said to the others, "Please pluck that plum. Our master's liberation is very important. If that plum falls into evil hands then he will continue to get rebirth and his condition will be worsened." So the plum was plucked and the master was carefully removed from that fruit. Then the soul left the body and a brilliant light emerged and he obtained *moksha.*

["So in this way" Shuklaji said, explaining the point of the story, "at the time when the soul leaves the body, attachment is formed with whatever is immediate, be it son, friend or wife. This is *karma* and *sanskar."*]

As is illustrated in Figure 7.2, the amount or degree of desire at death, is the key to the future. In the same way that *moksha* is brought about by having no desire, according to Shuklaji, so ghosthood is brought about by untimely and accidental deaths which leave people full of strong, unfulfilled desire. A small amount of desire results in rebirth as a human or worse, as in the story above, as a nonhuman.

Good Deeds and Good Company

One's last thought determines what happens after death and being free of desire is the means by which one can focus on particular thoughts at that difficult moment when life leaves the body. However, ultimately it is good work *(accha karma)* that is the key to achieving freedom from desire and thus *moksha*. Good work consists of "living well, eating good food, keeping good company, doing good behavior and the influence of previous lives." Good work, in turn, operates by leading to knowledge:

> Of course we do not know if there is no desire, but the *jivatman* and *paramatman* know. If there are desires [*iccha*] then rebirth is taken. If the soul has good destiny [*accha sanskar*] then he will be reborn with a willingness to learn [*jiggyasa*] and will later take *moksha*. This is not the result of one birth but of many births. It is dependent on the accumulation of many good deeds [*acche karma*].

Shuklaji believes that from one birth to another, a person's situation can become higher. Good deeds result in higher births, bad deeds in lower births. So one tries to do good deeds, such as "hard work, exercising a thousand times, taking God's name a thousand and four hundred times." Knowledge of *moksha* is one of the paths to *moksha* but it depends on the accumulation of the results of deeds done since birth and in previous lives. And if one is blessed to be brought up in a good situation, then one will get the results of the good deeds of parents and teachers. Reading religious books and having *darshan* (sight) of God lead directly to knowledge. But as important is keeping the company of good people who will increase your curiosity and knowledge. Good thoughts are obtained when in contact with good people. Eventually when a soul has accumulated enough good *karma* it will be in a position to acquire enough knowledge to remain free of desire at the time of death and then it will get *moksha*. The chain of logic, in sum, is something like this: good deeds leads to higher birth and good company, which leads to more good deeds, which leads to knowledge, which leads to freedom from desire, which leads to ability to concentrate on God during death, which leads to *moksha*.

How the Muktibhavan Helps

> If the dying person hears and takes the name of God, he will be able to see the form of God and he will attain full belief. And with his good destiny, he will come to a full understanding. But the attraction for this world is very strong. Even the people with very good *karma* feel attraction toward the world at the last moment. Thus it is good if the workers and the family members chant the name of God and show him God's picture.

Shuklaji is not expecting everybody to get *moksha* in this particular death from dying in Kashi. Some do, some do not. It is impossible to tell: "Whether a dying person had any desires or not at the time of death is very difficult to ascertain, as is the fate of his soul after death. The priest-workers only know that they have done good work for him and helped him toward *moksha* by improving his destiny."

Shuklaji's conception of *karma* is one in which good deeds are transferable. In the story, Gokarna's brother managed to destroy Gokarna's sins, and, as Shuklaji said, keeping good company leads to good thoughts and a good destiny. Hence, the Muktibhavan can still have an effect for an unconscious person; "A good destiny is made in the company of good people and a bad destiny is made in the company of bad people." So the dying person's destiny will be helped a lot by the good work being done in his or her presence and the good company being kept at the Muktibhavan. Alternatively, if the wrong types of activities occur *in the presence* of the dying person, or the wrong people are there, desire can remain. Thus at the Muktibhavan, people cannot be dying bad deaths, they cannot be behaving badly, and they cannot be the "wrong type" of people.

Muktibhavan Morality

In what follows I will give several examples of the manner in which Shuklaji's moral and spiritual understandings have an impact upon the running of the Muktibhavan and, ultimately, upon who can die in the Muktibhavan and what types of death they can die.

The priest-workers are under some strict behavioral controls. Shuklaji told me that he almost had to get rid of one of the younger *karmacharya* a few months earlier: one of the man's relatives had come to visit and, together, they had gone to see a movie. The priest-workers are forbidden to see movies because "it has a bad effect on their character." Nobody knows what kind of movies they will see. It is also not how they should be spending their limited amount of money. Shuklaji explained that the priest-worker would become more and more interested in seeing movies, and, as he does not have enough money, he would have to resort to robbery and stealing. It seems that he was on the brink of a moral abyss; Shuklaji told me that before coming to the Muktibhavan he had been in the "type of society that eats onions and drinks tea from shops," though he has left all that now. Drinking tea in the shop is bad because the glasses are not clean and the ingredients are not pure. In other words it is not *satvik* (virtuous). The priest-workers must all be pure and can be defiled by the wrong types of behavior. Ultimately this will affect their ability to help the dying people toward their spiritual goals.

The families of the dying are also under some strict behavioral controls. Shuklaji said that, many times, he has had to remove some families for bad behavior. For instance, he kicked some people out because they were smoking *ganja.* Generally, however, the wrong type of people are not allowed entry in the first place. Often, the people who are (supposed to be) refused entry are not those that would necessarily *behave* badly but those who appear to be morally problematic in some other sense. For instance, as a rule, they do not allow people to come to the Muktibhavan to die who do not have a family. "If his family members are not interested to do his service, then what is the use of keeping that type of person here?" Just as the care of a dying person is an act of benevolence which will ultimately benefit the recipient (see Figure 7.4), in Shuklaji's view, having nobody willing to care for you in old age is a result of bad *karma* either during this life or a previous life.

FIGURE 7.4

Small card often given out to people staying at the Muktibhavan (translated from Hindi)

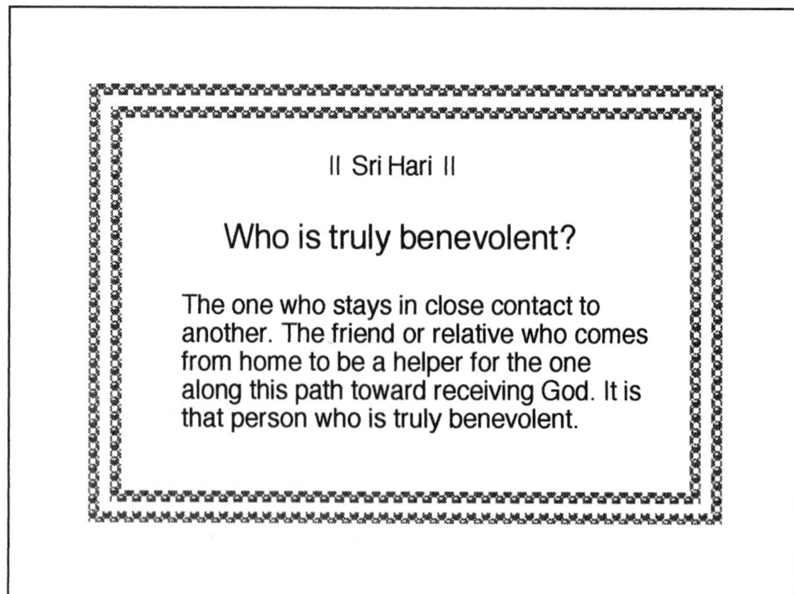
II Sri Hari II

Who is truly benevolent?

The one who stays in close contact to another. The friend or relative who comes from home to be a helper for the one along this path toward receiving God. It is that person who is truly benevolent.

Caste

Another indicator of bad *karma* in a previous life is being born an "untouchable." The written rule of the Muktibhavan, which states that one must be a member of the Hindu *varnashrama,* is ambiguous as to whether or not people belonging to untouchable *(acchut)* castes are allowed to stay at the Muktibhavan. Dalmia said that the untouchable castes are perfectly welcome. Shuklaji, on the other hand, interprets the rules as excluding them. He says that *acchut* (untouchable) people —which he also calls *niche jati wale* (low-caste people) and Harijans— are not allowed. Several times a year, he has to deal with such people who have come looking for a place to stay. He told me of one incident which, to him, was quite amusing because he had been fooled:

> One time a man came who hid his caste. He was a manager of some hotel and his name was Lalu Singh. His name made me think he was a Kshatriya, and also he kept himself and spoke like a Kshatriya. He was staying in the Ramakrishna Mission hospital, and in the very last stages of his life, they sent him here. At the time it was full so we could not take him. But after a couple of days a place was open and I called him and they brought him here. Now there were some village people with him and they were living here but conducting themselves very badly. One of the *karmacharyas* who was here at the time asked them which caste they belonged to. They said they were Harijan [Shuklaji laughs]. The *karmacharya* asked them who gave them permission to stay! They told the *karmacharya* that it was *me* who had given them admission! [laughing]. After hearing about this I went to them and said: "Why didn't you tell me which caste you were from? There is a different place for you people. We can arrange it for you." Then I sent them down to the place at Manikarnika ghat [Ganga-labh Bhavan].

The reasons given for excluding Untouchables is the same as for excluding Muslims and Christians; they have different beliefs, and they have different habits. "If they come here and start behaving as they do in their households then the other people will object": they would be disturbing to the orthodox Hindus trying to die in a spiritual environment.

The difference between castes, according to Shuklaji, is the stage of purity or holiness *(pavitrata):* "Each varna is made for a purpose and each maintains a certain degree of ritual purity. A new temple

[Vishvanath] had to be built after the Harijans entered it and defiled it. Their living standard is different and nobody knows how pure they will keep themselves. If they come and they do not keep themselves clean then the atmosphere will be bad." I speculate that the restriction of *acchut* castes from coming to the Muktibhavan is also a restriction against morally bad deaths. People are thought to be born into untouchable castes because of their bad *karma* and so their caste is a flag signaling some kind of past morally reprehensible behavior. According to Shuklaji's thinking such a person would necessarily die a bad death.

The *desire* to exclude untouchables also manifests as inconsistencies in the records. I heard from the priest-workers that members of untouchable castes do die there occasionally, but there are no records of untouchable castes in the Muktibhavan's records.[5] Either the pilgrims have hidden their caste to gain access to the Muktibhavan or the Muktibhavan is simply refusing to officially acknowledge that they have been there.

Morality and the Muktibhavan Records

Originally, I had thought that the records of the *muktibhavans* would simply provide a quantitative backdrop to my largely qualitative research. However, they have proved to be even more valuable. While still in the field, I began to suspect that some aspects of the records were not as factual as they could be. I spent some time observing the procedure by which they were recorded and compared my conversations with people to the records describing them. What I found were several systematic problems with a couple of the categories of information which seemed to make these records quantitatively useless. However, I began to recognize that these so-called quantitative problems were actually telling a qualitatively interesting and useful story. The story that they tell is of morality and of what is a morally good death. They tell of the pilgrims' desire to die—and the institution's insistence that they die—a morally good death.

Age

Figure 7.5 shows the distribution of reported ages of the people who died in the Muktibhavan during a one-year period in 1990–91. The first thing to notice is that the reported ages tend to end in either zeros or fives. In fact, over 80 percent of reported ages end in a zero or a five. This type of pattern suggests that people do not know their ages and so are estimating them. This is not surprising as the older people who live in small villages probably do not have documents recording when they were born and probably have no need to know exactly how

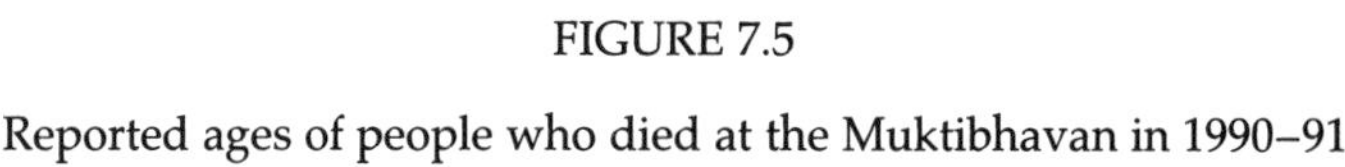

FIGURE 7.5

Reported ages of people who died at the Muktibhavan in 1990–91

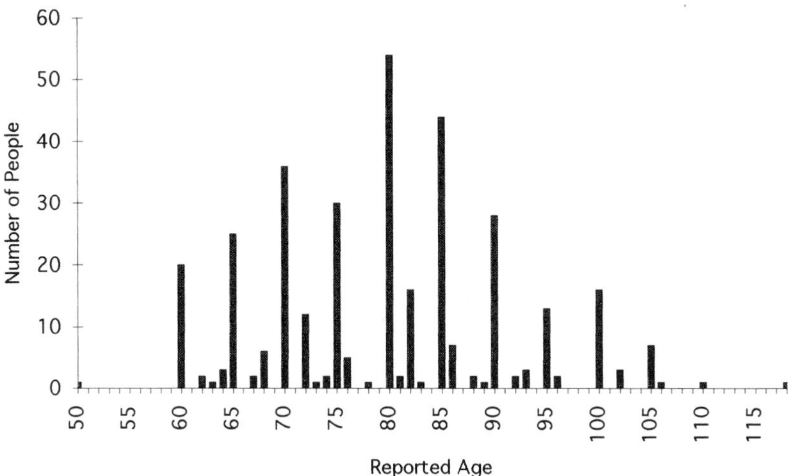

old they are. Checking into the Muktibhavan, the dying person, more often than not, can no longer speak and it is even less likely that a son or daughter would know the person's exact age.

A distribution of reported ages such as this indicates that there is ample opportunity for people to under- or overestimate their ages. My feeling is that the reported ages are not only estimates but that they are also systematically overestimated. Shuklaji, who agreed that many people did not know their exact ages, did not agree at all with this suggestion. However, I believe that the data and what they show of the magnitudes of the ages supports my theory. For instance, there is only one person whose reported age at death is less than sixty years. The oldest person to die there was reported to be one hundred and eighteen years. Eighteen people died at one hundred years and almost ten percent were one hundred years or more. Finally, the largest peak at eighty years also represents both the average and median ages of death. These are all higher than would be expected, even considering that this population is special and not representative of the population at large. According to Fries and Crapo (1981), the human life expectancy for North America, a figure estimating the expected age at death taking into account mortality rates from disease, is only 73, and the age of death of the longest-lived person for whom there is documentary proof is only 115.

Exaggeration of ages appears to be done by both the families and the institution. On several occasions, I saw people shrug their shoulders when asked the dying person's age, at which time the recorder would base a guess on the dying person's appearance. One man who was reported to be 105 had a son who was 36 and a grandson who was 8. These are not impossible figures but are highly unlikely, especially given how often this pattern occurs.

Though Fries and Crapo (1981) made the observation that age exaggeration is as prevalent amongst the very old as is age reduction amongst the middle-aged, I think in this case the reasons behind the exaggeration of age are quite specific. This is seen in the explanation as to why there is virtually nobody below the age of sixty dying at the Muktibhavan. It turns out that there is an unwritten rule that entry into the Muktibhavan for the purpose of dying is restricted to those who are sixty years of age or older. The reason that Shuklaji gave for this rule is that people *should not* die before they are sixty years old. Such a death is considered to be *akal mrityu* (untimely death). If you die an untimely death it is because of bad *karma*—of past sins. It is a morally bad death because it is caused by morally bad behavior. Shuklaji does not want such people to die there. Further, it appears that the longer one survives past sixty, from both the institution's and the family's perspective, the more it is a good reflection on the dying person's morality.

Sickness

Now I will turn to a related category in the records which is labeled "sickness" and implies "cause of death." According to the Muktibhavan records, almost 100 percent of the pilgrims who go there to die, die of the "sickness" known as "old age" *(burhapa)*. Less than one percent died of other sicknesses such as "paralysis" and "burst liver." A high number of deaths from old age, that is death from an unknown proximate cause, might be expected considering that the population is old and is not dying in a medical environment where a cause of death could be determined. But also there seems to be a clear policy, as far as the records go, that everyone dies of "old age." However, it is clearly not true, even given the broad possibilities for interpreting what "old age" might mean. For instance, a fifty-five-year-old woman came in one day straight from a nearby hospital, her IV tube still in place. She had been under treatment for several weeks but it had not helped. As she appeared to be close to death, her sons had decided to move her to the Muktibhavan. She died after a couple of pain-filled hours and her death was recorded as one of "old age."

One of the Muktibhavan's written rules states that people with infectious diseases such as tuberculosis, smallpox, plague, and cholera are not permitted to die at the Muktibhavan. The reason for this is, ostensibly, that it will put others—the priest-worker staff and the families of other dying people—at risk. However, it seems to go beyond this as well. I asked Shuklaji if there had ever been a problem with infectious disease and if a priest-worker had ever become sick? His response was, "There is no effect, only the effect of the God."

People with cancer are also not permitted to die at the Muktibhavan. In fact, I met several people who were there and were not hiding the fact that they had cancer. But as far as Shuklaji is *officially* concerned, people with cancer are not allowed. He said that, often, when cancer patients come, they are not admitted and he suggests that they try the Ganga-labh Bhavan—a place which he sees as being lax in its standards. The reason that Shuklaji gave for refusing pilgrims who are dying of cancer is that cancer is an infectious disease, "because it is a disease which spreads from the touch and other people will get it." But also, according to Shuklaji, it is because they try to keep the atmosphere pure and a cancer patient, though he could get *moksha,* will disturb the *saphai* (purity) of the place. Cancer is an *acchut bimari* (untouchable sickness) which implies both that it is infectious and that, like the *acchut* castes, it is essentially impure and polluting.

Cancer is not, of course, generally considered to be an infectious disease, but it is according to Shuklaji's way of thinking. The way he understands cancer as infectious is in terms of *karma* and cancer's familial relationship to other infectious diseases through *karma.* According to him, you get such diseases on the basis of your past actions. The etiology of infectious disease—in fact the very meaning of infectious—in this view, is that it is the result of bad *karma.* And so cancer too *is* infectious. If you are dying of an infectious disease, it is because either in this life, or a previous life, you have done something to deserve it. Dying of an infectious disease, therefore, reflects rather badly on your moral status and from this perspective it does not look like a morally good death. But, as Shuklaji said, "There is no hatred for people with these diseases. It is for the other people who are staying here. They would be *disturbed* by these diseases."

Good Deaths and Bad Deaths

It was difficult for me to ask Shuklaji about what I saw as inconsistencies in the records, but I felt that the possible confrontation might be revealing. "Why are all deaths recorded as being of 'old age'?" I asked him one day. He said, "it is because young people do not come here." I challenged him with several cases I had observed, including the woman with cancer from the hospital who had died there and whose sons had told me she was fifty-five years old. Why was her age recorded in the record books as being sixty and why was her sickness recorded as "old age"? Shuklaji beamed; his student had finally figured something out. "What can you do?" he laughed. "Sometimes such cases come and either they know one of the *karmacharya* or they die before anything can be done. In such a case, the record is kept in the mind not on paper. If it were recorded in the record book like that it would countervene the rules."

These "rules" are unwritten and, normally, unspoken. The rule underlying all the rules is that you must die a good death *(acchi maut)* to die at the Muktibhavan. When I asked directly, Shuklaji agreed, "Yes, it could be said that people must die a good death. Otherwise they cannot come here. *Akal mrityu* (untimely death) is not a good death, though there are some rituals *(narayan bali)* the family can do afterwards"

Death by "old age" is always a timely death and a timely death is a good death. The question is, what is old age?

> People who come of their own desire and who are interested to die, come because they are feeling sick. Old age is both the sickness and the reason for the sickness. So the cause of death is old age.

According to Shuklaji, the *varna* system prescribes sixty years as being the onset of old age. His point is that a sixty-year-old man is regarded as old in Indian society. "If a sixty-year-old man fell down, and somebody asked you who fell, what would you say?" he asked me. "You would answer that an old man fell—an old man died." Mostly, old people die timely deaths but not always: being old does not guarantee a death of old age. A ninety-year-old man who was killed by being struck by a car would not be considered to have died of old age, according to Shuklaji. It would be an untimely death *(akal mrityu)* "because that man's time of death may be two years hence. It is a death by accident." Old age is what is left over when there has been no accident and no disease, with the proviso that you are over sixty.

Many people, including Shuklaji, hold the idea that there is some predetermined length of time that a person should live. If he or she lives to that age, then he or she will die a timely and good death. If not, it reflects badly on the person's life, or even one of his previous lives, in a moral sense. It is thought to be *karma* that has caused whatever situation that has resulted in the bad death. In contrast, old age and a natural death are good evidence that somebody has lived out his or her allotted time, and that the person's *karma* is not bad.

Conclusion

Dalmia maintained that there are no restrictions on who can come and die in the Muktibhavan provided the person *is* dying and is a Hindu who believes in rebirth and *moksha*. Shúklaji, however, is reticent to accept people of untouchable castes. He maintains that people must be over sixty years of age to be eligible to stay at the Muktibhavan and is concerned that people are dying timely, good deaths. Shuklaji's concern for whether or not people are dying morally good or bad deaths relates, in part, to his understanding of the importance of being in association with the right kind of people. In his words, "A good destiny is made in the company of good people and a bad destiny is made in the company of bad people." Morality can rub off, and not just in the sense of learning bad behavior. Similarly, he said that if you give assistance to a sinner, even a bit of food, you accumulate some of his or her bad *karma*. A person dying a morally bad death—a person dying in a way that suggests his or her bad *karma* is responsible for his or her situation—in this view, would have the potential to interfere with the quest of others for their spiritual goals. A person dying a morally bad death would interfere with the religious atmosphere which is conducive to full spiritual reward for others.

In the end, however, what are excluded are not morally bad deaths but what *appear* to be morally bad deaths too much to be ignored: when somebody comes to the Muktibhavan who looks to be a little less than sixty, he or she will be raised up to sixty, or made to appear not to have been there at all by exclusion from the record book. Unless it is obvious, people are not asked why they are dying. Shuklaji said there is no need; they are dying of old age.

From another perspective, the appearance of a death is important because you cannot otherwise know what the fate of a person is. Nobody really knows who is good and who is bad because they cannot know what happens to the soul after death. The only way that they can judge is on the basis of how the person *appears* to be dying. This is as much a popular belief as an "institutional" one: several family members told me that it was a good sign that there is no evidence of disease at the time of death. The *Garuda Purana* warns several times of the diseased death that awaits the sinner. The person who sins, it says, suffers while in the body and has a death by sickness:

> Having collected the good and bad work of previous births, if some inauspicious works remain in balance, the human body will become full of disease. Without getting the result, bad *karma* will not go away. Those who hope for a long life, for them the mental and physical pain will ride on their head like a black snake. (GP, 1:19–20)

8

Physiological Dying

> O Garuda, at the time of death *(pranyatra ka samay)* the dying person must keep a hunger strike *(anashan)* and eat nothing. If his mind has become detached, he can take *sannyas* in the time of death.
>
> —*Garuda Purana* Ch 9:34

My analysis of the Muktibhavan and Ganga-labh Bhavan records turned up some interesting trends in terms of the length of time between a dying person's arrival at one or the other *muktibhavan* and that person's death. I will begin this chapter by presenting several graphs derived from the records and discussing their implications. The data raise questions about how death is predicted and about the timing of the departure from the village and arrival in Kashi. They also suggest a common type of physiological process of dying which is directly tied into cultural understandings of the nature of spiritually and morally good deaths.

Some Trends in the Records

The Muktibhavan has recorded the date of entry and the date of death for all the people that have died there since it began operation. I was thus able to calculate for all records the number of days between people's arrival and their eventual deaths. Figure 8.1 shows the survival time for the 319 people who came to the Muktibhavan between July 1990 and June 1991 who died and for whom the records were complete. The first column on the graph represents the people who died on the same day (or first day) that they arrived at the Muktibhavan and column two represents those people who died the day after arriving, and so on.

The graph shows that, generally, people die quite quickly after arriving at the Muktibhavan. After one week, 84 percent of the people had died and virtually everybody had died by the seventeenth day,

FIGURE 8.1

Deaths by number of days from arrival to the Muktibhavan in 1990.

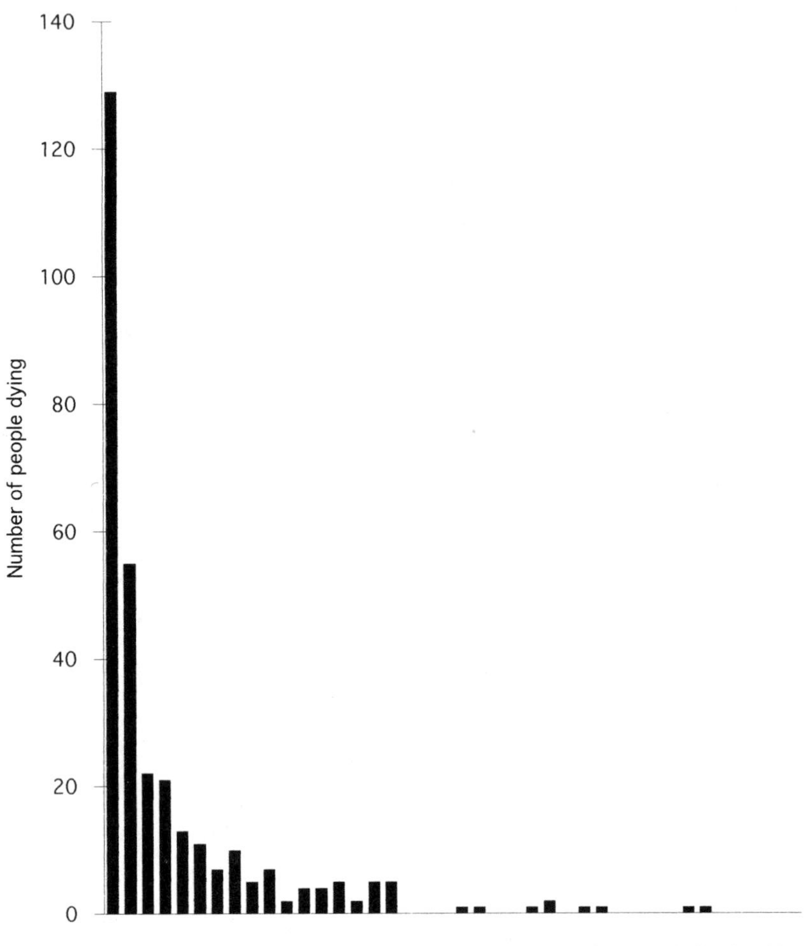

after which the graph shows a distinctive drop indicating that very few people stay more than this length of time. This corresponds reasonably well with the Muktibhavan's written rule, a rule that is generally unenforced, which states that fifteen days is the maximum allowable stay. The break does not correspond to an increase in people leaving the Muktibhavan and "returning home" as would be the case if people were being asked to leave after this fifteen day time limit is up. The roughly 10 percent of people who return home alive generally do so well before this limit.

The short stays are no surprise to the Muktibhavan staff. They give out rooms, according to Pandey "only to people who look as though they will live three to four days." The families also expect that people will die very quickly having reached the Muktibhavan and often the family will come thinking they will be away from their home for just a short period. As Pandey said: "A lot of people come thinking that their sick person *(rogi)* will die very quickly and so bring only a limited amount of money. Sometimes they have to go home because they have no money on which to live."

Perhaps the most striking feature of the graph in Figure 8.1 is the first column which shows that 129 people, or 40 percent of all people who died at the Muktibhavan, died on the very same day that they arrived there. Though not shown graphically, this phenomenon is even more striking when calculated in hours:[1] it turns out that 158, or almost 50 percent of all people, died within twenty-four hours of arrival at the Muktibhavan.

Figures 8.2 and 8.3 show survival times in hours for the first seventy-two hours and the first six hours respectively. Figure 8.2 shows the number of people dying within six hour time increments over the first three days. As can be seen, most of the people dying on the day that they arrived, in fact died within six hours of arriving at

FIGURE 8.2

Deaths which occurred within seventy-two hours of arrival to the Muktibhavan in 1990, by six-hour increments

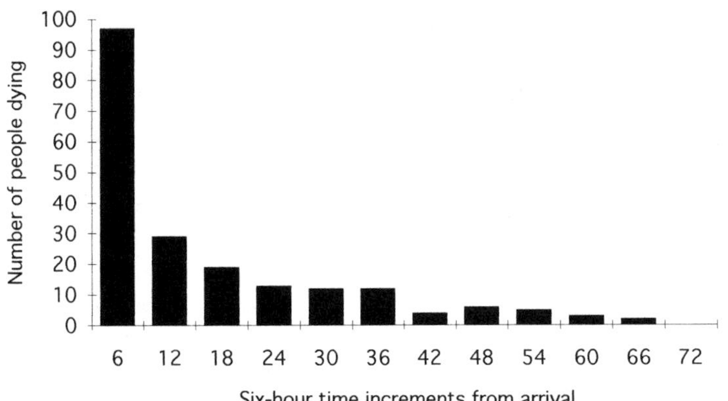

FIGURE 8.3

Deaths which occurred within six hours of arrival to the Muktibhavan in 1990, by one-hour increments

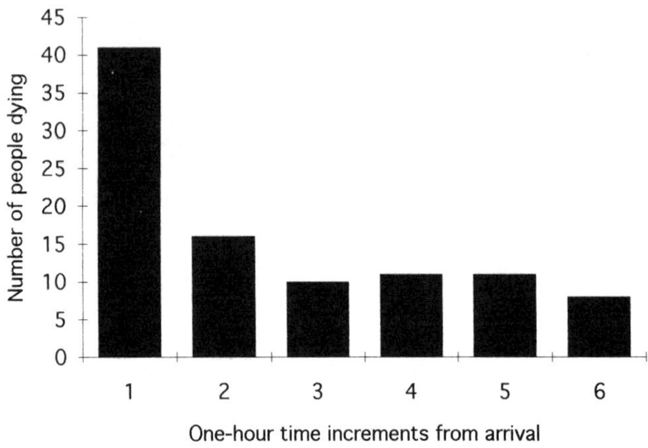

the Muktibhavan. Ninety-seven people, or 30 percent of all arrivals, survived for six hours or less. Figure 8.3 shows the first six hours divided into one hour increments. Forty-one people, or 13 percent of all people who died at the Muktibhavan, are recorded as having died within one hour of their arrival there.

The large proportion of people dying very quickly at the Muktibhavan is not reflected at the Ganga-labh Bhavan where only about 15 percent of people who died in 1990 died on the day that they arrived. Also, looking backwards through time, the high number of Muktibhavan "first-day deaths" seems to be a new phenomenon. Figure 8.4 shows the percentage of people who died on the day of their arrival at the two *muktibhavans* over a period of decades. It appears that in the past at both the Ganga-labh Bhavan and the Muktibhavan, and presently just at the Ganga-labh Bhavan, the proportion of people dying on the day of their arrival is generally between 12 and 16 percent. Sometime between 1980 and 1990, and only at the Muktibhavan, this proportion, and the absolute number of people, dying on the day of their arrival rose dramatically.

Figure 8.5 shows the median number of days stayed before death at both *muktibhavans* for the same years. This chart indicates that over the last thirty years at the Muktibhavan, there has been a gradual decrease in the length of time people stay before dying. Comparing this chart to that of Figure 8.4, it can be seen that the trend toward a

FIGURE 8.4

Proportion of people dying on the day of their arrival in different years

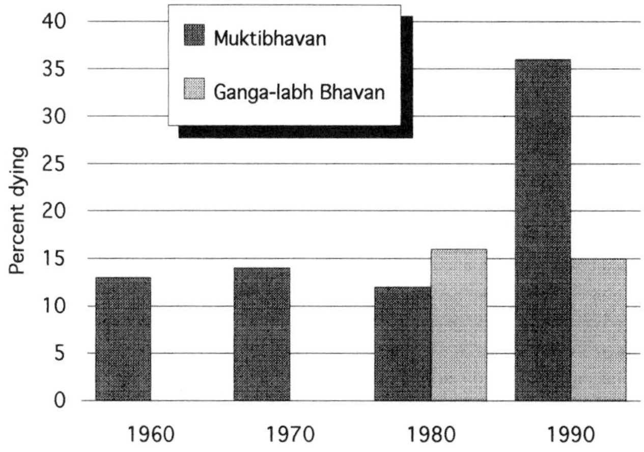

shorter median stay at the Muktibhavan can only be accounted for by an increase in people dying on the first day in the case of 1990. In the other years the decrease in median number of days stayed was unaccompanied by an increase in first day deaths.

FIGURE 8.5

Median number of days stayed before dying in selected years

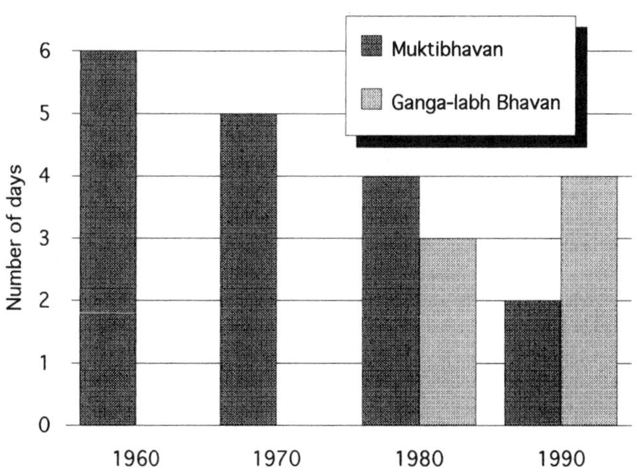

Towards an Explanation

I have found myself drawn to try to explain three aspects of what the records seem to reveal about the timing of arrival and how long people live after ensconcement in the Muktibhavan. The recent increase at the Muktibhavan of people dying on the day that they arrive may involve changes in transportation or hospital policy. On the other hand, the fact that almost thirteen percent of arrivals die within one hour may have quite a different explanation, one that may involve either "holding on" on the part of the dying person or "interpretation" on the part of the relatives. Finally, it seems remarkable to me that the vast majority die within one week, and virtually everybody dies within two weeks, and I believe this implies both prediction and causation. I will deal with these possibilities in order.

I cannot fully explain the first two trends. In general, the people whom I had the opportunity to meet, get to know and interview were those who stayed at the Muktibhavan for several days at least. My "ethnographic sample" is biased toward people who stayed a long time and away from those who died very quickly. Although many times I was aware of people arriving and dying very quickly, until I analyzed the records I had no idea that they represented such a significant proportion of the people who died at the Muktibhavan.

The survey questionnaire does adequately represent the people who died very quickly upon arrival. The guardians for fourteen people who died within one hour—an oversampling of about 50 percent of what would be expected in a random sample—and thirty people who died on the same day that they arrived, filled out the questionnaire. However, the questionnaire indicates that there are few immediately obvious differences between, for instance, those who died in one hour and those who survived longer than one day. The proportion of people who knew about the Muktibhavan before coming, or had actually been there before, is the same for both groups. Average reported age also does not differ between those people who died very quickly and those who died more slowly. The most noticeable difference is that people who died within an hour have more accompanying relatives (average 6.6) than do people who survive longer than a day (average 4.4), but due to the large variance even this difference is far from significant.

The cases of the very few people who I met and talked to—families who had brought somebody to die at the Muktibhavan who had died just hours after arriving—proved more helpful in understanding the trends in the records. I will describe two such cases. They

FIGURE 8.6

Rogi marnewala with his daughter and grandson at Kashi Labh Muktibhavan

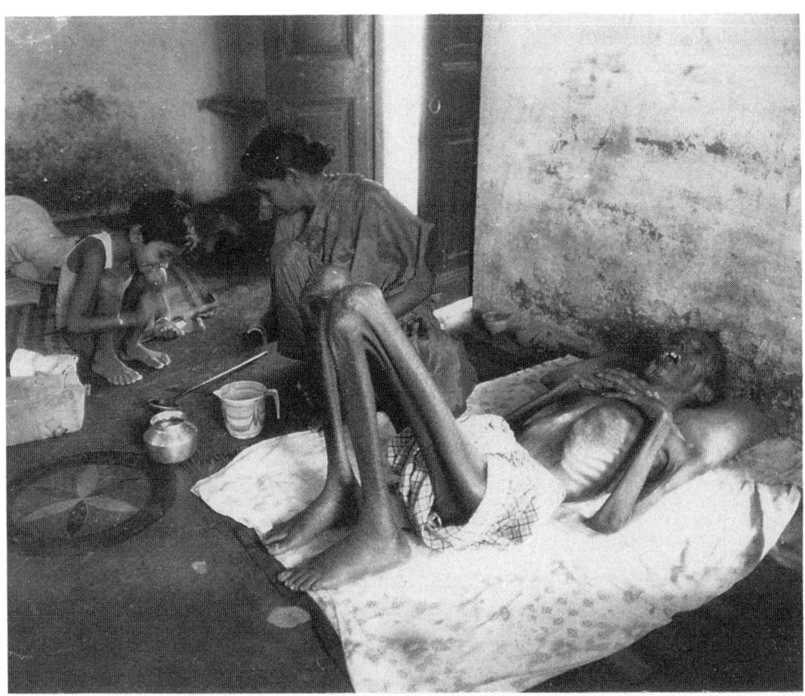

suggest that at least some of the people who died very quickly had been brought directly from a hospital after the late stages of the dying process had begun.

The Increase of Hospital Referrals

Lalita Devi

One afternoon in September, an auto-rickshaw was let in through the gate and pulled up in front of the Muktibhavan. In it were three men, and lying across their knees (the only way to move a horizontal body in a rickshaw), was a very old and decrepit woman. It was obvious she had just come from a hospital; there was an IV catheter still in place in one of the veins of her hand and an empty IV bag was lying across her chest. The men carefully negotiated themselves out from under her and into positions where they could lift her out of the rickshaw. She was in a great deal of pain. She was moaning loudly with every movement and tossing her head from side to side.

The staff of the Muktibhavan, many of whom were sitting around the courtyard, did nothing to demonstrate any concern or even awareness of this new arrival. Pandey was the only one to react. He quickened his generally slow gait ever so slightly and he led the three men, who were carrying the old woman, around to the rear entrance. Pandey found them an empty room and the three men took her in and laid her on the floor.

The three men were her grandsons. The youngest was a student at Banaras Hindu University. Talking just outside the door, he told me that the old lady's name was Lalita Devi and that she came from a village named Chudradeo Raj in the district of Rohtas in the state of Bihar. Her husband was still alive but at ninety-eight was "too old to be with his wife" and so had remained in the village. Lalita Devi had been at the Banaras Hindu University hospital for a month, where her grandsons who resided in Kashi had been attending to her. She had been under both Ayurvedic and "English" medical care for a "peptic ulcer" which was also "an early sign of stomach cancer."

"It is our belief," he said, "it is the opinion of the people, mine and all people's, that in such places as this, one can get *moksha*. Especially in Kashi. But the Banaras Hindu University hospital is outside of the boundaries of Kashi. *Moksha* is not available there." The surgeon at Banaras Hindu University hospital had told the three brothers that there was no chance of her being cured and that they should take her back to the village to die. However, the decision was made to bring her into Kashi instead. Had this been her own decision? "No, it was my decision, the decision of my brothers and also my culture's decision." His grandmother had always wanted to die in Kashi, he said, and that now that she was there she was extremely happy. While hearing her painful moans and seeing her frightened eyes, he told me this, calmly and smiling.

In the room Lalita Devi was being attended to by her two eldest grandsons. She was lying on a thin blanket on the cement floor. She had a dirty pillow under her head and a hole-filled, grey blanket over her lower body. The only source of light was a window behind her head and a diffuse beam of sunlight reflecting off the neighboring brick buildings highlighted the wrinkles of her face and the grey of her hair. A monkey sat at the bars on the window looking in disinterestedly. The grandsons were sitting on either side of her, one holding her hand and the other gently stroking her belly. She was in pain. She was moaning and trying, within a limited scope of movement, to find a more comfortable position. Her eyes were open wide and darting around the room though most of her attention was focused on her two grandsons.

One of the brothers motioned me to come in. Sitting with them on the floor, they turned their attention completely upon me and talked away, smiling and laughing, about how good it was that I was so interested in their culture. I learned from them that they had not really known about the Muktibhavan when they left the hospital. They tried another place, the Mumukshu Bhavan near Asi ghat, and the manager there directed them to the Muktibhavan. The eldest of the two grandsons lived in the village with his family. It was he who had brought Lalita Devi from the village to the hospital and it was primarily his responsibility to deal with whatever happened. He said: "Either she will die within a week or she will be in a position to survive and I will return to the village with her. In the case that she dies, I will cremate her here."

Periodically Lalita Devi would reach out her hand and hold on to one of her grandson's legs. She was trying to say something but the grandsons insisted that she was saying nothing. She was only expressing her pain, they said. In spite of her open eyes, the two grandsons agreed that she was "unconscious." The eldest said that Kashi was important only to his grandmother; to the rest of them there was no difference between whether she died at home or in Kashi. What was important was that she believed she was in Kashi. He would take her home after a week, he said, and she would not know the difference.

Alternating Hindi and English, across their grandmother's prostrate form, the two brothers explained the details of her sickness. The only solution to her problem it seemed would have been to operate. But she was "anemic" and of a "rare blood type" and therefore the chances of survival would have been very low. The decision was made not to try. The eldest brother would stay with her for a week or so in Kashi and, if she survived, would take her back to the village. This was the second time that they had told me this and both times it struck me as strange. Clearly she was not going to survive. She had been taken off the IV that had been sustaining her body for the last month and was now going to receive nothing but *tulsi* leaves and Ganga water. She was already starting to gurgle as she drew in breath. They must have known it was a matter of minutes.

The conversation stopped and attention was focused back on Lalita Devi by her going into a fit of choking. I helped them roll her on to her side so she would not aspirate, but this obviously hurt her a great deal. After this they gave her some Ganga water and a dark brown, opaque substance, kept in a glass jar. Then they gave her a little of some medicine from the hospital which they said was for peptic ulcer. What was important now, however, was only the Ganga water: "During the last time of life, Ganga water and the leaves of the *tulsi* plant must be provided in the mouth," one of the grandsons told me. She would be given no more food, as "her time for eating is over."

Moments later, Lalita Devi went into another crisis; her eyes wide open, she started moaning more loudly and frantically. One grandson started shouting to her, " *'Sita Ram' kahe!"* meaning that she should say *"Sita Ram."* He yelled at her, *"Ram! Ram! Ram! Sita! Ram! Sita! Ram! . . . Aum nama Shivai!, Sita! Ram! Sita! Ram!"* As he was yelling these things into her ear, the other grandson was calmly explaining to me that she must hear and recite these names as she dies.

After some time several other relatives arrived. They turned out to be another grandson and an aunt and her servant. I left them sitting around Lalita Devi, massaging her legs and gently stroking her inflamed abdomen. The grandsons insisted that I come back tomorrow. When I arrived the next morning the room was occupied by some new people, who stared back at me through their open door. Lalita Devi had died early the previous evening, just a couple of hours after arriving at the Muktibhavan. By then she had been burned and her ashes were floating many miles down the Ganga.

A Man at the Gate

One day during the very hot part of the year, I arrived at the Muktibhavan to find a dead man lying on the cement near the gate. The dead man was covered with an old sheet, and was unattended. His relatives, the man's brother, and his son and another man whose relationship I do not know, were off buying the necessary funerary items.

Upon returning the family began preparing the body. The dead man had a urinary catheter in place which his brother could not pull out, though he tried his best. They washed the body using well water with a little *charnamrit.* Then they tied a kind of special cloth around his lower region. His old sacred thread was removed and a new, bright yellow one, was put in its place. The body was wrapped in a large piece of thin white cotton and tied on to a bamboo frame with heavy cord. A colorful *pitambari* and strings of flowers were draped over the body and incense was burned all around it. As soon as preparations were complete the relatives recruited a priest-worker to help them and loaded the bier on to their shoulders. Chanting *"Rama nam satya hai,"* they set off toward the burning ghat. No more than one hour had passed from their arrival at the Muktibhavan to their departure.

The family told me that the dead man had been ninety years old, but I thought he was much younger as his beard and hair were only partially grey and his skin was not very wrinkled. They said that the dead man had died at the very instant that they came through the gate of the Muktibhavan. Previously, I had been told stories by several of the priest-workers of this happening occasionally, but I had never before been around at such a time. The priest-workers seem to take the relative's reports of "deaths at the gate" at face value and tell the stories as though they demonstrate the wonderful properties of the Muktibhavan. I thought at the time that probably he was dead on arrival.

Both Lalita Devi and the man described above had been brought straight from the hospital. Both of them seem to have been brought in something of a rush, judging from the fact that they both still had tubes attached to their bodies. It is likely that the family made a decision to leave the hospital in the very late stages of the dying process, and rushed the dying person into Kashi. It is likely, too, that they had medical assistance in determining imminence of death and possibly, though neither of the above cases indicate this, advice on where in Kashi to take the dying person.

The questions that I cannot fully answer are: what proportion of the people that die at the Muktibhavan come directly from a hospital? And to what extent can these "hospital referrals" account for the large proportion of people that die on the day of their arrival at the Muktibhavan? Shuklaji and Pandey both estimated that about 40 percent of the dying people—"those that are rich"—have first tried to recover in a hospital, though not all of these would be rushed from a hospital at the last minute. It is possible that the increase in the number of people that die on the day of arrival at the Muktibhavan, as seen in Figure 8.4, is due, in part, to an increase in "hospital referrals," such as Lalita Devi, who have been brought from the hospital only when death is imminent. Though I have no other evidence suggesting that more people than before are being rushed from the hospital as they are dying, it is a simple way of explaining the recent increase of very quick deaths at the Muktibhavan. Leaving the hospital and whatever life support they had been on might be expected to speed up the dying process.

On the other hand, not one of the guardians of the thirty people who died on the day of their arrival, and who filled out the questionnaire, indicated that they had come on the advice of a doctor. The more gradual decrease in the number of days before dying which people stay at the Muktibhavan, as seen in Figure 8.5, may better be explained by the increased ease of transportation for some people. Especially, the growing number of privately owned vehicles may increase people's ability to set off from their village at a very late stage in the dying process of the person they are bringing.

Interpreting Death and Holding On to Life

Pandey, who registers most of the people arriving at the Muktibhavan, estimated that 60 percent of all people have come straight from the village without having first gone to a hospital. I accept this figure as roughly accurate, primarily because Pandey has a real sense of what is going on at the Muktibhavan and his estimates, such as of the number of people who return home alive, have proved to be accurate on other occasions. It is, however, impossible for me to estimate what proportion of the people who died within one or two hours of arrival came straight from the village, though I am confident not all these quick deaths are accounted for by people rushing from hospitals. Both Shuklaji and Pandey told me stories of people coming from the villages who died before getting to Kashi. To the extent that people coming directly from the villages are leaving such a narrow margin of time, it is likely too that many people arrive just in time.

It is likely too that some of the first-hour deaths are, in fact, people who have died before arriving at the Muktibhavan. If dying is regarded as a process, there is an event, usually the cessation of breathing, which people generally recognize as the end of life. It is possible that the endpoint may be understood as occurring at a different time than the cessation of breathing such that people might be talking about death occurring, say, with the completion of a goal related to dying. Alternatively, families may be simply pretending. Once they arrived with the story that the person had died just on coming through the gate, however, it is likely that they would be registered at the Muktibhavan as the priest-workers would not question their story. To the extent that this is happening, it speaks of the importance to the family that the dying person not only die in Kashi, but *officially* die in Kashi by being recorded as having died at the Muktibhavan.

It is not possible to account for those people who, for instance, died between two and six hours of arriving at the Muktibhavan in the same manner. In 1990 there were fifty-six people, or almost 20 percent of all people dying at the Muktibhavan, who survived more than one hour but less than six hours. The families of the dying people who are recorded as having died within the first few hours, or in some cases the dying people themselves, may have very accurately predicted their deaths and set off for Kashi at just the right time. Alternatively, the rigors of the journey may in some way contribute to the dying person's quick deterioration. A third possibility is that the dying person, his or herself, may have managed to hold off their deaths until reaching the Muktibhavan or Kashi. In most cases, dying in Kashi is of enough importance to the dying person that they are willing to give up kith and kin and their familiar surroundings to go there to die. As I have shown, not reaching Kashi before dying has both spiritual and moral implications to the extent that rebirth will be taken in nonhuman form and it will be obvious to all that the reason Kashi was not reached was an accumulation of bad *karma*. To whatever extent is possible, then, I speculate that people would generally have the *will* to survive the journey and die only once Kashi has been reached,[2] though this must be considered a matter for further investigation.

The Predictable Death

Up to this point I have concentrated on possible explanations for the very quick deaths, for which I have scant information, having identified the phenomenon from the records only after the fact. Now I will back up one step and look at the larger picture and another process which suggests a relationship between culture and the physiological dying process. As can be seen graphically in Figure 8.1, the vast majority of people manage to time their arrival at the Muktibhavan to within just days of their deaths. As it was the people who lived for at least several days at the Muktibhavan before dying whose families I got to know, I have a much clearer idea of the processes underlying this phenomenon.

Ram Lal Singh

I met a man one day when I went down to the Muktibhavan. He was sitting outside on a bench in the sun reading a newspaper. He had come to the Muktibhavan with his father-in-law, Ram Lal Singh, who was dying. They had been there for twelve days already. The son-in law was quite used to the place and had a regular routine of bathing in the Ganga early in the morning and then sitting in the Muktibhavan's courtyard, either reading or chatting. Inside, Singh was being attended to by his daughter and his wife.

The son-in-law told me that Singh was 105 years old. He looked pretty old but not particularly feeble compared to many of the other people there. The color of his face and hair had converged giving him a look of near lifelessness, but his arms, though quite thin and a little drawn, were not covered with loose wrinkled skin like many others. The son-in-law told me that he was not unconscious but he had stopped speaking. He could still hear and understand what was going on around him. He was in some pain from being in bed but "not the type of pain that medicine can have any effect on." He could not be moved to go to the bathroom and he had been incontinent for some time.

Singh was a Kurmi by caste. He lived in a village in Rohtas where he owned about six acres of land, which he had worked all his life. His daughter and son-in-law lived in a nearby village. Singh's wife was his second; his first wife had died more than fifty years ago, they said. His new wife was only about fifty years old and had two daughters and several grand-daughters. Singh had been educated up to a primary standard and could read and write.

The family had been the first to recognize that he was dying. They say that they saw his condition and realized. They never saw a doctor; the family came to the conclusion themselves and Singh, himself, agreed. They knew he was dying because Singh had stopped eating food. He gave it up six days before leaving for Kashi, eighteen days before I met him. The son-in-law explained that "his soul *(atman)* is no longer demanding the food." Slowly the *atman* has "given this answer, because he is very old." He did not *decide* to stop eating, according to the son-in-law, he just lost his desire for food.

The family made the decision to come to the Muktibhavan two days before they set off, when they saw that he was nearing the last stage. Singh, at this time, had been off food for four days. From the time he arrived at the Muktibhavan, he took only the *charnamrit* that the priest-workers bring around and the water from the Ganga that his son-in-law brought back after his morning bath. The son-in-law considers both these things to be very purifying. He also insisted that Singh had no sickness whatsoever. The family took this to be a very good sign because it meant that he was very purified.

Singh had never been a religious man or done any religious work, according to his son-in-law. He neither went to the temple nor prayed. But the family was not surprised that he wanted to go to Kashi because "he has seen many people go off to Kashi to die. He has heard many stories of people who have done so." Many of the old people from the village go to Kashi to die, I was told. But it is only a small percentage of deaths as most people die when they are young.

Singh's son-in-law thinks this is the reason that people come to Kashi: "They come because if in their lives they have done some bad work, in Kashi it can be corrected. Then the future life will become perfect." His father-in-law has not knowingly done such bad work, he said, but it is still good to come. A good future life means "his next birth will have to be good" but he cannot tell what the details of this improved next birth might be. "It is unfathomable," he said.

Before leaving the village many people came to see him off. They said, "Now you are going to Kashi and nobody knows if you will come back to be with us." They asked him to forgive any mistakes they had made and to give them his blessing. They all touched his feet. Singh had told his visitors to live a long life and to be healthy. He and his family then caught a bus to Kashi. They came to the Muktibhavan because "all the facilities are guaranteed and if people will die here their future is guaranteed." This is because Kashi is in the city of Vishvanath and because in the Muktibhavan the name of God is chanted twenty-four hours a day.

Originally, Singh had wanted to come to Kashi and had demanded that he be brought. His desire had been to die very quickly. His wife was in favour of bringing him. However, after four or five days, when he had not died, he decided that he wanted to go home. The son-in-law said that Singh believed that if he went home he would die more quickly and he wanted to die as soon as possible. His family shared in this desire that he would go quickly. "When somebody becomes useless, everybody agrees that it is better if God takes them quickly," his son-in-law explained. But they did not want to take him back to the village. "We have to listen to the words of such an old man," the son-in-law said, "so we will take him back . . . if he survives for a month. We will wait here for one month. We do not want to take him back. He is old and he changes his mind. We are interested in improving his future life."

The son-in-law, since coming to the Muktibhavan, had been spending a lot of time talking to one of the priest-workers. He thought this priest-worker was very knowledgeable and called him Panditji. Panditji had told him that his father-in-law would die within four or five days. "Panditji told me that he will leave his body soon. He is in the last stage *(antim samay),"* the son-in-law said. In fact, Singh lasted another thirteen days. He gradually became weaker and weaker and after being in the Muktibhavan for 25 days and off food for 31 days, he "left his body." The family burned the body in Kashi at Manikarnika ghat. Singh's brother's son's son "gave the flame" as Singh had no direct male descendants.

It is hard to know what was "family opinion" and what the priest-worker had taught the son-in-law over the time that he was there. It is likely that he had taught him quite a bit because the son-in-law had some pretty "accessible" ideas of what a good death is. The following is from our discussion about what are the characteristics of good death *(acchi maut):*

> The person whose soul leaves from the top of the body, that is a good sign. If the next birth is going to be a good one, then this will be a sign. This depends on good *karma.* This is a good death. If the soul leaves from the bottom part of the body, then that is a bad sign. The person should be remembering the name of Rama at the time of death. If he does the future will be much better. . . . There is no sleep around the time of death. . . . At the last moment the breathing system changes. . . . People automatically do not desire food and water as their death approaches, it is not a good thing to eat just before dying.

The case of Singh is representative of many other cases in several respects and I have included it here because his *decision* to not eat was made particularly clear and was significant to his son-in-law, who told me his story. And yet, in an important way, it is not typical; Singh stayed twenty-five days at the Muktibhavan before dying. More generally, families are able to accurately recognize signs that allow them to anticipate correctly when someone will die. They are able to do so because the type of death they are dying, one of steady deterioration after giving up sustenance, is known and predictable. In the case of Singh, the family brought him "early" in the dying process. Most families wait until later.

As I discussed in chapter 7, the people who are dying at the Muktibhavan are old and perceived to be disease free. From the perspective of the Muktibhavan staff, everybody is dying a "good" death, which in this case means they are dying of old age. But when I asked Pandey to describe the dying people, he began with the following words: "The people who come to this place are those whose final stage has come and who have stopped eating and drinking."

It is an accepted and unremarkable fact to the priest-workers that, for the most part, those people coming to die at the Muktibhavan are no longer eating or drinking and, generally, have given it up quite some time before coming. It is accepted because it is common; it is unremarkable because, as I will discuss in chapter 9, it is thought to have no effect.

To reiterate, the vast majority of guardians who answered my questionnaire indicated that the dying person they had brought was eating nothing and often the people I interviewed indicated that the dying person had not been taking food or drink for as long as several

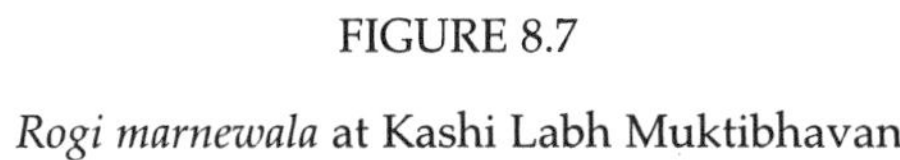

FIGURE 8.7

Rogi marnewala at Kashi Labh Muktibhavan

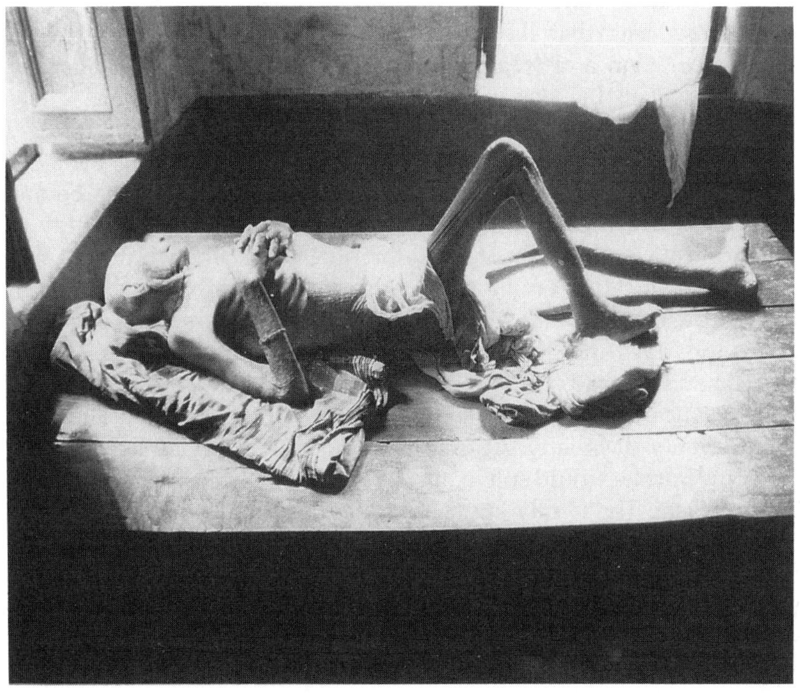

weeks or a month. In what follows, I will review some of the pertinent features of several of the deaths I have already described to show that, while they are all quite varied, there is also an underlying pattern.

Mishra, whose case I described in chapter 4, tried several times to be cured in hospital and by himself with Ayurvedic medicine. Then he decided that he would die and started to take Ayurvedic herbs which would help him to die as soon as possible. He immediately did a *gau dan*—the gift of a cow, done when death is approaching. Only when he became very weak did he declare that he wanted to die in Kashi. Mishra stayed at the Muktibhavan for fourteen days. He gradually stopped talking and became unconscious for a larger and larger percentage of his days. One night, he became quite lucid and the family helped him into sitting position. He drank a glass of milk, the first food that he had taken in weeks, then he died.

Dubey's mother (chapter 5) was fine until she announced to her son that she had decided to do the donation of a cow *(gau dan).* Within a couple of days she became "slightly paralyzed on one side" and started to eat less and less rice and stopped being able to speak very well. Dubey said that she quickly "became very old" and started to experience "pain and weakness." They set off for the hospital but it was decided on the way not to attempt a cure. She became totally uncommunicative just after reaching Kashi.

The Ojha family said they knew it was time to bring their old aunt to die because, though she has been sick many times before, she could always communicate. This time she also lost the ability to communicate. A doctor confirmed their belief that she would not survive. She was eating only a few grapes a day. When I talked to them they predicted their aunt would live three or four more days. She lived three more days and died after ten days at the Muktibhavan.

Anandi Prasad's grandmother (chapter 6) had been undergoing some medical treatment for six months, but she gave it up and died about twenty days later. At first they had tried to make her take the medicine but she would spit it out. She gifted a cow ten days before they left for Kashi. The family knew it was her last time *(antim samay)* "because she stopped eating and was taking only juice." She abandoned food the day before she did the *gau dan.* Her body became weaker and weaker. She did not eat anything up until the day before her death when she asked for some *kicheri,* which she ate with her own hands.

Uppadhya, whose story has not been presented, said of his uncle, "His stomach is full so he has stopped taking food. He is taking only water." They went to a hospital in Bukar and spent one thousand rupees but there was no result. The doctor said it was no use and discharged them. So then they came to Kashi and went to the hospital at Banaras Hindu University. He wanted to die in Kashi but they tried to see if they could find a cure at this hospital first. However, they could not help him either. He became very weak and could not speak "because he has not been taking any food." By the time he died he had not eaten in thirty-three days.

Kapil Deo Singh (chapter 6) told me that the family knew his mother was dying "because in old age when the senses stop working there is no use to eat. So she has decided like that." They had also talked to a doctor who had said "medicine is of no use. Now you must do service *(seva)* for her." At the Muktibhavan she was drinking water with some vitamins—no food and no medicine. She had not eaten in two weeks before coming to the Muktibhavan.

The theme which I have stressed in these narratives of peoples' deaths is a relationship between the dying process and the abandoning of food. In some cases, such as that of Mishra, the cessation of eating occurred after an attempt to find a cure and a recognition on the part of the dying person that a cure was not forthcoming. In other cases, food was given up after a self-recognition of being in the dying process, as signaled by the dying person's desire to do a *gau dan* ritual. In only one case, that of Uppadhya, was it thought that the cessation of eating was a natural sequela of a particular physiological problem, such as digestive failure.

The priest-workers recognize the cessation of eating as a signal to the families that a person has begun the dying process. Pandey says that people recognize that someone is dying by these criteria:

> They are in their last stage of life *(chautha pan),* meaning seventy to eighty, or even ninety years old so their last stage of life has come. They suddenly become weak and they are not eating. Those like this show all the symptoms of the dying.
>
> They cannot do any work with their hands and they do not speak. These are signs that, though they do not have any serious illness, their time for *moksha* is near.
>
> Slowly they get all the symptoms of the dying. All activity stops. Their extremities do not work and they cannot sit up, so they become entirely helpless. At this time, it is thought that they will die very soon.

Tikka Baba described the recognition of the onset of the dying process and various steps along the way in the following manner:

> He is not eating food and he is not drinking water. So they understand that he will die. In the Kali Yuga, food is the basis of life. The person who does not eat or drink for two or four days will become unconscious. He will not be in his senses. He has stopped eating and drinking. He does not even drink milk. What happiness does he have? His breath is being drawn and he will die quickly. So they think that they should bring him to Kashi. After two or four days he will die. . . .
>
> At the very end, the breathing becomes very fast. They see that he is now getting hiccups. When he gets hiccups, he will definitely die. He will die within one hour. Now his breath is fast. He will die soon. Now he has died. . . . These are the symptoms. Everybody understands this.

Tikka Baba said that if a young person stops eating, he will go to the hospital. But this will not happen when old age has been reached. Old age, he says, starts at forty years and is signaled by the whitening of the hair. "Look at my son Amernath," he said. "He has two more years, then his hair will become white. Already his beard has started to become white. After that it will all become white. In *Kali Yuga* life can end at fifty years though some people will live to one hundred and twenty-five."

The Value of a Predictable Death

Khare (1967) collected and analyzed a series of narratives from Brahmins in western Bihar in which the dominant theme was the prediction of death. He stated that "Hindus attach considerable importance to the prediction of death, as the last moments of one's life are thought to determine the nature (human or nonhuman) of one's next incarnation" (1). He said that the Brahmins rely on "a language of prediction," a set of symbols which indicate the impending death of a friend or relative.

I know of no such symbolic predictors being used in determining the upcoming deaths of the people dying at the Muktibhavan, and yet prediction is an important element in the process. The dying people themselves are very often predicting their own deaths, and acting upon the prediction by gifting a cow. The family of the dying person is doing a different type of prediction whereby they are watching the dying person's deterioration and trying to accurately gauge when they should set off for Kashi. The families seem to be using physiological signs for their prediction of the stage on the dying process, a system of prediction which is developed in Ayurvedic medicine.[3]

One of the prime goals of Ayurveda is the enjoyment of a long life and the reaching of old age. Great emphasis is put on the ascertainment of life expectancy. In fact, according to some texts, the first thing a physician should do is ascertain how long the patient can expect to live (Kutumbiah 1962, 101). The life expectancy of a patient can be determined from the reading of a long list of prognostications of death which are known as *aristhas.*

Often among the people coming to the Muktibhavan to die, the cessation of eating begins a predictable process of deterioration whereby the old dying person becomes weaker and weaker, until at some point they become uncommunicative. In several cases, this was the signal for the family that it was time to take the dying person to Kashi. In other cases, the person was brought before the uncommunicative stage. In either case, however, this seems to have been an important marker in the dying process for the people involved, signaling that death was just days away. Finally, several people described a period of lucidity just before the person's death. In two cases this was accompanied by a request for food which the dying person consumed just before dying.

The pattern which I have just described is one that I recognized through my exposure to a number of families who had brought people to die. This pattern is also recognized to varying degrees by the families themselves, but especially by priest-workers such as Tikka Baba and Pandey. Shuklaji, too, knows this pattern and understands it as a morally proper way of dying.

When I asked Shuklaji why they had a limit of fifteen days, he said it is used to prevent abuse of the system. Most people who are really dying, he says, will die in just a few days, but sometimes it takes fifteen days or longer. If they are the "proper" people their time can be adjusted to the situation. But sometimes people come and they improve, and sometimes people will want to stay for a month or two months. This rule encourages them to go. But sometimes people do stay for long periods. Years before, a person stayed for ninety-five days. Dalmia was in Kashi at the time and objected, but the person who had come from Madhya Pradesh was not eating or drinking. "What can you do if someone is not eating or drinking?," Shuklaji asked. Though there is no rule at the Muktibhavan about whether or not people can eat, people are expected not to eat and it is apparent that not eating or drinking is taken as evidence of one's commitment to dying and thus an indicator of being the right type of person to die at the Muktibhavan.

There is another type of "predictable" death which the priest-workers told me about, but that I never myself witnessed. Sometimes, they say, it is the dying person him or herself who decides when to come to Kashi and remains in control to the end. Sometimes these people are extremely accurate at predicting their deaths. In Pandey's experience about ten percent of people are very accurate. Pandey related the following two stories to illustrate this point.

> An old woman came a while back. At that time it was very crowded here. The situation was such that many people were staying on the verandahs because all the rooms were full. So we told her "We do not have any space. Please go to the Ganga-labh Bhavan at Manikarnika ghat." But she did not want to go there. She said that her husband had died in this very place and she

> wanted to die at the exact spot where her husband had left his body. We told her family that it would be very problematic as there was no room. But the old lady just walked right in. She went to the very spot where her husband had died. She lay down there and died just at that very moment.
>
> Once a man was here and his family was concerned because he seemed to be getting better. He was walking around and drinking milk and eating. He could talk and knew who everybody was. His family was poor and so they thought they should take him home. I said that you should ask the patient his opinion. They did this in front of me, when I went to give the morning *arti.* I heard the *rogi* say "No, I will not return to the village. I will stay here and hear about God. I will die after four or five more days." He died on the seventh day after saying this.

These stories are told with much regard for dying people who can predict their deaths. The ability to predict is considered a sign that the person is a spiritually advanced person, and the death is a good one. A death in which there is this kind of control by prediction is far removed from an uncontrolled accidental death with its moral implications and spiritual sequelae.

9

Good Death and the Dying Process

> People want to die very quickly after reaching Kashi and often we priest-workers are asked: "Please give me some blessing that I may attain *moksha* quickly—so that I will reach God's abode quickly." We console them by saying "We are doing what is most needed by you and your family. We are offering prayers, reciting from the *Gita,* and chanting the name of Rama. This we can do. But when *moksha* will come, that is in the hands of God."
>
> —Hridyanand Pandey

In this chapter I show how spiritual and moral ideas of what it means to die a good death are implicated in the type of physiological dying process discussed in the last chapter. I start with the story of Tivari whose case, though unique in some ways, illustrates and weaves together many of the meaningful elements of dying at the Muktibhavan.

I met Tivari's son one day when he approached me in the Muktibhavan courtyard to see what I was doing there. He told me he was from a small village in Bihar and was a farmer. He had brought his father to die.

I asked him why they had come to Kashi. "The Veda," he answered, "is the oldest book in the world. It says that Kashi is Kailashpuri (the place of Shiva), and is different from the rest of the world. If you die in Kashi, the lord Vishvanath says '*Rama, Rama'* into your ear and, when you hear the name of God at the time of death, you go to God and attach to God." "Is this your own personal belief?," I asked him. He replied, "It is the belief of our holy books, which I support. I have faith that all the books are right." Then he asked me a question: "How many creatures have a soul?" My shrug worked, and he himself answered that cows, dogs, trees, and even I had a soul and that God was in all of us. "Creatures come and go but *atman* never dies. *Atman* is light and light is never finished. When *moksha* is attained the light goes into another light . . . God." Any creatures who can remember God at the time of their death can get *moksha,* he said. Even coming from Canada and saying "God, God, God" I would get *moksha.*

As most people who were dying at the Muktibhavan had stopped communicating, I was used to talking mostly to relatives like Tivari's son. I was thus surprised when I asked him a question about his father and he replied: "Come with me. You can ask him yourself." I walked into their upstairs room to find a frail old man sitting cross-legged on the edge of the bedframe wearing a black woolen ski mask, the type with one hole for the face, pulled down over his head. Out through the opening stuck a short grey beard and a pair of intense, sparkling eyes. On the ground in front of him was a large bucket of ash which he used for spitting in. I introduced myself in Hindi and inquired after his health. He let out a combination belch and growl that shook paint off the wall and then replied in raspy English that his health was "very bad."

"Very bad" turned out to be one of the few things that Tivari could say in English though, apparently, he could read the language; Tivari was an educated man and had had a career as an inspector for the water-works. We smiled at each other as his son explained to him who I was. I learned a few things about Tivari during that first visit. He had been at the Muktibhavan for ten days. He was eighty-six. He wanted to die very quickly but it was not happening. When he died his body would be burned, but not in the new electric crematorium. His body would die, but his *atman* would continue: "It will go to God," he said, "light into light."

I came back, several times, bringing Omji to interpret but several days passed before Tivari felt well enough to talk. Shuklaji was interested enough to sit in and the three of us and Tivari's son sat in a semicircle on the floor facing the old man on the cot. Early in the interview he growled a complaint: "You are asking questions like in a court case!" "It is not me," I said, "it's that translator." Tivari was very pleased with my response and laughed himself into a coughing spell. Red-faced and smiling, he said he was very happy.

"I have no need to stay in this world. I want to go," Tivari said of why he came to Kashi. Fifteen years before, in the village, Tivari had had an astrological horoscope *(kundali)* made. It was made by a pandit who lived in his village but the pandit had died many years ago. The *kundali* was written in Sanskrit which Tivari could not read. On the *kundali,* it was written how many more years he would live. This year, he believed it said, his time was up.

This prognosis was confirmed by "many doctors," Tivari said. He was at that time taking medicine for cough, his stomach and for fever. He showed me his cough syrup, a bronchodilator, and "heart palpitation pills." His son added "Here, God is his doctor and his medicine is *charnamrit.*" A doctor in the village had told him that there was no chance of saving him. Tivari, himself, also felt that it was his time to die.

Tivari thought that many people from his village would want to die in Kashi but not everybody could; only two or three people would manage to come every year. Tivari, himself, has brought several people to die in Kashi. He brought his mother to die in 1957 and they stayed at the Ganga-labh Bhavan. She died within two hours of arriving. He also brought some man from the village who was not a relative. Finally, Tivari brought his wife on the 6th of July 1985, to the Muktibhavan. She died right away so they didn't stay there the night. Now, for the first time, he was there to die himself.

Tivari said that he wanted to die in Kashi because, "it is written in our Hindu scriptures that whatever bad man, bad soul, comes and falls under Vishvanathji, then he will get *moksha.*" He himself has read this in the *Ramcharitmanas.* Sometimes, too, people had come to the village and told stories about such things. Tivari had came to Kashi to die in order to avoid another birth and another miserable life:

> There is a lot of sorrow in the world, it is a type of hell. You take birth and then die, you take birth and then die. The whole life is miserable. All human beings are unhappy . . . there are many difficulties. Unhappiness always follows happiness. When the soul joins the supreme power, *then* there is happiness.

Tivari said he was not afraid to die because, for the *atman,* there is no death. The body merely changes and he would get a new body. "My body has become very weak," he said. "My death should come quickly. My body should *change.* It has become fully weak and now it is of no use. The *atman* should *change* quickly." This answer surprised me as minutes before he had spoken of never being born again, not taking a new body through rebirth. How was Tivari able to hold these seemingly contradictory ideas? When I asked him he laughed and said that he could not really know what would happen after death: "Only somebody who has gone there and come back could tell you that," he said with a mischievous grin. He continued:

> Whether or not there will be a new birth, nobody has the power to know, because those who have gone have never come back and told. The scriptures say that dying in this place, in Kailash-puri where Shiva lives, the soul will stay there and will not be born again. It depends on *individual* faith.

The exact meaning of *moksha,* precisely what awaits the soul or life force, was not all that important for Tivari. *Moksha* was a goal *traditionally* sought after. Not only was Tivari aware of the complexities of his beliefs about *moksha,* he also clearly recognized the tension between the texts and custom. This is best illustrated by his answer to my question as to whether or not it is necessary to do the post-death rituals for somebody who has died in Kashi. He replied, "There is popular custom *(lokachar)* and there is the tradition *(vedachar),* two routes. According to the *shastras,*" he explained, "one need not celebrate the *shraddha,* but society forces you to do the rituals." On the one hand there is personal belief, but on the other there is what society expects.

Both "society" and Tivari, himself, have strong ideas of what is right and what is wrong. Tivari, like others, is influenced by the tradition of Hindu morality *(dharma).* Ultimately, he feels it is good work *(accha karma),* such as "reading sacred stories, the holy scriptures, and things that do not make others feel bad," that results in *moksha.* If one does bad work, then one will go to hell. If one does good work, then one will get enjoyment (*bhog*). The sinner will not get *moksha* in Kashi, Tivari said. The sinner will not be allowed to die in Kashi. He will be kept out by his *karma* and Lord Bhairav. Further, he believed that only human beings can get *moksha* because animals cannot do the type of ritual work that improves their lives. Life as a human being is the last chance to improve the future. Thus, for Tivari, there is an urgency in getting *moksha.* "If one has done bad work, he will be born again as a different creature like horse, donkey, cat or insect," he said. Hell *(nark),* for Tivari and many others, is, literally, rebirth in animal form.

Tivari refused to tell me what good work he had done in his life toward getting *moksha.* "Whatever good work I have done, I cannot say. I cannot speak of that. It will lose its power. What I have done is due only to the grace of God." He would not speak of his sins either. I asked him if he died *outside* Kashi, whether he thought he would get *moksha.* Much to everybody's amusement, he answered that if he knew that he could get *moksha* outside of Kashi, then why would he have come?

I asked Tivari what it meant to die a good death. He paused for a moment and then came up with what I have found to be almost a direct quote from the *Garuda Purana:* "It is best to die on the ground which has been purified with cow dung and spread with a mattress of *kusha* grass," he said. He continued:

> It is said in the *Gita* by Lord Krishna that at the time of death, a person should keep his senses, focus on God and say the sound "Aum." [He demonstrated a few times: "Aum, Aum, Aum".]

> Then God will invite him near. The person who does not do like that, he will remain far from God and will take birth again and again. All the things in the world, all the beautiful things, will come to mind at the time of death. There will be much attachment. Reading the *Gita* and saying "Aum" will make you detached from all the temporary things in the world.

It is good to be aware of your upcoming death, he said. If not, how could you take Ganga water and *tulsi* leaves? It is not good to die in your sleep, he said, and it is better to die with an empty stomach: "An empty stomach is absolutely purified. If there is nothing inside the stomach when a person dies, that is much better."

Tivari, himself, was eating almost nothing and said he had no desire to eat. He said he had no taste remaining in his tongue and his stomach was always full. He took a small piece of a *chapati* (unleavened bread) once a day. But he had no hunger. "Everything tastes like clay," he said. He did not believe that not eating would speed up his death: "If the time is not completed, then a man cannot die, whether he is eating or not."

Tivari did not die at the Muktibhavan. He and his family returned to their village two days after our interview through a strange set of circumstances. A local astrologer came and checked Tivari's astrological chart, which had not been read for fifteen years. The astrologer said that according to the *kundali,* his time was not finished. There had been some mistake and Tivari had three more years before his time was up. On the other hand, apparently there were many bad planets in the horoscope that could kill him before this time, and so he didn't know when he would die. At any rate, on the basis of what the astrologer said, Tivari and his family began making plans to return to the village.

I went to see them in their room the night they were leaving. The old man was asleep on the cot. Tivari's daughter was squatting in the corner cooking something on a small stove. Her husband and Tivari's son were stretched out on their backs on blankets, looking a little bored and staring at the ceiling. I poked my head in the door and was immediately invited in by the simple motion of spreading out the blanket so there was enough room.

Tivari's son told me that everybody in their small village had a *kundali,* and that they were very accurate. His said that he would live until he was eighty-five, another twenty-seven years. He was confident his father would live for three more years. The train trip home would be difficult, he said, because the old man needed enough space to sleep and the local trains are very crowded. From the station they would have to go a further five kilometers by horse-drawn cart *(tamtam).* Tivari woke from his sleep and I asked him how he was. "Very bad," he growled back to me in English.

Tivari's case illustrates many of the elements of dying at the Muktibhavan which I have used to form the structure of this analysis. Tivari came from a small village in which there is a tradition of going to Kashi to die. He believed that all the old people in the village have the desire to die in Kashi. His family, too, had a tradition of dying there; he, himself, had brought his mother and his wife to die in Kashi.

Tivari believed that dying in Kashi resulted in *moksha,* though he did not really have a clear idea of what *moksha* is. Most importantly, it is a way of avoiding the hell of a long series of non-human rebirths from which there is no escape. There were several inconsistencies in what Tivari told me he believed, though he was quite aware of these. At first he had said that even a sinner who died in Kashi would get *moksha,* a thought which he attributed to the *Ramcharitmanas.* Later, he said that a sinner would not get *moksha* from dying in Kashi, because he would not be able to die in Kashi. Tivari could also say that he desired both *moksha* and getting a new body because he recognized both as possibilities.

As I see it, the inconsistencies arise because Tivari had many sources of information from which, throughout his life, he had been able to pick and choose. In addition to all that he had learned as a member of many levels of culture, he had had the opportunity, like many others, to get to know several scriptural texts—texts from diverse periods of history and philosophical streams. Like many people dying at the Muktibhavan, he explicitly mentioned the *Ramcharitmanas* and the *Bhagavadgita* and he quoted almost directly from *Garuda Purana* in telling me what a good death was. The apparent contradictions, as I understand it, are inherent in Hinduism. According to some ways of thinking, it is the very difficulty in resolving the contradictions of Hinduism, which lead to the ultimate reward of Hinduism; an understanding of the "unmanifest."

Inconsistencies or not, Tivari had come to Kashi to die and he was, in fact, dying. He believed he was dying and so did the people around him. He had said good-bye to friends and family and had left his village and his home. He had also stopped eating, although he attributed this to always feeling full and to his loss of the sense of taste. Like many other people dying at the Muktibhavan, he was well into the dying process from physiological, psychological and social perspectives. Unlike many other people, however, these interactive processes were initiated, in part, by his belief that his time was up as predicted by his astrological chart. The importance of the astrological chart's role in initiating the dying process is underlined by the fact that, when it was reinterpreted to predict he had another three years to live, he decided to go home to his village.

The astrological prediction of death may have actually initiated or accelerated the physiological dying process. Tivari, himself, did not associate his cessation of eating with his will to die; he stopped eating, he said, because he had no appetite and food no longer had taste. On the other hand, he also said that he believed that whether one ate or not, one would still die at a predetermined time. He said that, in terms of purity, it was much better to die on an empty stomach, and he may have stopped eating, in part, for this reason. I do not know whether or not he began eating again after leaving the Muktibhavan, or how long he has survived.

Timely death *(Kal Mrityu)*

Several people that I interviewed made comments to the effect that a dying person would not die until his or her time was up. For the most part, I attached little meaning to these statements. And yet, for some, the comments were meant quite literally and referred to the common distinction between timely and untimely deaths *(kal mrityu* and *akal mrityu).* Tivari is an example of a man who believes that there is a predetermined time to die, and that a good death *is* a timely death occurring at that predetermined time. Tivari acted on these beliefs to the extent that his decision to come to Kashi to die was based, in part, on the astrological prediction of the time when he would die. His decision to leave Kashi was similarly based on a reevaluation of the astrological chart which essentially showed that there had been a misreading of the chart and he had three more years to live.

The predetermined time of death does not mean that people have predetermined life spans. It does not mean, therefore, as Wellenkamp (1991, 119) reported for some Toraja, that one need not be worried about dying when undertaking a dangerous journey because death cannot come before its time. Rather, Tivari's understanding was that he could not live *past* the predetermined time. On the other hand, there were several bad planets in his chart which made it doubtful whether he would make it the extra three years.

An astrologer *(jyotishi)* I talked to in Kashi reiterated to me that, from his perspective, the date and time of timely death are predetermined. Nobody can live a moment longer than what is allotted him or her. On the other hand, one can easily die *before* this set time. Astrology can predict accurately, in theory, the time and date of a person's death, providing it is a timely death. It cannot predict an untimely death, but can provide certain information to avoid one. The astrologer told me that if, for instance, the chart indicates a potential problem with drowning, the person might be advised not to swim.

I knew several people in Kashi who had predictions about the time at which they would die *(mrityu samay).* Shuklaji said, with a very pleased look, that he had another fifty years and would live to be an old man at ninety-two. A friend's father died, as predicted, at seventy-four. That same friend's mother was making plans to live until eighty according to her *kundali.* She said that almost everybody knows when they will die, but generally people refuse to tell others. Another friend, Manoj, showed me his Kundali and told me that he will live to be seventy-two . His wife, however, had never had one done because, she said, the exact time of her birth is not known; unless it is exactly known, the prediction may be way off.

There seems to be some variability as to how seriously the predictions of death times are taken. Omji said that, often, *kundali* predictions are shown to be inaccurate and then it is assumed that the time of birth must have been inaccurate by a minute or more. Manoj, who will live to seventy-two, has little faith in the predictions for the reason that he believes the times of birth are never known accurately enough for a true prediction. On the other hand, the mother of another friend said she was budgeting her remaining time on the assumption that she would live ten more years.

Among the people dying at the Muktibhavan, I believe that *kundalis* are not generally important. Although Tivari's son said everybody in his village had one, Masterji said that most people in his village do not. Only the richer folk have them, he said, because they are expensive to have made. He did not have one, himself, as his parents had lost interest after spending a lot of money on the *kundalis* of the twins born before Masterji. One had died as a child, and his parents, not knowing whose was whose, threw both of the twin's *kundalis* into the river. Masterji thought that the main use of *kundalis* would be to diagnose sickness. They would be taken to an astrologer who would look at them and then recommend certain rituals *(pujas).* He thought that generally, the prediction of time of death would not be taken too seriously by people unless they were experiencing other problems; that it would not be too common that somebody would expect to die just on the basis of their *kundali.*

The Good Death

Though astrological predictions of the time of death may not be important among the people coming to die at the Muktibhavan, the underlying principle, that there is an individual predetermined maximum life span, is widespread. This seems to be a fundamental idea of dying a good death. A good death occurs when you do not get killed before your allotted time. The allotted time is determined by the planets, but reaching your allotted time is determined by the good deeds you have done or by the grace of God. A good death occurs when you have reached your allotted time, or, practically speaking, when you are old enough that nobody has a problem accepting it as such.

From friends in Kashi, I heard many ideas about good and bad deaths. Monday is considered to be a good day for dying in Kashi and it is, more generally, good to die on the eleventh day of each Hindu

FIGURE 9.1

Man massaging the legs of his dying father at Kashi Labh Muktibhavan

month; at full moon; and from about 3:30 a.m. to 5:30 a.m. Eleven at night to about 3:00 a.m. is a bad time to die, as it is the time of evil beings. Its also bad to die drunk, eating meat, during sex, or child delivery. There are, I was told, vast lists of good and bad ways of dying mentioned in "technical" texts such as the *Preta Mangeri.* These texts are essentially instructions for priests and are not generally known, though it is probable that ideas trickle out of them.

There is no question that the people I talked to make a definite distinction between "good" and "bad" deaths *(acchi maut* and *buri maut).* These terms are used and are generally meaningful. The more common distinction, however, is between timely and untimely death *(kal mrityu* and *akal mrityu).* There is general agreement that a timely death is a good death and that such deaths are deaths of old age. Beyond that, there is less universal agreement and the information stops being volunteered. The following is from a conversation I had with Kapil Deo Singh:

CJ: What is a good death?
Singh: One of old age. A person who will die according to his own time, his death time.
CJ: Should one be conscious?
Singh: It is impossible.
CJ: Should one be asleep?
Singh: Death never comes to a sleeping person. It is impossible.
CJ: Should one be taking God's name?
Singh: That is very important. The name of God and donations are the two most important things.
CJ: Should the stomach be empty or full?
Singh: The stomach of somebody dying a good death will always be empty because they will not eat at that time.
CJ: What are bad deaths?
Singh: *Akal mrityu,* like falling down from something or being killed by somebody. They are bad deaths because . . . [long pause] because they are the result of bad *karma.* Someone who dies an untimely death can still get *moksha* but their relatives must first do the Gaya *shraddha.*

There are many ideas about what is a good or a bad death. The ideas I am dealing with here are only those commonly held by the people dying at the Muktibhavan. From the perspective of the analytical realms I have been using, a good death can be spiritually rewarding, morally correct, physiologically good or simply in line with the way other people die. The good death is one that leads to *moksha* and so occurs in Kashi, in a religious environment, concentrating on God and sipping Ganga water with *tulsi* leaves. The good death is one in which there is no trauma or other indication that a store of bad *karma* is enacting its punishment. And the good death is one that occurs at as old an age as possible, free from disease, with an empty stomach, awake, and that is expected. Or a good death can simply be one that is traditional: the way the other villagers, or maybe even the rich high caste villagers, die. Ideas of good and bad deaths encompass a range of possibilities which can be differentially stressed, unreflectively accepted or arranged in idiosyncratic combinations.

The interesting thing is how the ideas all fit together. At one level, core principles can be flushed from all their manifestations. As I have argued, the core idea seems to be that a good death is a death when one's time is up. At another level, these various ideas can be shown to have an interactive arrangement when they are acted upon. It is to this that I now turn.

It seems that ideas of good death which are about spiritual reward, or the moral implications of dying, have primacy over and may even be said to be causal of, ideas in the physiological realm. Specifically, I want to make the argument that ideas of spiritual reward and morality logically result in the desire to die a death that is perceived by self and others, to be at an old age, free of disease, controlled, and predicted. This desire leads, in turn, to specific behaviors around dying, one of which is the giving up of food early in the dying process. I am not suggesting that this connection is consciously made, though in some cases it is recognized.

The Good Death and Not Eating While Dying

When I asked Masterji how long he thought his mother would live, he said he thought another one or two months, "because she sometimes takes milk, orange juice and bananas. If she did not take food then she would die sooner," he said. His mother did not want to die and so she continued to eat. But that is not all. The words of Masterji illustrate how people can well understand the relationship of eating and living, but see connections at other levels too. The following is a piece of a conversation with Masterji just before his mother's death:

CJ: If your mother wanted to die would she stop eating?

Masterji: Yes, anyone (would). But sometimes we see that people have not taken food in two or three months and they live, so we can't say that (one) will die.

CJ: Is this common in Hindu society? I have heard that older people stop eating?

Masterji: No, not because they wish to. The digestive system stops working so they stop taking food.

CJ: But I have heard that if you have food in your stomach it makes it harder to obtain heaven.

Masterji: Yes, that is the reason. If you have power in the body then the *pran* (vital breath) does not go quickly from the body, you struggle. So it is difficult. And if you are very weak, the *pran* will go very easily.

Life, Masterji was saying, when food has been forsaken, leaves without a fight. This is one of the *signs* of a good death.

The giving up of food early in the dying process has the effect of making death predictable, and therefore controlled. Death by malnutrition and dehydration has a recognizable pattern. It is this, I believe, which is largely responsible for people being able to arrive at the Muktibhavan so close to death. Among the people dying at the Muktibhavan, an important sign family members very often used as a signal to leave for Kashi was the dying person ceasing to communicate. Death, it was said, was then only hours or days away.

Not eating and drinking for some time before death probably results in a lowered chance of incontinence at the time of death. The absence of incontinence is evidence that the life's breath has escaped through one of the holes of the head which, in turn, indicates that the soul has achieved *moksha*.[1] If there is incontinence at the time the *pran* leaves the body it indicates a bad fate. Turned around, the desire that the life breath appears to exit through the upper region may be one of the reasons that there is a textual prescription that people should not be eating at the time of their deaths. The desire to appear to have died a good death could also be a more direct motivation to stop eating as death was perceived to be approaching, though I have no evidence that this is the case.

Not eating or drinking during the time of dying can also be considered an aspect of a general detachment from the material world, a spiritual goal of classical Hinduism and an idea that many people seem to share. I see many of the aspects of the pilgrimage to Kashi to die, such as leaving the familiar surroundings of home and village, and leaving one's friends and relatives, as enabling detachment from the material world.[2] Many people understand the value of material detachment in terms of allowing for full-time spiritual endeavor, but do not necessarily see the cessation of eating in this manner.

I have argued that the question of why people who die at the Muktibhavan give up food and die a particular type of physiological death finds an answer in the spiritual and moral ideas of what it means to die a good death. Here, I will look more broadly at some aspects of the symbolic importance of eating in Hinduism.

There is an obvious relationship between food and life, though it is one that is culturally mediated everywhere. The ancient Ayurvedic medical system is a pervading source of such mediation in India (Kakar 1982, 219). Health, in Ayurveda, consists of maintaining a proper balance in the body of such things as the five elements, the three humors, and heat and coolness. Foods are infused with these properties and have the ability to throw off or restore the body's balance. The *control* of food intake is day-to-day body maintenance. Fasting is one aspect of controlling physiological processes. Many people believe that the control of eating is important for longevity. People who eat less live longer than those people who eat a lot, and if one wants to live longer, one should maintain fasts.

There is also a cultural relationship between eating and dying. According to Mahantji, the man who keeps the small place for dying pilgrims at Tulsi ghat, hunger striking—"thinking I would like to leave this earth so I will do a hunger strike and die"—is generally considered to be a very good way of dying. Though suicide is considered to be a great sin, he said, leaving the body by such yogic practices is considered to be a very great thing. He explained: "If somebody was going into battle and knew they would probably die, would you call that suicide? No. In the same way, we don't consider death from hunger strike suicide."

Though several of my *banarsi* friends were surprised that people dying at the Muktibhavan were not eating, most were not. I was told by one man that not eating at the time of death was widespread. Many old people in their homes, he said, also stop eating when they are going to die. The reason, he said, is that "having milk and fruit and such things in the stomach at the time of death is not helpful for getting into heaven."

Conclusions

The manner in which people die, having made the pilgrimage to Kashi and the Muktibhavan, bears some superficial resemblance to the several deaths of "certain old, enfeebled" aboriginal people described by Eastwell (1982, 12) in his attempt to argue by analogy that the mode of voodoo death is dehydration. Amongst both Eastwell's old, dying people and those going to the Muktibhavan, the initiation of the dying process is ritually recognized and the process of dying is facilitated by the cessation of nourishment. There is, however, a significant difference between Eastwell's understanding of the deaths he has reported and my understanding of the process of dying at the Muktibhavan. Probably because Eastwell was using these cases as an analogy for voodoo death, he sees them as either euthanasia or "senilicide" and does not recognize the possibility that the elderly person could be involved in initiating the process. Further, the process he describes allows the old person no room in determining the course of the process of dying. He stated that: "The social behavior of beginning the obsequies while the patient-victim is alert *defines* the role of the dying person and *prescribes* the person's behavior" (17, emphasis added).

The pilgrimage to die in Kashi is not generally one that is driven by the social group. It is the dying individual who decides, or recognizes, that it is time to die and initiates the cessation of taking nourishment. The relatives, upon recognition that death is inevitable, do not consider the person socially dead, nor do they withdraw. Rather, they go to great trouble and expense to bring the dying person on a final pilgrimage to Kashi. Far from being considered either euthanasia or senilicide, the deaths at the Muktibhavan are very much self-controlled.

Fasting is an everyday part of religion for many people in India. Many of the people dying at the Muktibhavan had reportedly undertaken fasts during their lives in pursuit of *moksha.* If a fast to death is not considered to be suicide but, instead, is auspicious and purifying, and if it is thought to aid in the ability to concentrate on God at the time of death, then it is possible that people *decide* to stop eating early in the dying process for one or another of these specific reasons. However, to the best of my knowledge, this idea would not ring true to the dying people at the Muktibhavan. In general, the families I talked to said their dying relatives did not actively decide to stop eating. They considered not eating a natural corollary of dying—a sign, not a cause, of moving toward death.

I am suggesting that many of the behaviours surrounding dying, especially those around not eating, are, in some complicated manner, connected to the scriptures. At the textual level, the logical connection between dying a good death and not eating certainly exists: not eating is specifically prescribed in at least one text *(Garuda Purana* 9:34). More generally, the broader cultural context does not provide sanction against not eating while dying and the Muktibhavan expects, and may subtly encourage, giving up food while dying. Although some people who are not eating while dying might not associate the cessation of eating with dying a good death, the connections are still there: people are both *allowed* and *encouraged* to not eat during the dying process.

Cultural ideas of what good death is, and what it looks like, can affect people's eating behaviour in a number of ways. Not eating as death approaches is thought to allow life to slip away with the minimum of struggle. The process of dying is predictable and thus controlled. A lowered chance of incontinence at the moment life slips away corresponds with a greater chance that the death will appear good. And not eating at the time of death is evidence of a detachment from the material world. Giving up food with the perception that the dying process has begun, both ensures that the dying process *has* begun and participates significantly in the construction of the physiological as well as other aspects of the dying experience.

Afterword

In 1983 Vinoba Bhave, a famous disciple of Mahatma Gandhi, had a heart attack while in his late eighties. After the heart attack, he refused any medication and soon gave up food. He died a few days later in his hermitage. The death, as Madan describes it, was "a paradigmatic death, surcharged with dignity"(1992; 431). However, many of the major Indian newspapers ran editorials following Bhave's death charging that the doctors involved were guilty of professional misconduct in allowing him to die in such a manner. That the medical profession should have some interest or control over such a man and his choice of the time and manner of his death is at odds with what I consider to be at the basis of dying at the Muktibhavan. While the pilgrimage to die in Kashi is but one cultural form of a diversity of Hindu deathways, it is generally fair to say that professional bodies and institutions have not rested control of death from the individual and family. One of the useful things about learning how dying is understood and experienced by others is that it can elucidate the potential for responding to and shaping the biological universal of dying. And as Madan (1992) put it, other cultural perspectives on dying have the potential to temper our excesses and reintroduce a measure of humanness in our treatment of old, sick, and dying people.

In the first chapter I pointed out that Western thanatological literature is generally focused on young people who are dying premature deaths. Furthermore, the qualitative distinction between these deaths and death at the end of the life cycle is not generally recognized. However, among the people who make the pilgrimage to Kashi to die, and embedded in the rules and operation of the Muktibhavan, is a clear distinction between a natural, timely, and good death at the end of the life cycle and an unnatural, untimely, and bad death which occurs at a young age. Such a distinction is generalizable and useful. The meaning of death is said to be "ambiguous" in North American society, though I suspect that the concept "meaning" is largely at the basis of the ambiguity. Certainly there is something about our understanding of death that allows, and likely derives from, interventionist action in the dying of others. It may be that our ideas about death are overly accommodated to premature deaths (which are becoming increasingly rare). It is thus death at the end of the life cycle which must be understood as extant systems of meaning are not necessarily relevant for people dying of old age.

For the people dying at the Muktibhavan, being old is a prerequisite for dying a good death. Other than this, many elements of a good death are related to awareness and control. These seem to be generalizable features of good deaths in many cultural settings (Counts and Counts 1983–84; Bloch and Parry 1982). In this respect, allowing people in North American society to die better deaths would involve taking control of dying away from the medical and legal systems; allowing people more freedom to die as they see fit; and, as both individuals and families, taking control of the process by which we die. To some extent this is happening in the area of palliative care but not within the context of natural death at the end of the life cycle.

Is the process of dying at the Muktibhavan an acceleration of the dying process? The concept of acceleration begs the question: accelerated with regard to what? The point of reference, I believe, would have to do with a particular set of ideas relating to "natural" physiological process. We tend to strive to do what we think of as natural, and to see as natural that which we do. It is quite possible to see the cessation of eating in advanced old age or in the end stages of lingering illness as a natural physiological process. In this case it would make little sense to see dying at the Muktibhavan, or any other examples of dying at the end of the life cycle by starvation or dehydration, as accelerated.

There is a small body of literature which focuses on appetite loss among elderly people. It is generally accepted that food intake decreases with age and that often elderly people report a decrease in appetite (Rolls 1992, 442).[1] Often, the researchers assume that these changes are problematic and it has been suggested that they may be a result of increased depression in old age (Olsen-Noll and Bosworth 1989, 142). The literature also assumes that it would be good to restore "normal" eating behavior and some of it (i.e. Winograd and Brown, 1990) takes the restoration of appetite in the elderly as a primary focus. There seems to be general agreement that *dying* people, as distinct from elderly people, lose their appetites and do not eat much on their own (Lynn and Childress 1986, 215). There are anecdotes of animals, such as dogs and cats, that stop eating many days before their deaths, and it seems that the cessation of eating, as a part of a general withdrawal preceding death, is common in domesticated animals. Though this is only suggestive, the implication is that the cessation of eating before dying is a "natural" process because it occurs without cultural mediation.

Considering the cessation of eating early in the dying process as at least within the range of "natural" physiological process would have some significant theoretical and practical implications. For instance, we might understand the social and cultural context, in which dying people on their way to Kashi are quitting food, as one which allows nature to take its course. On the other hand, we would have to see North American cultural norms as nonconducive to dying a 'natural' death. That is to say that cultural norms which allow either force-feeding or the gentle encouragement of a non-hungry, dying person to eat—and which encourage the dying person, him or herself, to always continue eating—act to "unnaturally" extend the dying process.

The necessity of feeding and hydrating gerontological and terminally ill patients has developed into a controversial ethical and legal issue in North America (see Sandstead 1990). In the home environment, there is often pressure from family members that the old person continue to sustain him or herself by eating and drinking. In the hospital, where the vast majority of people in the West die of old age and lingering terminal disease, nutrition and hydration have been provided as a matter of course (cf. Zerwekh 1983; Michaelson et al. 1987). When they are not, staff feel pressure from family members to provide nutrition and hydration, thereby "unnaturally" extending the dying process as well as exacerbating certain physiological problems (Zerwekh 1983, 49).

One realm of cultural understanding that seems to be significant here is that related to subtle meanings of food and nutrition. In the Western literature dealing with the ethics of dying, for example, are statements such as "food and water are not only the goods that preserve life and provide comfort; they are also symbols of care and compassion" (Lynn and Childress 1986: 226), and "[t]he feeding of the hungry . . . is the most fundamental of all human relationships" (Callahan 1986, 232). According to Callahan, while Karen Ann Quinlan's father was fighting to have his daughter taken off her respirator, he was amazed when asked if he wanted her intravenous feeding stopped too. "Oh no," he reportedly said, "that is her nourishment" (1986, 231). Taking her off the respirator would have been letting her die, but stopping her feeding would have been killing her.

In the West, death by "not eating" seems to be regarded as akin to suicide, which implies an unnatural process. The issues of feeding and hydrating lie between the blurred ethical and legal boundaries of "artificial medical intervention" and "natural life support." The naturalization of this type of death—that is moving toward thinking about it as within a range of natural—has significant ramifications in shifting these boundaries and making forced nutrition and hydration in dying people seem artificial and interventionist. There is thus a significant need for research with elderly and dying people to elucidate the extent to which appetite loss can be tied to natural physiological processes, to meaningful cultural connections between food and life, and to societal factors which encourage, until the end, the continuation of bodily sustenance.

Appendix: Survey Questionnaire and Compilation of Responses

Survey Questionnaire
Questions and Answers
Answer Yes or No—Fill in the Empty Spaces

Name of *Rogi* Register # ______
Rogi's District State City / Village ______
Date of Entry

Education: Primary Middle High Graduate None

Rogi's business or occupation ______

Who made the decision to come here? ______

Has a doctor told the *rogi* he will not recover? Y N

Was all the family agreed to admit the *rogi?* ______

Does the *rogi* desire that he will not be saved? ______

With whose help was this Muktibhavan found? ______

Before coming did you know about this Muktibhavan? Y N

Before coming did you know any Muktibhavan workers? Y N

Who brought *rogi,* how many times has he brought others? ______

Is the *rogi* happy to leave his body in Kashi? Y N
Does the *rogi* feel fear of death? Y N
Does the *rogi* want to attain mukti very quickly? Y N

Which food and medicine is being taken now?
Is the *rogi* presently eating anything? Y N

Is the *rogi* taking any medicine?	Y	N
Is the *rogi* feeling relief from pain?	Y	N
Has *rogi* done other things in his life to obtain *moksha?*	Y	N
Which things		
In the view of the *rogi:*		
Only in Kashi you get *moksha* just from dying?	Y	N
Is it necessary to not eat just before dying?	Y	N
Should you be aware of your own death?	Y	N
Is it necessary to be in control of your own death?	Y	N
(like grandfather Bhisma)?	Y	N

Compilation of Responses

Education	
None	62
Primary	11
Middle	2
High	3
Graduate	9
Business or occupation	
farmer/householder	77
teacher	3
businessman	2
shopkeeper	1
laborer	1
service-worker	1
earthenware maker	1
Who made the decision to go there?	
dying person	67
family	17
neighbour	1
doctor	1
village	1
Has a doctor told the *rogi* he will not recover?	
Yes	74
No	11
Was all the family agreed to admit the *rogi?*	
Yes	84
No	3

Does the *rogi* desire that he will not be saved?	
Yes	83
No	2

With whose help was this Muktibhavan found?	
knew from before	62
named individual	25

Before coming did you know about this Muktibhavan?	
Yes	73
No	13

Before coming did you know any Muktibhavan workers?	
Yes	47
No	39

Who brought *rogi*, how many times has he brought others?	
Never	37
Once	17
Twice	15
Three times	3
Four times	3
Eight times	1
Many times	2

Is the *rogi* happy to leave his body in Kashi?	
Yes	85
No	1

Does the *rogi* feel fear of death?	
Yes	10
No	75

Does the *rogi* want to attain *mukti* very quickly?	
Yes	85
No	0

Which food and medicine is being taken now?	
Nothing	60
Water	19
Milk	6
Tulsi leaves	3
Fruit	2
Light food	2
Medicine	1

Is the *rogi* presently eating anything?

Yes	6
No	81

Is the *rogi* taking any medicine?

Yes	4
No	82

Is the *rogi* feeling relief from pain?

Yes	86
No	1

Has *rogi* done other things in his life to obtain *moksha?*

Yes	82
No	1

Which things?
See Figure 6

In the view of the *rogi:*
Only in Kashi you get *moksha* just from dying?

Yes	71
No	7

Is it necessary to not eat just before dying?

Yes	50
No	27

Should you be aware of your own death?

Yes	68
No	11

Is it necessary to be in control of your own death?

Yes	12
No	67

Glossary of Commonly Used Hindi Terms

acchi maut: good death
akal mrityu: untimely death
antim samay: one's last time before death
antyesthi sanskar: last rites, funerary rites
arti: worship with display of camphor flames waved before deities
ashrama: stage in life; hermitage
atman: self, the essence of life, the essence within a person
Aum: the universal sound
banarsi: local culture of Kashi (Banaras)
Bhagavadgita: "Song of God," part of Mahabarata, Krishnas's teaching to Arjuna about duty
Bhagavan: God; common honorific title for God
Bhairava yatna: punishment meted out by Lord Bhairav to those sinners who die in Kashi
bhajan: devotional recitation, collective hymn singing
bhakti: devotion to a personal deity
bhavan: mansion, house
Brahman: the Absolute, the essence of life, the source of everything
bhut: a spirit, ghost, or demon
brahmacharya: first period in life; studenthood
burhapa: old age
charasi lakh yoni: 8,400,000 life forms or births to be lived before taking human birth
charnamrit: holy water, made by washing the feet of an image of Vishnu
darshana: auspicious sight, usually of a deity
deva lok: the realm of the gods, heaven
dharma: religion; moral duty
Dharmashastra: collection of lawbooks which outline religious and moral duty
dharmsala: resthouse for pilgrims, often free of charge

dom:	caste who control Manikarnika burning ghat
Ganga jal:	water from the Ganga, given as medicine at the Muktibhavan
Ganga-labh:	the spiritual profit from dying near the river Ganga
Garuda Purana:	eschatological scripture read publicly after death
gau dan:	the gift of a cow
ghat:	landing places along a coast or river, steps down to the water
ghee:	clarified butter
grihastya:	second stage of life; householder
kal mrityu:	timely death
karma:	doctrine of the consequences of one's actions either in this life or subsequent lives
karmacharya:	worker
Kashi-labh:	the profit or benefit of dying in Kashi
Kashi-vasa:	residence in Kashi
kirtan:	religious singing
kundali:	astrological chart
labh:	benefit, profit
Mahabharata:	one of the great Indian epics
mahapatra:	funeral priest
mahasmashan:	the great cremation ground, synonym for Kashi
mahatmya:	literature of glorification or praise
mahant:	head of a monastic establishment
marnewala:	dying person, one who is about to die
moksha:	liberation from cycle of birth, death, and rebirth
mukti:	liberation from cycle of birth, death, and rebirth
muktibhavan:	"mansion of liberation," place for people to die
nark:	hell
pandit:	learned man, scholar
pap:	sin
pinda dan:	ritual offering of rice balls made to nourish the dead
pitr:	ancestor
pitri paksh:	fortnight of the ancestors, period of time auspicious for conducting rites for the ancestors
pran:	life's breath
pret:	a spirit, ghost, or demon
puja:	worship, generally including offerings to a deity
Ramayana:	one of two great Indian epics, featuring Lord Rama
Ramcharitmanas:	local Hindi version of Ramayana
rogi:	sick or afflicted person
salokya:	residence in the same world as God

samipya:	residence in the vicinity of God
samsara:	cycle of birth, death, and rebirth
sannyasa:	fourth stage of life, asceticism, material renunciation
sarupya:	taking the same form as God
sayuja:	merging with God
shraddha:	rites for the dead performed after cremation
svarg:	heaven
tarak mantra:	what Shiva is said to whisper in the ear of a dying person in Kashi which results in *moksha*
tirtha:	crossing place, pilgrimage center
Vaitarni River:	mythical river full of horrors that must be crossed on the after death journey
vanprasthya:	the third life stage, "forest dweller," period of material withdrawal
vatavaran:	atmosphere, as in religious places
yatra:	pilgrimage
yatri:	pilgrim
yuga:	an age or immense span of time in Hindu cosmogony

Notes

2. Kashi

1. Generally, Kashi is very linguistically forgiving as pilgrims with many language backgrounds are constantly arriving there. Almost all the people coming to die at the Muktibhavan are speakers of Bhojpuri—a dialect of Hindi —who can understand and speak standard or "pakka" Hindi when necessary. My Hindi became good enough that I could meet and carry on a basic conversation with a patient Hindi speaker, but I could not pick up the subtle meanings which I was interested in. During interviews I could ask questions but relied on Omji for immediately interpreting answers, and ultimately, on transcription and careful translation of tapes.

2. I recorded a sample of 5 percent of all the records. Additionally I recorded every record from one year each decade, so that I have 100 percent of the records for 1960, 1970, 1980, and 1990. I chose these years because I was in Kashi in 1990. As I was there from July, I started collecting my full-year samples starting July 1 and ending June 30th. The full year of records which I am calling 1990, for instance, is everything from 1 July 1990 to 30 June 1991.

3. Dying in Kashi

1. Bhardwaj (1973) in a study conducted in Himachel Pradesh showed that there is huge variation in what Hindus consider the preeminent *tirtha.*

2. Often a husband and wife will enter this stage and come to Kashi together. But the important thing here is that they have left behind, for the most part, the connection to larger family. I did, however, meet several people who had come to Kashi as *vanprasthis* who maintained correspondence with and sometimes visited their families.

3. Probably in the past, as well as now, there are a significant number of such people who come to Kashi for dying but have a private place to stay such as with friends or relatives or with a *panda* who is responsible for their region or family.

4. There are a number of types of place where pilgrims coming to Kashi can stay including *ashrams, mathas* and *dharmsalas. Mathas* are for only those who are devotees of the mahant of the *matha.* In *ashrams* the public can stay.

Dharmsalas are also for the public, but they are usually for people of a particular region or religion. In a *dharmsala* one can stay for only three or four days and no food is provided. Some *pandas* have their own *dharmsalas* where their groups stay, for example, the pilgrims that come *en masse* for *pitri paksh.*

5. The year *vikram sanvat* 1990 overlapped with AD 1932.

6. The figures graphically represented and discussed in the text are the numbers of people who were registered at the *bhavans* and not the number of deaths. This distinction was not made in the records for all years.

4. Kashi Labh Muktibhavan

1. Almost all of my data is, in a sense, "proxy" data, as interviews with dying people proved to be very rare. I will discuss the general validity of this data in chapter 6.

2. For example, according to the *Bhagavadgita,* dying when the sun is on its Northern path (roughly 21 June to 21 January) will result in *moksha,* whereas dying in the other half of the year even a yogi will return to another life.

5. Dying as Tradition

1. More properly, people gave forty-two different responses to the question of their caste which is asked routinely during registration. A research assistant identified several records (though a small percentage of the total) in which the name suggested a lower caste than that which was stated.

2. These are "as the crow flies" distances and say little of the difficulty of making the journey. It may be more difficult for somebody in nearby Rohtas who is a long way from the railway station, than for somebody further away from Kashi but closer to a station.

3. There are three main dialects of Hindi spoken in Bihar: Bhojpuri, Maithili, and Magadhi. Brass 1974 (55–116) argues that the speakers of each dialect have distinctive economic and cultural characteristics.

4. In the years for which I have complete records for the Muktibhavan: in 1960 three people came, in 1970 two people came. In the years for which I have complete records for both places, in 1980 five people came (two to Ganga-labh Bhavan, three to the Muktibhavan) and in 1990 three people came (one to Ganga-labh Bhavan and two to the Muktibhavan). Also, three records from the years between 1980 and 1990 were captured by the 5 percent sample of the intervening years.

6. Dying in a Spiritual System

1. When I look at all the responses in the order in which they were collected, some interesting patterns emerge in terms of what people are doing to obtain *moksha.* When something is mentioned once, then it very often is mentioned again very soon after. I think it is pretty clear that, in some cases, the priest-workers supplied those people who had nothing much to say with the "correct" answer.

2. *Mukti* is used interchangeably with *moksha.*

3. These ideas, which several people I talked to had heard of, had no apparent effect on the number of people dying at the Muktibhavan at particular times of the day, month or year, according to the records.

7. Dying and Morality

1. *Karma,* famous as the doctrine of cause and effect, exists as a concept in many textual and popular variants. However, Fuller (1992, 245–50) argues that in popular Hinduism *karma* is not as important as its fame might suggest, but is more important with the socio-religious elite—high-caste, educated men who are comfortably settled in the world.

2. For Dalmia the most important attribute of the people coming to die at the Muktibhavan seemed to be that they are poor as well as being dying Hindus. In his view, the type of people who use the place are those who cannot afford treatment, as people who could afford treatment would go elsewhere.

3. *Atman,* while translated in the dictionary I am using as "soul, spirit," is often carefully distinguished from the Western conception of soul by scholars of Hinduism who tend to define it as "self" (Klostermaier 1988, 512). It is often used interchangeably with *jiva* (life) and *jivatman* (individual life force) in reference to that which survives death.

4. I find this an insightful account of the transfer of knowledge and the ethnographic endeavor.

5. In the year 1990–91, two pilgrims marked as being Brahmins had personal caste names which a Banarsi friend thought indicated that they were, in fact, from an Untouchable caste.

8. Physiological Dying

1. In 1984 the Muktibhavan had started to record the time of death in the record books, and in 1989 they started to record the time at which people

arrived. Thus, only for 1990, I was able to calculate to the hour the length of time inbetween a person's arrival at the Muktibhavan and their deaths. While 129 people were recorded as having died on the same date as they arrived, 158 people were recorded as having died within twenty-four hours of arrival. The Muktibhavan changes its date at 3:00 a.m.; anybody who arrived at midnight and died six hours later would be counted as dying on the second day because of the date change.

2. This raises the question as to why people wait so long before setting off for Kashi. I can only speculate that it is due to the fact that the trip is both costly and inconvenient to the family and the longer they are away the more money and farming time it will cost them.

3. Ayurvedic texts, though ancient and generally unknown, prescribe understandings and behaviors that resonate strongly with day to day life. As Sudhir Kakar (1982, 220) says, Ayurveda is "the principle repository of the Indian cultural image of the body and concept of the person." He describes how he discovered his own deep-seated cultural ideas when he first went through the texts: "In Ayurveda, I discovered the source of my unvoiced suspicion that the twig from the *neem* tree with which I brushed my teeth as a child . . . did infinitely more than just clean the teeth. Here I found the source of my reluctance to eat radishes and guavas at night, the origin of my reverence for the beneficial properties of honey and clarified butter, and of my secret respect for many herbs and roots, especially if they are from (or are said to be from) the Himilayas."

9. Good Death and the Dying Process

1. This is written in the *Garuda Purana.* Several people told me that this is the only indication of what had happened to the *atman* after death.

2. This line of thinking can be taken quite far. Focusing on God could be seen as a metaphor for complete detachment from the material world. Many of the things which are observable can be explained in terms of a rejection of the body, including the more or less rough handling of the dying person's body by the relatives, the injunction that the person should die on the ground, and especially the fact that the person has not eaten in some time.

Afterword

1. Sensitivity of taste and smell decline progressively with age, but this has not been linked to appetite loss and elderly people seem to report no corresponding decrease in appreciation of food (Rolls 1992, 423). There is some evidence that natural regulatory changes with aging may affect hunger and

food intake, however. Older rats have been shown to have decreased opoid peptides in the hypothalamus, a factor which has been linked to the palatability of food (Morly and Silver 1988). Elderly human subjects have shown reduced ability to experience the sensation of thirst after dehydration, due in part to changes in receptors in the central nervous system (Philips et al. 1991).

References

Ariès, Phillipe

1974 *Western Attitudes toward Death from the Middle Ages to the Present.* Johns Hopkins University Press, Baltimore and London

1981 *The Hour of Our Death* Alfred A. Knopf, New York

Bachofen, J. J.

1967 "An Essay on Ancient Mortuary Symbolism" (transl. E. Mannheim). In *Myth, Religion and Mother Right.* Routledge and Kegan Paul, London.

Badone, Ellen

1989 *The Appointed Hour: Death, Worldview, and Social Change in Brittany.* University of California Press, Berkeley.

1990 *Religious Orthodoxy and Popular Faith in European Society.* Princeton University Press, Princeton.

Baltes, M.

1977–78 "On the Relationship between Significant Yearly Events and Time of Death: Random or Systematic Distribution?" *Omega* 8. 2: 165–72.

Bakker, Hans

1986 *Ayodhya.* Egbert Forsten, Gröningen.

Bardis, Panis

1988 *The History of Thanatology.* University Press of America, Lanham, MD.

Basedow, Herbert

1925 *The Australian Aboriginal.* Adelaide, F.W. Preece.

Bayly, C. A.

1981 "From Ritual to Ceremony: Death Ritual and Society in Hindu North India since 1600." In *Mirrors of Mortality: Studies in the Social History of Death.* St. Martin's Press, New York.

Becker, E.

1973 *The Denial of Death.* New York: Free Press.

Bhardwaj, Surinder Mohan

1973 *Hindu Places of Pilgrimage: A Study in Cultural Geography.* University of California Press, Berkeley.

Biardeau, Madeleine
1989 *Hinduism: The Anthropology of a Civilization.* Oxford University Press, Delhi.

Blauner, Robert
1966 "Death and Social Structure." *Psychology* 29: 378–94.

Bloch, Maurice and Jonathan Parry (eds.)
1982 *Death and the Regeneration of Life.* Cambridge University Press, Cambridge.

Blumer, H.
1969 *Symbolic Interactionism.* Prentice Hall, Englewood Cliffs, NJ.

Bowker, John
1991 *The Meanings of Death.* Cambridge University Press, Cambridge.

Brass, Paul R.
1974 *Language, Religion and Politics in North India.* Cambridge University Press, Cambridge.

Callahan, D.
1986 "On Feeding the Dying." In R.F. Weir (ed.), *Ethical Issues in Death and Dying.* Columbia University Press, New York.

Cannon, W. B.
1942 " 'Voodoo' Death." *American Anthropologist* 44: 169–81.

Carol, Lucy
1977' " 'Sanskritization,' 'Westernization,' and 'Social Mobility': A Reappraisal of the Relevance of Anthropological Concepts to the Social Historian of Modern India." *Journal of Anthropological Research* 33.4: 355–71.

Carse, James
1980 *Death and Existence: A Conceptual History of Human Mortality.* John Wiley and Sons, New York.

Charlsely, Simon
1987 "Interpretation and Custom: The Case of the Wedding Cake." *Man* 22: 93–110.

Chaudhuri, Nirad C.
1979 *Hinduism: A Religion to Live By.* Chatto and Windus, London

Cohen, Lawrence
1995 "Toward an Anthropology of Senility: Anger, Weakness and Alzheimer's in Banaras, India." *Medical Anthropology Quarterly* 9.3: 314–34.

Counts, David A.

1976–77 "The Good Death in Kaliai: Preparation for Death in Western New Britain." *Omega* 7: 367–72.

Counts, David A. and Dorothy R. Counts

1985a "Introduction: Linking Concepts, Aging and Gender, Aging and Death." In D.A. Counts and D.R. Counts (eds.) *Aging and Its Transformations.* ASAO monograph no. 10. University Press of America, Lanham, MD.

1985b "I'm Not Dead Yet! Aging and Death: Process and Experience in Kaliai." In D.A. Counts and D.R. Counts (eds.), *Aging and its Transformations* ASAO monograph no. 10. University Press of America, Lanham, MD.

Counts, Dorothy R. and David A. Counts

1983–84 "Aspects of Dying in Northwest New Britain." *Omega* 14: 101–13.

1991 *Coping with the Final Tragedy: Cultural Variation in Dying and Grieving.* Baywood Publishing, Amityville, New York.

Danforth L. M.

1982 *The Death Ritual of Rural Greece.* Princeton University Press, Princeton, NJ.

Davis, Wade

1988 *Passage of Darkness: The Ethnobiology of the Haitian Zombie.* University of North Carolina Press, Chapel Hill.

De Coppet, D.

1981 "The Life-Giving Death." In H. C. Humphrys and H. King (eds.), *Mortality and Immortality: The Archaeology and Anthropology of Death.* Academic Press, London.

Eastwell, H. D.

1982 "Voodoo Death and the Mechanism for Dispatch of the Dying in East Arnem, Australia." *American Anthropologist* 84: 5–18.

Eck, Diana L.

1981 "India's Tirthas: 'Crossings' in Sacred Geography." *History of Religions* 20.4: 323–44.

1983 *Banaras: City of Light.* London: Routledge and Kegan Paul.

1991 "Following Rama, Worshipping Siva." In Diana Eck and Francoise Mallison (eds.), *Devotion Devine: Bhakti Traditions from the Regions of India.* École Française D'Extreme-Orient, Paris.

Elias, Norbert

1985 *The Loneliness of the Dying.* Basil Blackwell, Oxford.

Fabian, J.
1973 "How Others Die—Reflections on the Anthropology of Death." In A. Mack (ed.), *Death in American Experience.* Schocken Books, New York.

Fries, James F. and L. M. Crapo
1981 *Vitality and Aging: Implications of the Rectangular Curve.* W. H. Freeman, San Francisco.

Fuller, C. J.
1992 *The Camphor Flame: Popular Hinduism and Society in India.* Princeton University Press, Princeton, NJ.

Gangadharan, N.
1972 *Garuda Purana—A Study.* All India Kashiraj Trust, Ramnagar Fort, Varanasi.

Gennep, A. van
1960 *The Rites of Passage.* University of Chicago Press, Chicago.

Glaser, B. G. and A. Strauss
1965 *Awareness of Dying.* Aldine, Chicago.
1968 *Time for Dying.* Aldine, Chicago.

Glascock, A. P.
1983 "Death-Hastening Behaviour: An Expansion of Eastwell's Thesis." *American Anthropologist* 85: 417–20.
1990 "By Any Other Name, It Is Still Killing: A Comparison of the Treatment of the Elderly in America and Other Societies." In Jay Sokolovsky (ed.), *The Cultural Context of Aging: Worldwide Perspectives.* Bergin & Garvey, New York.

Good, Byron
1994 *Medicine, Rationality and Experience.* Cambridge University Press, Cambridge.

Goody, J.
1971 "Death and the Interpretation of Culture: A Bibliographic Overview." In D. Stannard (ed.), *Death in America.* University of Pennsylvania Press, Philadelphia.

Harrison, A. A. and N. E. A. Kroll
1985–86 "Variations in Death Rates in the Proximity of Christmas: An Opponent Process Interpretation." *Omega* 16.3: 181–92.

Harrison, A. A. and M. Moore
1982–83 "Birth Dates and Death Dates: A Closer Look." *Omega* 13.2: 117–25.

Havell, E. B.
1905 *Benaras, the Sacred City: Sketches of Hindu Life and Religion.* Blackie and Sons, London.

Hertz, Robert
[1909] 1960 *Death and the Right Hand.* (Translated by R. C. Needham) Cohen and West, Aberdeen.

Hopkins, Thomas J.
1992 "Hindu Views of Death and Afterlife." In Hiroshi Obayashi (ed.), *Death and Afterlife.* Greenwood, New York.

Huntington, R. and P. Metcalf
1979 *Celebrations of Death: The Anthropology of Mortuary Ritual.* Cambridge University Press, Cambridge.

Jackson, C. O.
1977 "Death Shall Have No Dominion: The Passing of the World of the Dead in America." *Omega* 8: 195–203.

Kane, P. V.
1973 *History of Dharmashastra,* vol. 4. Bhandarkar Oriental Research Unit, Poona.

Kakar, Sudhir
1982 *Shamans, Mystics and Doctors: A Psychological Inquiry into India and Its Healing Traditions.* Oxford University Press, Delhi.

Kalish, Richard and David K. Reynolds
1976 *Death and Ethnicity: A Psychocultural Study.* University of Southern California Press, Los Angeles.

Kastenbaum, R. and R. Aisenburg
1976 *The Psychology of Death.* Springer Verlag, New York.

Keesing, Roger
1982 *Kwaio Religion.* Columbia University Press, New York.

Khare, R. S.
1967 "Prediction of Death among the Kanyo-Kubja Brahmins." *Contributions to Indian Sociology* 2(1): 1–25

Kinsley, David
1986 *Hindu Goddesses: Images of the Divine Feminine in the Hindu Religious Tradition.* University of California Press, Berkeley.

Klostermaier, Klaus K.
1989 *A Survey of Hinduism.* Munshiram Manoharlal, New Delhi.

Kubler-Ross, Elisabeth
1969 *On Death and Dying*. MacMillan, New York.

Kumar, Nita
1986 "Open Space and Free Time: Pleasure for the People of Banaras." *Contributions to Indian Sociology*, n.s., 20.1: 41–60.
1992 *Friends, Brothers and Informants: Fieldwork Memoirs of Banaras*. University of California Press, Berkeley.

Kumar, Pramod
1984 *Moksha: The Ultimate Goal of Indian Philosophy*. Indo-vision, Ghaziabad.

Kutumbiah, P.
1962 *Ancient Indian Medicine*. Orient Longmans, Madras.

Lachman, S. J.
1982–83 "A Psychophysiological Interpretation of Voodoo Illness and Voodoo Death." *Omega* 13.4: 345–60.

Lifton, R. J.
1979 *The Broken Connection: On Death and the Continuity of Life*. Simon & Schuster, New York.

Lynn, J. and J. F. Childress
1986 "Must Patients Always Be Given Food and Water?" In R. F. Weir (ed.), *Ethical Issues in Death and Dying*. Columbia University Press, New York.

McKellin, W. H.
1985 "Passing Away and Loss of Life: Aging and Death among the Mangalese of Papua New Guinea." In D.A. Counts and D.R. Counts (eds.), *Aging and Its Transformations*, ASAO monograph no. 10. University Press of America, Lanham, MD.

Madan, T. N.
1987 *Non-renunciation: Themes and Interpretation of Hindu Culture*. Oxford University Press, Delhi.
1992 "Dying with Dignity." *Social Science and Medicine* 35.4: 425–32.

Malinowski, B.
1929 *Magic, Science and Religion*. Faber and West, London.

Mandelbaum, D. G.
1965 "Social Uses of Funeral Rites." In H. Feifel (ed.), *New Meanings of Death*. McGraw-Hill, New York.

Marshall, Vic
1980 *Last Chapters: A Sociology of Aging and Dying*. Brooks and Cole, Monterey.

1985 "Conclusions: Aging and Dying in Pacific Societies: Implications for Theory in Social Gerontology." In D.A. Counts and D.R. Counts (eds.), *Aging and Its Transformations,* ASAO monograph no. 10. University Press of America, Lanham, MD.

Mauksch, H. O.
1975 "The Organizational Context of Dying." In E. Kubler-Ross (ed.), *Death: The Final Stage of Growth.* Prentice Hall, Englewood Cliffs, NJ.

Michaelson, Eva, Astrid Norberg, and Bo Norberg
1987 "Feeding Methods for Demented Patients in End Stage of Life." *Geriatric Nursing* March/April, 69–73.

Moller, David Wendell
1990 *On Death without Dignity: The Human Impact of Technological Dying.* Baywood Publishing Co., Amityville, NY.

Morly, J. E. and A. J. Silverman
1988 "Anorexia in the Elderly." *Neurobiological Aging* 91: 9–16.

Olson-Noll, Cynthia and M. F. Bosworth
1989 "Anorexia and Weight Loss in the Elderly." *Postgraduate Medicine* 85.3: 140–44.

Ortner, Sherry
1984 "Theory in Anthropology since the Sixties." *Comparative Study of Society and History* 26.1: 126–66.

Palgi, Phyllis and Henry Abramovitch
1984 "The Anthropology of Death." *Annual Review of Anthropology* 13: 385–417.

Palmore, Erdman
1983 "Cross-Cultural Research: State of the Art." *Research on Aging* 5: 45–57.

Parry, Jonathan
1980 "Ghosts, Greed and Sin: The Occupational Identity of the Banaras Funeral Priests." *Man* 15.1: 88–111.
1981 "Death and Cosmogony in Kashi." *Contributions to Indian Sociology* 15: 337–65.
1982 "Sacrificial Death and the Necrophagous Ascetic." In Maurice Bloch and Jonathan Parry (eds.), *Death and the Regeneration of Life.* Cambridge University Press, Cambridge.
1985 "Death and Digestion: The Symbolism of Food and Eating in North Indian Mortuary Rites." *Man* 20: 612–30.
1994 *Death in Banaras.* Cambridge University Press, Cambridge.

Peacock, James
1986 *The Anthropological Lens: Harsh Light, Soft Focus.* Cambridge University Press, Cambridge.

Phillips, David P. and Kenneth A. Feldman
1973 "A Dip in Deaths before Ceremonial Occasions: Some New Relationships between Social Integration and Mortality." *American Sociological Review* 38: 678–96.

Phillips, P. A., M. Bretherton, C. Johnson, and L. Gray
1991 "Reduced Osmotic Thirst in Healthy Elderly Men." *American Journal of Physiology* 261: 166–71.

Radcliffe-Brown, A. R.
1964 *The Andaman Islanders.* Free Press, New York.

Radhakrishnan, S.
[1948] 1982 *The Bhagavadgita.* Blackie and Sons, Bombay.

Riley, J. W.
1983 "Dying and the Meaning of Death." *Annual Review of Sociology* 9: 191–221.

Rivers, W. H. R.
[1926] 1978 "The Primitive Conception of Death." Reprinted in Richard Slobodin, *WHR Rivers.* Columbia University Press, New York.

Rolls, Barbara
1992 "Aging and Appetite." *Nutrition Reviews* 50.12: 422–26.

Sandstead, Harold H.
1990 "A Point of View: Nutrition and Care of Terminally Ill Patients." *American Journal of Clinical Nutrition* 52: 767–69.

Saraswati, Baidyanath
1975 *Kashi: Myth and Reality of a Classical Cultural Tradition.* Indian Institute of Advanced Study, Simla.
1983 *Traditions of Tirthas in India: The Anthropology of Hindu Pilgrimage.* Bose Memorial Institute, Varanasi.
1985 "The Kashivasi Widows." *Man in India* 65.2: 107–20.

Sarkar, R. M.
1978 "Social Anthropology and the Study of Complex Societies in India." In R. Srivastava (ed.), *Social Anthropology in India.* Books Today, New Delhi.

Saunders, C.
1977 "Dying They Live." In Herman Feifel (ed.), *New Meanings of Death.* McGraw-Hill, New York.

Scaletta, Naomi M.
1985 "Death by Sorcery: The Social Dynamics of Dying in Bariai, West New Britain." In D.A. Counts and D.R. Counts (eds.), *Aging and Its Transformations,* ASAO monograph no. 10. University Press of America, Lanham, MD.

Schulz, Richard and Max Bazerman
1980 "Ceremonial Occasions and Mortality: A Second Look." *American Psychologist* 35.3: 253–61.

Srinivas, M. N.
1966 *Social Change in Modern India.* University of California Press, Berkeley.
1976 *The Remembered Village.* University of California Press, Berkeley.

Sri Gaurudapuranam
nd. Prakashak-babu Bejnath Prasad Bukselar, Rajadarvaja, Varanasi.

Stannard, D.
1975 *Death in America.* University of Pennsylvania Press, Philadelphia.

Stevenson, Peter H.
1983–84 " 'He Died Too Quick!' The Process of Dying in a Hutterian Colony." *Omega* 14.2: 127–33.

Sudnow, D.
1967 *Passing On: The Social Organization of Dying.* Prentice Hall, Englewood Cliffs, NJ.

Tulsidas
1990 *Tulsidas's Sri Ramcharitmanus.* Edited and translated R. C. Prasad. Motilal Banarsidass, Delhi.

Turner, Victor
1967 *The Forest of Symbols.* Cornell University Press, Ithaca, NY.
1973 "Death and the Dead in the Pilgrimage Process." In F. E. Reynolds and E. H. Waugh (eds.), *Religious Encounters with Death: Insights from the History and Anthropology of Religions.* Pennsylvania State University Press, University Park, PA.

van Gennep, A.
1960 *The Rites of Passage.* Translated M. B. Visedom and G. L. Caffee. University of Chicago Press, Chicago.

Vidyarthi, L. P., Makhan Jha and B. N. Saraswat.
1979 *The Sacred Complex of Kashi (A Microcosm of Indian Civilization).* Concept Publishing, Delhi.

Warner, W. L.
1937 *A Black Civilization: A Social Study of an Australian Tribe.* Harper and Brothers, New York and London.

Watson, Wilbur H.
1976 "The Aging Sick and the Near Dead: A Study of Some Distinguishing Characteristics and Social Effects." *Omega* 7.2: 115–23.

Wellenkamp, Jane
1991 "Fallen Leaves: Death and Grieving in Toraja." In David R. Counts and Dorothy A. Counts (eds.), *Coping with the Final Tragedy: Cultural Variation in Death and Grieving.* Baywood Publishing, Amityville, NY.

Winograd, Carol H. and Ellen Brown
1990 "Aggressive Oral Refeeding in Hospitalized Patients." *American Journal of Clinical Nutrition* 52: 967–68.

Younger, Paul
1982 "Ten Days of Wandering and Romance with Lord Rankanatan: The Pankuni Festival in Sriranam Temple, South India." *Modern Asian Studies* 16: 623–56.

Zerwekh, Joyce V.
1983 "The Dehydration Question." *Nursing* 83, (January): 47–51.

Zusne, L.
1986–87 "Some Factors Affecting the Birthday-Deathday Phenomenon." *Omega* 17.1: 9–26.

Index